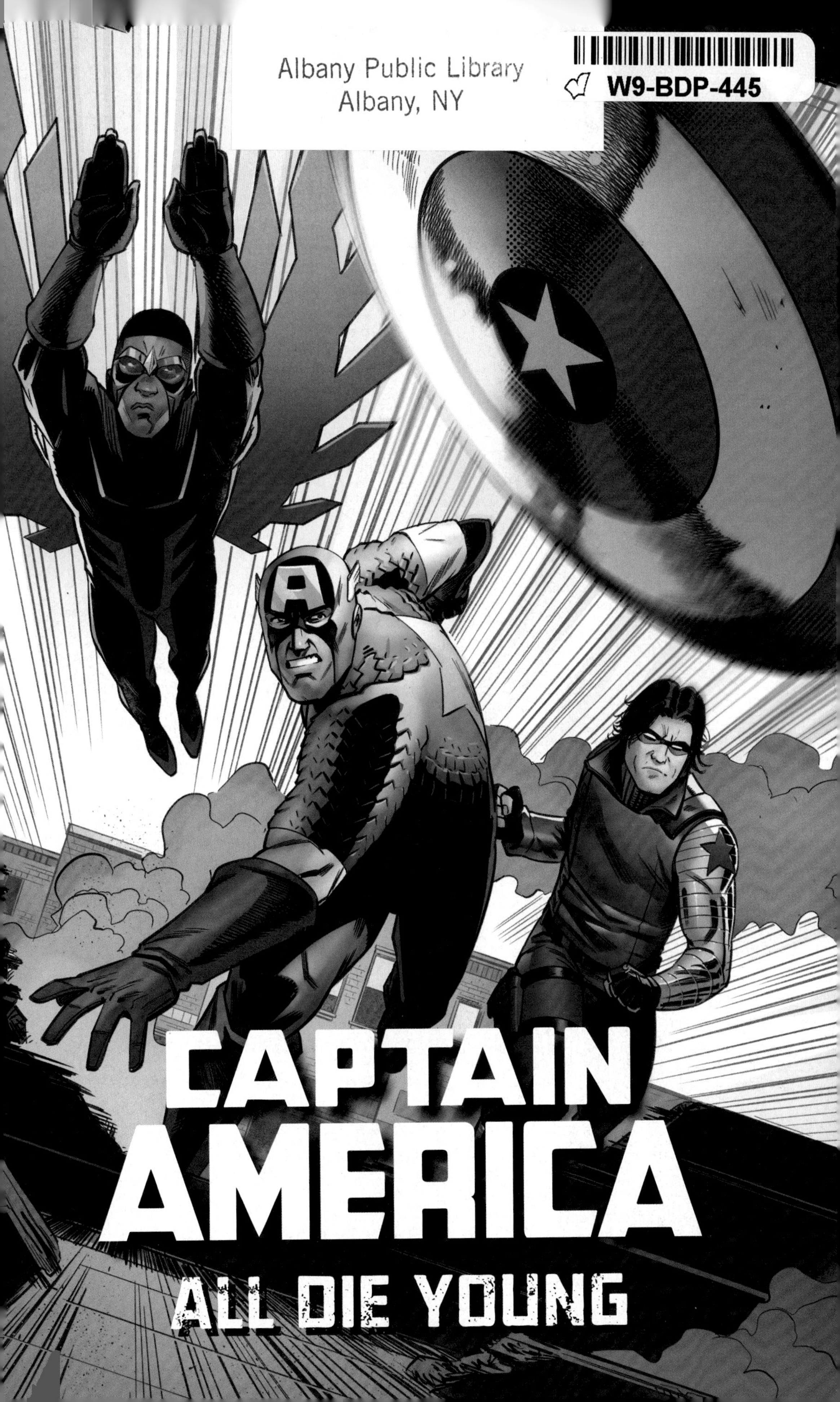
CAPTAIN
AMERICA
ALL DIE YOUNG

HYDRA CONQUERED THE UNITED STATES UNDER A LEADER WITH STEVE ROGERS' FACE. CAPTAIN AMERICA RETURNED, AND HYDRA FELL, BUT A NEW THREAT KNOWN AS THE POWER ELITE EMERGED AND DECLARED STEVE AND THE HYDRA SUPREME TO BE ONE AND THE SAME.

AFTER THE POWER ELITE FRAMED AND IMPRISONED STEVE FOR THE MURDER OF THUNDERBOLT ROSS, SHARON CARTER AND THE DAUGHTERS OF LIBERTY BROKE HIM OUT, HOPING TO PROTECT HIM LONG ENOUGH TO EXPOSE AND DEFEAT THE POWER ELITE.

STEVE DISCOVERED THAT THE MYSTERIOUS LEADER OF THE DAUGHTERS OF LIBERTY WAS NONE OTHER THAN PEGGY CARTER, AN OLD FLAME HE BELIEVED LONG DEAD. BUT THERE'S NO TIME FOR STEVE TO GRAPPLE WITH THIS REVELATION — PEGGY REVEALED THAT SELENE OF THE POWER ELITE STOLE A BIT OF SHARON'S SOUL, AND THEY NEED TO GET IT BACK BEFORE IT'S TOO LATE!

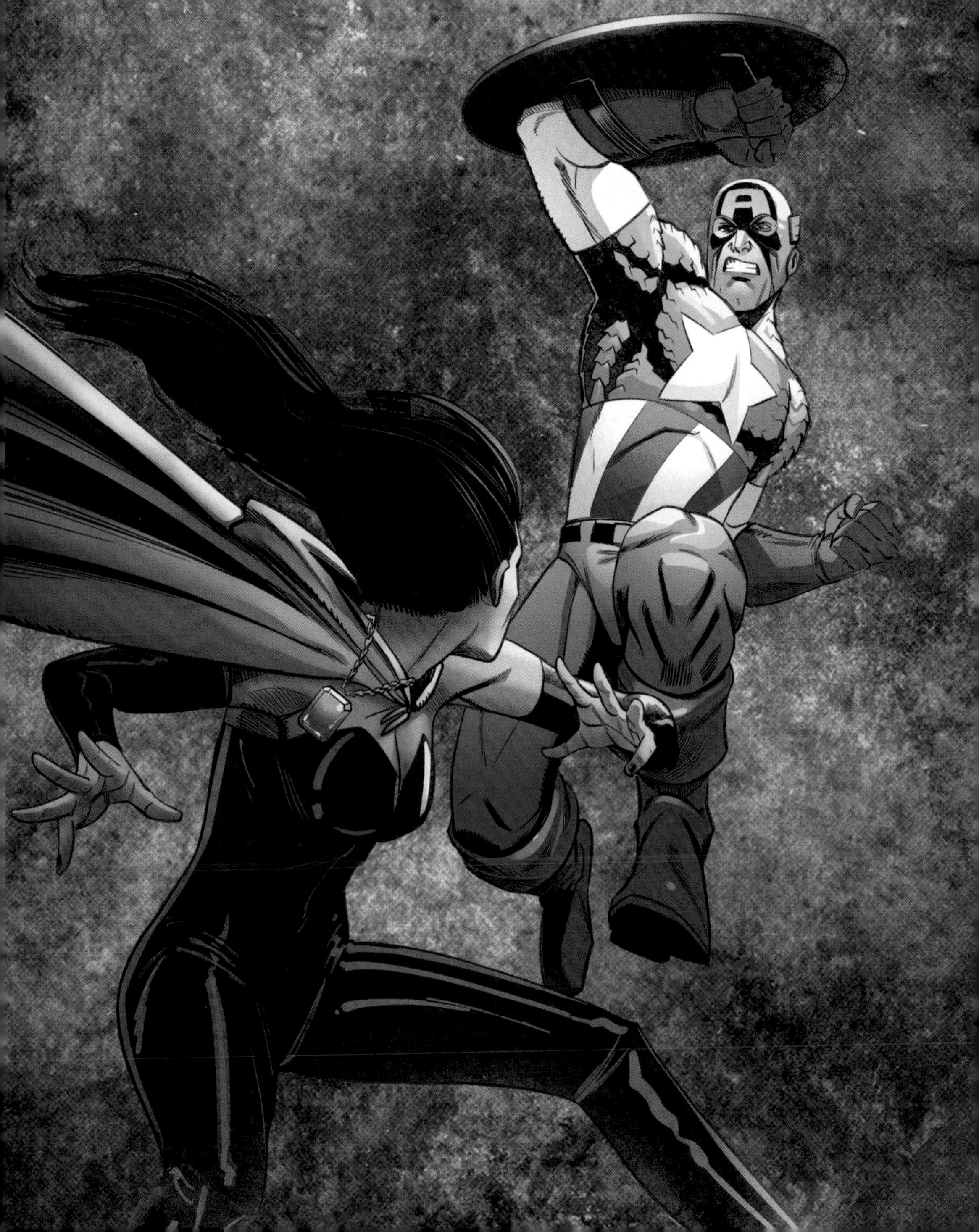

CAPTAIN AMERICA

ALL DIE YOUNG

Ta-Nehisi Coates
WRITER

Bob Quinn [#20-23], **Daniel Acuña** [#24] & **Leonard Kirk** [#25]
ARTISTS

Matt Milla [#20-23 & #25]
COLOR ARTIST

"THE PROMISE"

Anthony Falcone & Michael Cho
WRITERS

Michael Cho
ARTIST

VC's Cory Petit [#20] & **Joe Caramagna** [#21-25]
LETTERERS

Alex Ross
COVER ART

Martin Biro
ASSISTANT EDITOR

Alanna Smith
ASSOCIATE EDITOR

Tom Brevoort
EDITOR

CAPTAIN AMERICA CREATED BY JOE SIMON & JACK KIRBY

COLLECTION EDITOR **JENNIFER GRÜNWALD**
ASSISTANT EDITOR **DANIEL KIRCHHOFFER**
ASSISTANT MANAGING EDITOR **MAIA LOY**
ASSISTANT MANAGING EDITOR **LISA MONTALBANO**

VP PRODUCTION & SPECIAL PROJECTS **JEFF YOUNGQUIST**
BOOK DESIGNERS **STACIE ZUCKER** WITH **ADAM DEL RE**
SVP PRINT, SALES & MARKETING **DAVID GABRIEL**
EDITOR IN CHIEF **C.B. CEBULSKI**

CAPTAIN AMERICA BY TA-NEHISI COATES VOL. 4: ALL DIE YOUNG. Contains material originally published in magazine form as CAPTAIN AMERICA (2018) #20-25. First printing 2020. ISBN 978-1-302-92040-1. Published by MARVEL WORLDWIDE, INC., a subsidiary of MARVEL ENTERTAINMENT, LLC. OFFICE OF PUBLICATION: 1290 Avenue of the Americas, New York, NY 10104. © 2020 MARVEL No similarity between any of the names, characters, persons, and/or institutions in this magazine with those of any living or dead person or institution is intended, and any such similarity which may exist is purely coincidental. **Printed in Canada.** KEVIN FEIGE, Chief Creative Officer; DAN BUCKLEY, President, Marvel Entertainment; JOE QUESADA, EVP & Creative Director; DAVID BOGART, Associate Publisher & SVP of Talent Affairs; TOM BREVOORT, VP, Executive Editor; NICK LOWE, Executive Editor, VP of Content, Digital Publishing; DAVID GABRIEL, VP of Print & Digital Publishing; JEFF YOUNGQUIST, VP of Production & Special Projects; ALEX MORALES, Director of Publishing Operations; DAN EDINGTON, Managing Editor; RICKEY PURDIN, Director of Talent Relations; JENNIFER GRÜNWALD, Senior Editor, Special Projects; SUSAN CRESPI, Production Manager; STAN LEE, Chairman Emeritus. For information regarding advertising in Marvel Comics or on Marvel.com, please contact Vit DeBellis, Custom Solutions & Integrated Advertising Manager, at vdebellis@marvel.com. For Marvel subscription inquiries, please call 888-511-5480. **Manufactured between 12/4/2020 and 1/5/2021 by SOLISCO PRINTERS, SCOTT, QC, CANADA.**

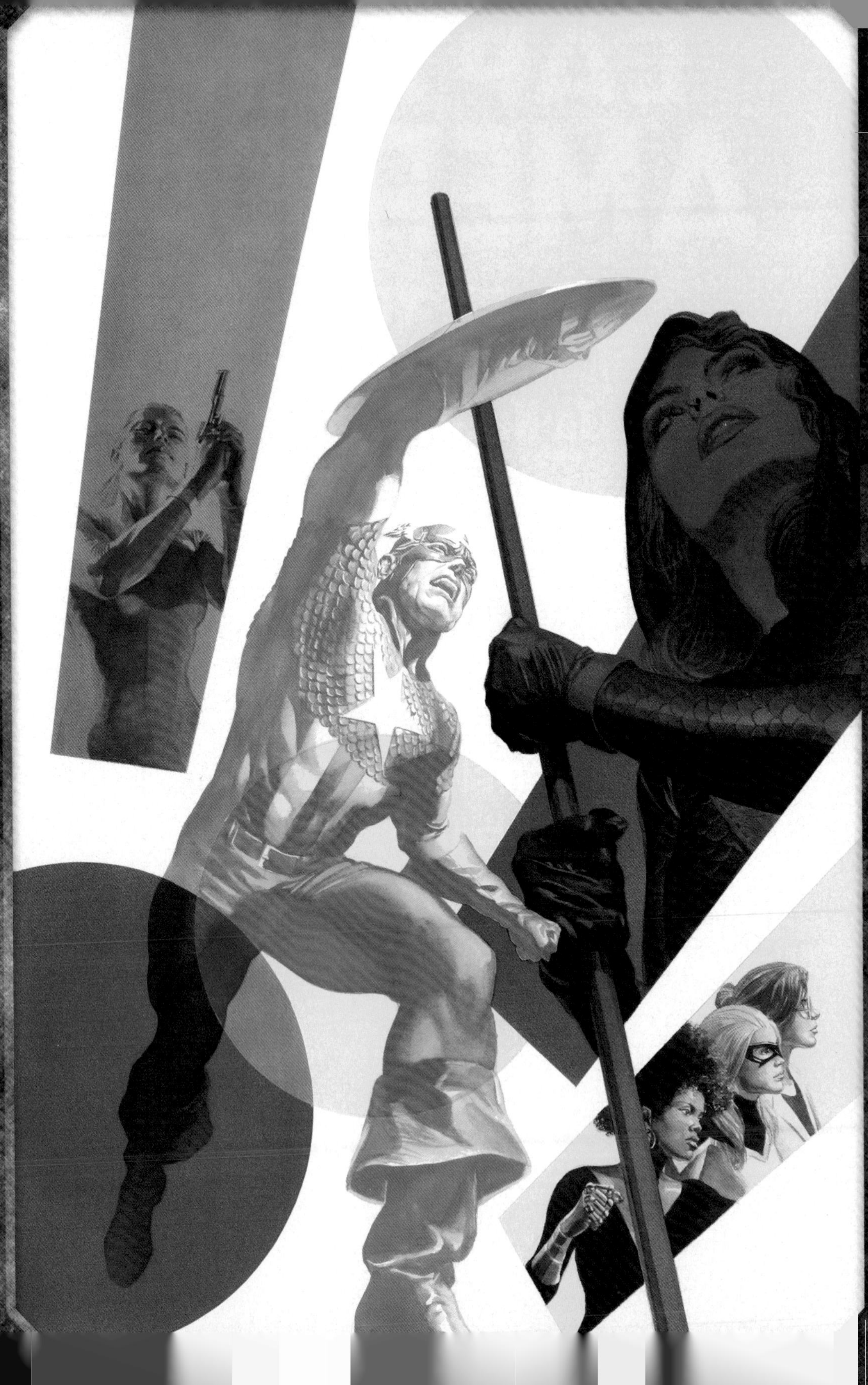

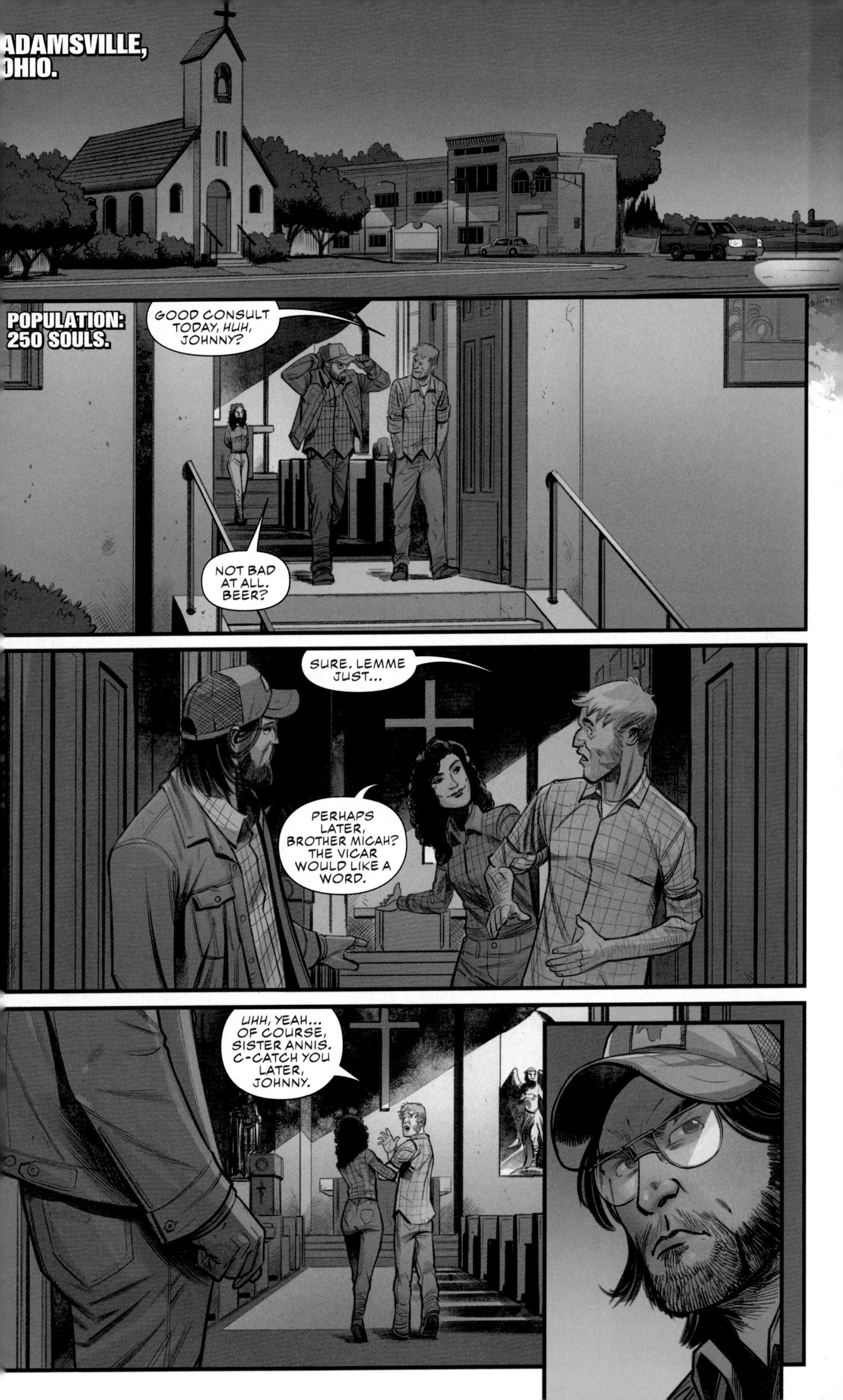
ADAMSVILLE, OHIO.
POPULATION: 250 SOULS.
GOOD CONSULT TODAY, HUH, JOHNNY?
NOT BAD AT ALL. BEER?
SURE. LEMME JUST...
PERHAPS LATER, BROTHER MICAH? THE VICAR WOULD LIKE A WORD.
UHH, YEAH... OF COURSE, SISTER ANNIS. C-CATCH YOU LATER, JOHNNY.

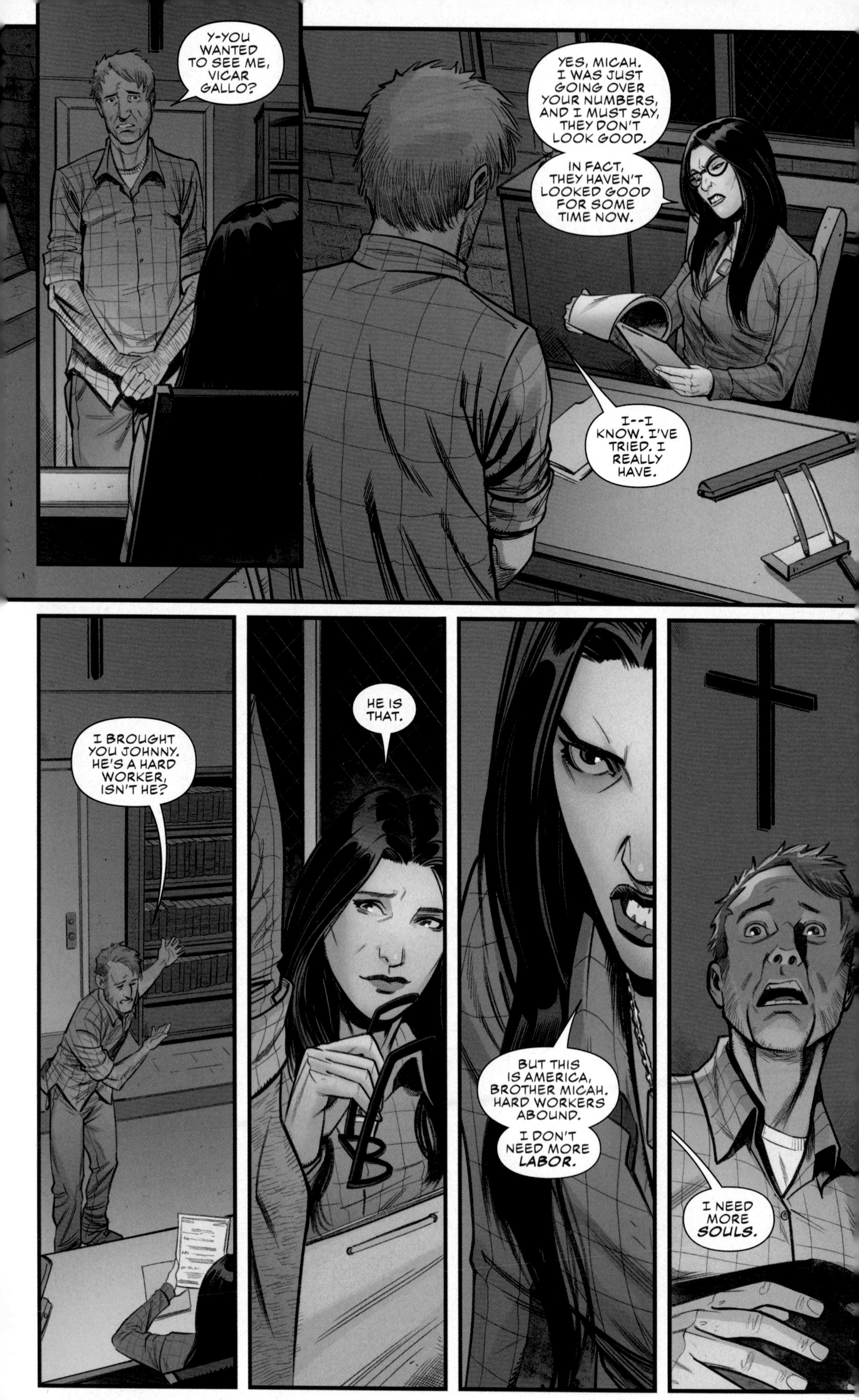
Y-YOU WANTED TO SEE ME, VICAR GALLO?
YES, MICAH. I WAS JUST GOING OVER YOUR NUMBERS, AND I MUST SAY, THEY DON'T LOOK GOOD.
IN FACT, THEY HAVEN'T LOOKED GOOD FOR SOME TIME NOW.
I--I KNOW. I'VE TRIED. I REALLY HAVE.
I BROUGHT YOU JOHNNY. HE'S A HARD WORKER, ISN'T HE?
HE IS THAT.
BUT THIS IS AMERICA, BROTHER MICAH. HARD WORKERS ABOUND.
I DON'T NEED MORE LABOR.
I NEED MORE SOULS.

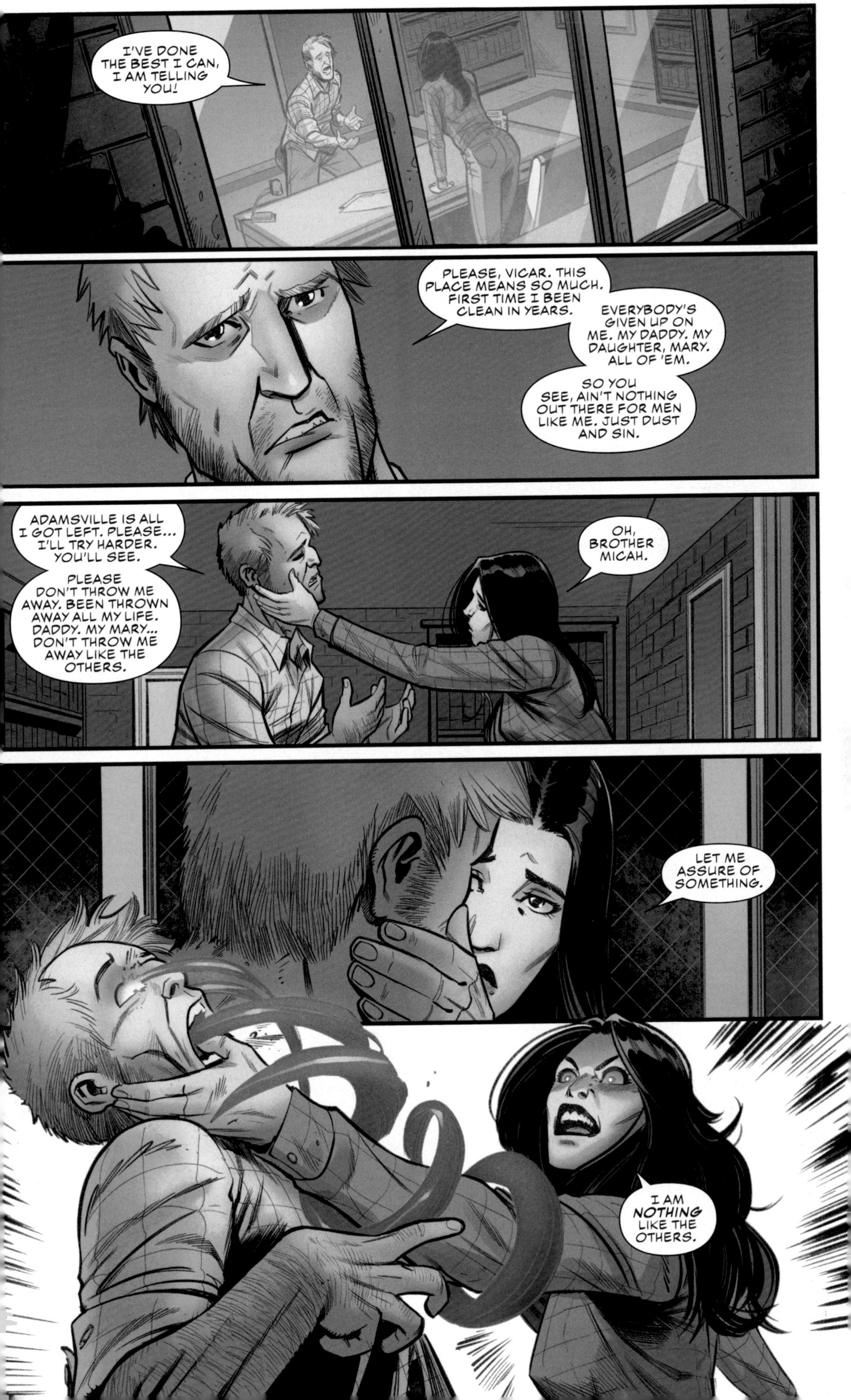

I'VE DONE THE BEST I CAN, I AM TELLING YOU!
PLEASE, VICAR. THIS PLACE MEANS SO MUCH. FIRST TIME I BEEN CLEAN IN YEARS.
EVERYBODY'S GIVEN UP ON ME. MY DADDY. MY DAUGHTER, MARY. ALL OF 'EM.
SO YOU SEE, AIN'T NOTHING OUT THERE FOR MEN LIKE ME. JUST DUST AND SIN.
ADAMSVILLE IS ALL I GOT LEFT. PLEASE... I'LL TRY HARDER. YOU'LL SEE.
PLEASE DON'T THROW ME AWAY. BEEN THROWN AWAY ALL MY LIFE. DADDY. MY MARY... DON'T THROW ME AWAY LIKE THE OTHERS.
OH, BROTHER MICAH.
LET ME ASSURE OF SOMETHING.
I AM **NOTHING** LIKE THE OTHERS.

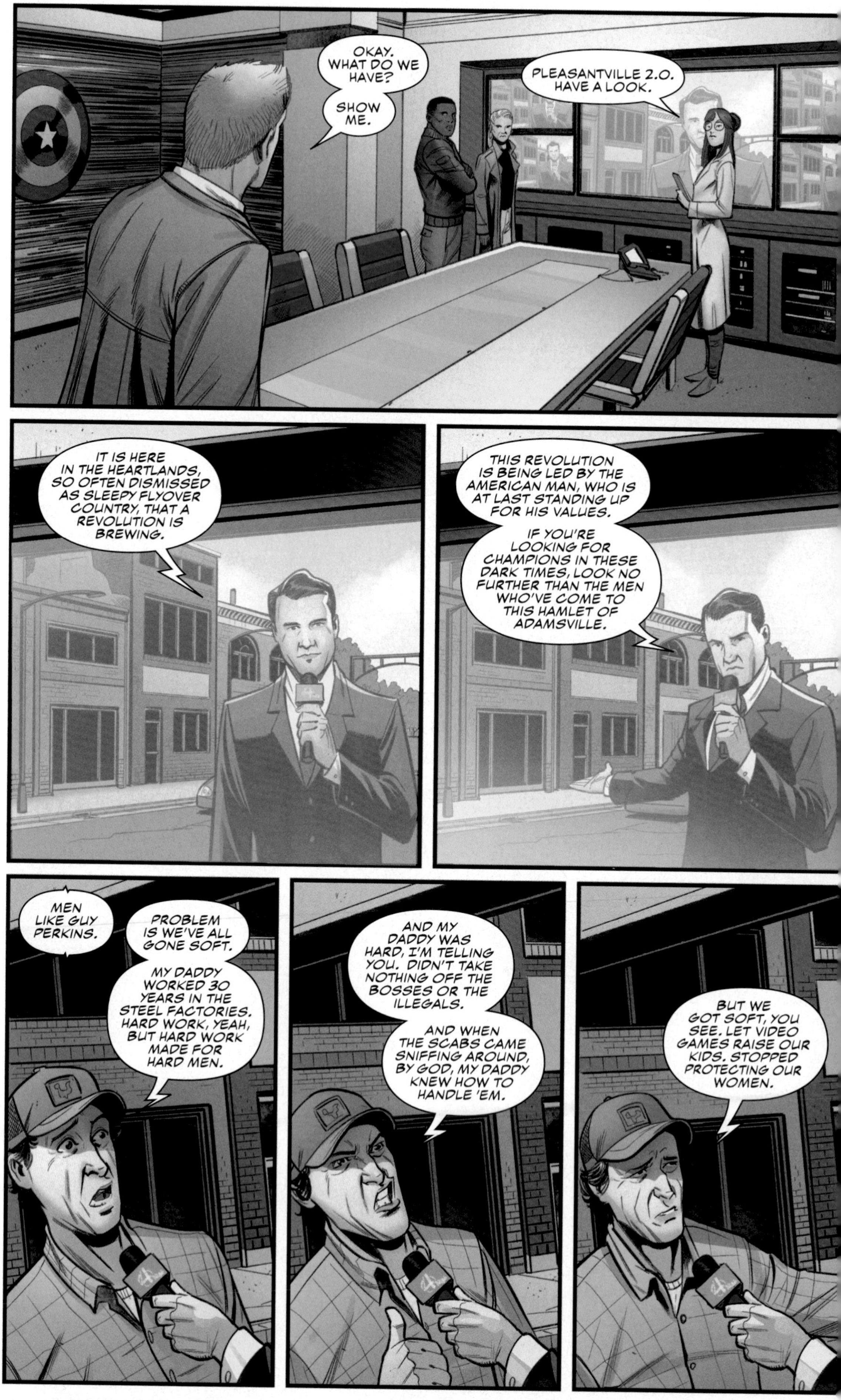
OKAY. WHAT DO WE HAVE?
SHOW ME.
PLEASANTVILLE 2.0. HAVE A LOOK.
IT IS HERE IN THE HEARTLANDS, SO OFTEN DISMISSED AS SLEEPY FLYOVER COUNTRY, THAT A REVOLUTION IS BREWING.
THIS REVOLUTION IS BEING LED BY THE AMERICAN MAN, WHO IS AT LAST STANDING UP FOR HIS VALUES.
IF YOU'RE LOOKING FOR CHAMPIONS IN THESE DARK TIMES, LOOK NO FURTHER THAN THE MEN WHO'VE COME TO THIS HAMLET OF ADAMSVILLE.
MEN LIKE GUY PERKINS.
PROBLEM IS WE'VE ALL GONE SOFT.
MY DADDY WORKED 30 YEARS IN THE STEEL FACTORIES. HARD WORK, YEAH, BUT HARD WORK MADE FOR HARD MEN.
AND MY DADDY WAS HARD, I'M TELLING YOU. DIDN'T TAKE NOTHING OFF THE BOSSES OR THE ILLEGALS.
AND WHEN THE SCABS CAME SNIFFING AROUND, BY GOD, MY DADDY KNEW HOW TO HANDLE 'EM.
BUT WE GOT SOFT, YOU SEE. LET VIDEO GAMES RAISE OUR KIDS. STOPPED PROTECTING OUR WOMEN.

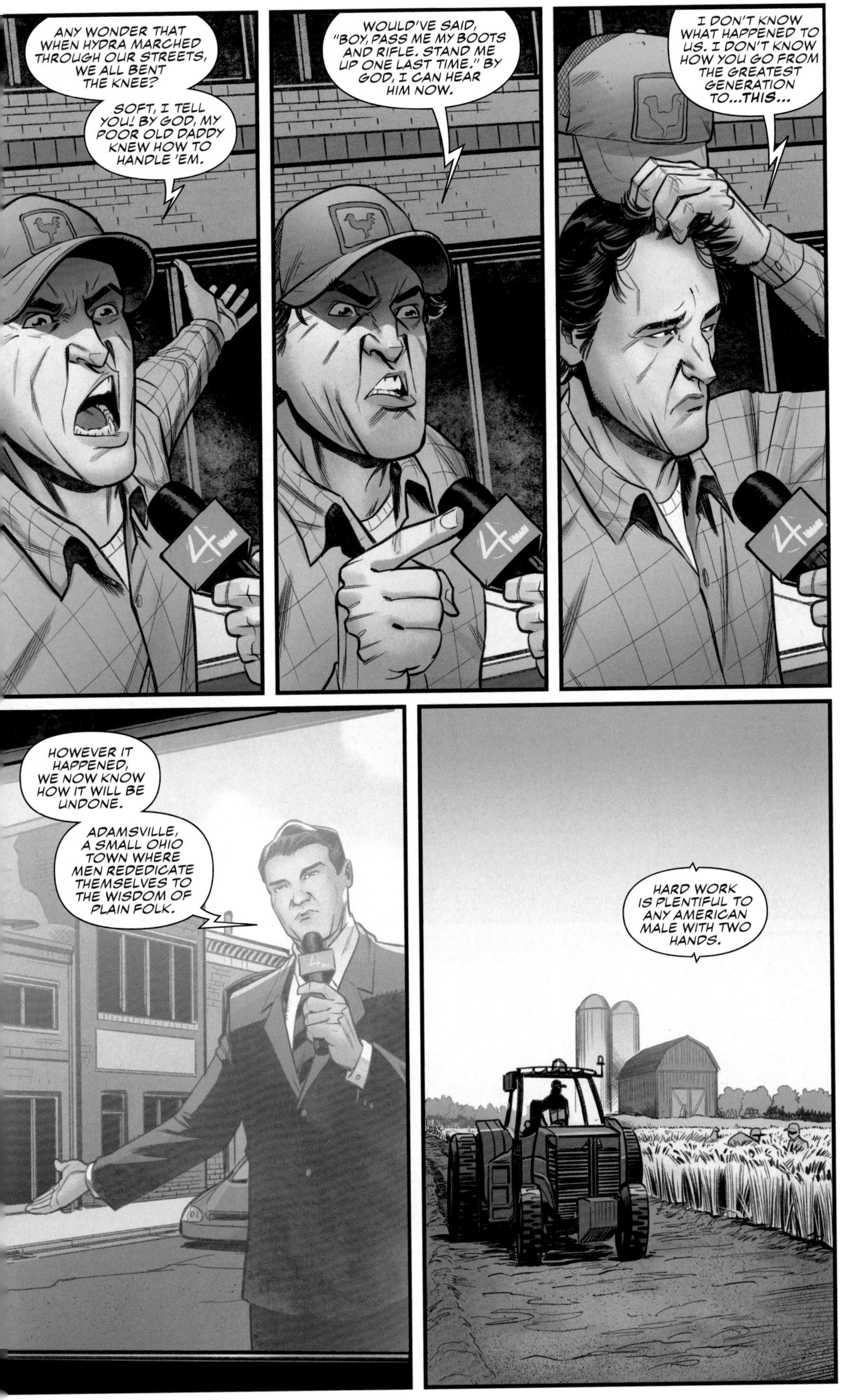

ANY WONDER THAT WHEN HYDRA MARCHED THROUGH OUR STREETS, WE ALL BENT THE KNEE?
SOFT, I TELL YOU! BY GOD, MY POOR OLD DADDY KNEW HOW TO HANDLE 'EM.
WOULD'VE SAID, "BOY, PASS ME MY BOOTS AND RIFLE. STAND ME UP ONE LAST TIME." BY GOD, I CAN HEAR HIM NOW.
I DON'T KNOW WHAT HAPPENED TO US. I DON'T KNOW HOW YOU GO FROM THE GREATEST GENERATION TO...THIS...
HOWEVER IT HAPPENED, WE NOW KNOW HOW IT WILL BE UNDONE.
ADAMSVILLE, A SMALL OHIO TOWN WHERE MEN REDEDICATE THEMSELVES TO THE WISDOM OF PLAIN FOLK.
HARD WORK IS PLENTIFUL TO ANY AMERICAN MALE WITH TWO HANDS.

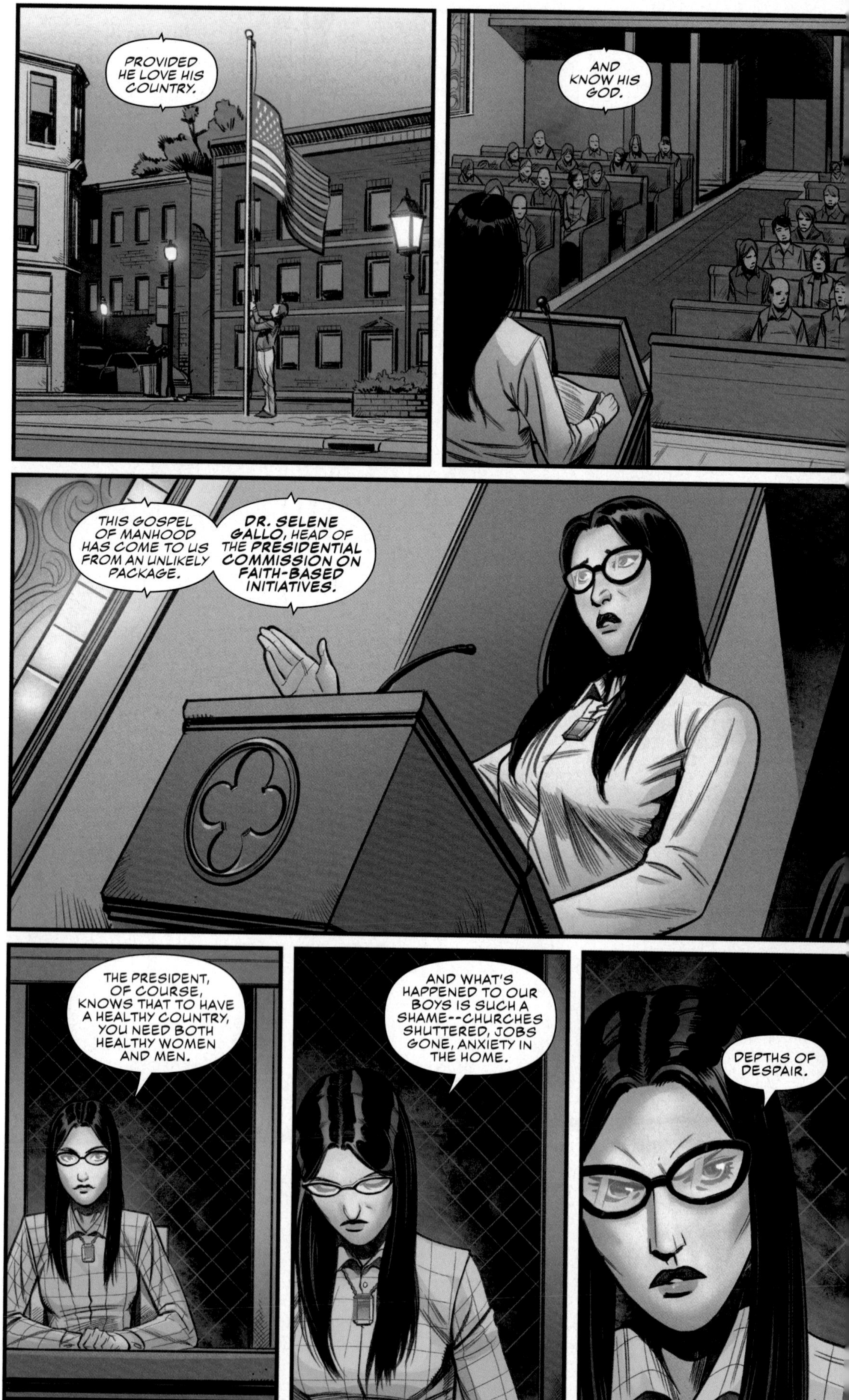

PROVIDED HE LOVE HIS COUNTRY.
AND KNOW HIS GOD.
THIS GOSPEL OF MANHOOD HAS COME TO US FROM AN UNLIKELY PACKAGE.
DR. SELENE GALLO, HEAD OF THE PRESIDENTIAL COMMISSION ON FAITH-BASED INITIATIVES.
THE PRESIDENT, OF COURSE, KNOWS THAT TO HAVE A HEALTHY COUNTRY, YOU NEED BOTH HEALTHY WOMEN AND MEN.
AND WHAT'S HAPPENED TO OUR BOYS IS SUCH A SHAME--CHURCHES SHUTTERED, JOBS GONE, ANXIETY IN THE HOME.
DEPTHS OF DESPAIR.

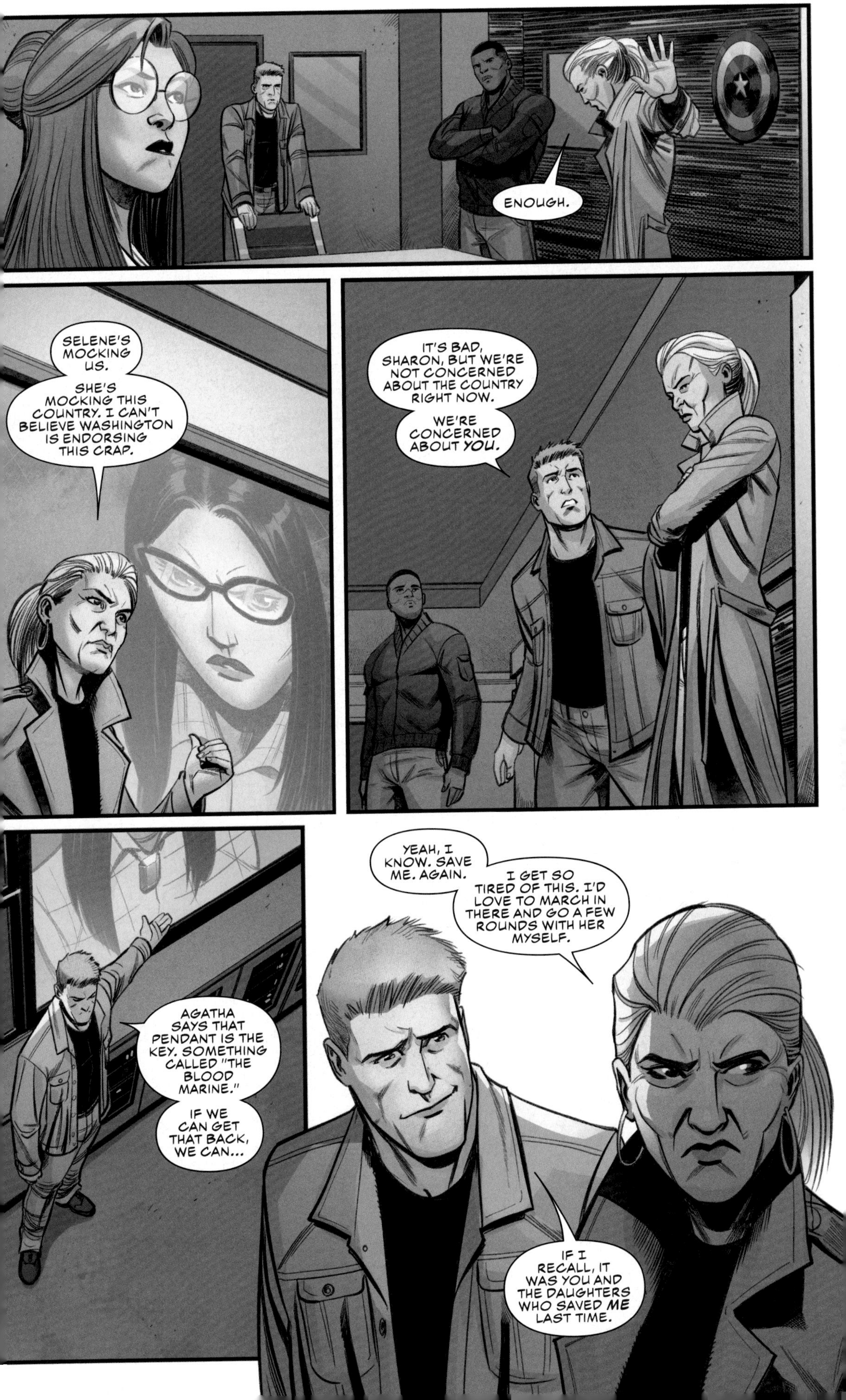

ENOUGH.
SELENE'S MOCKING US.
SHE'S MOCKING THIS COUNTRY. I CAN'T BELIEVE WASHINGTON IS ENDORSING THIS CRAP.
IT'S BAD, SHARON, BUT WE'RE NOT CONCERNED ABOUT THE COUNTRY RIGHT NOW.
WE'RE CONCERNED ABOUT YOU.
AGATHA SAYS THAT PENDANT IS THE KEY. SOMETHING CALLED "THE BLOOD MARINE."
IF WE CAN GET THAT BACK, WE CAN...
YEAH, I KNOW. SAVE ME. AGAIN.
I GET SO TIRED OF THIS. I'D LOVE TO MARCH IN THERE AND GO A FEW ROUNDS WITH HER MYSELF.
IF I RECALL, IT WAS YOU AND THE DAUGHTERS WHO SAVED ME LAST TIME.

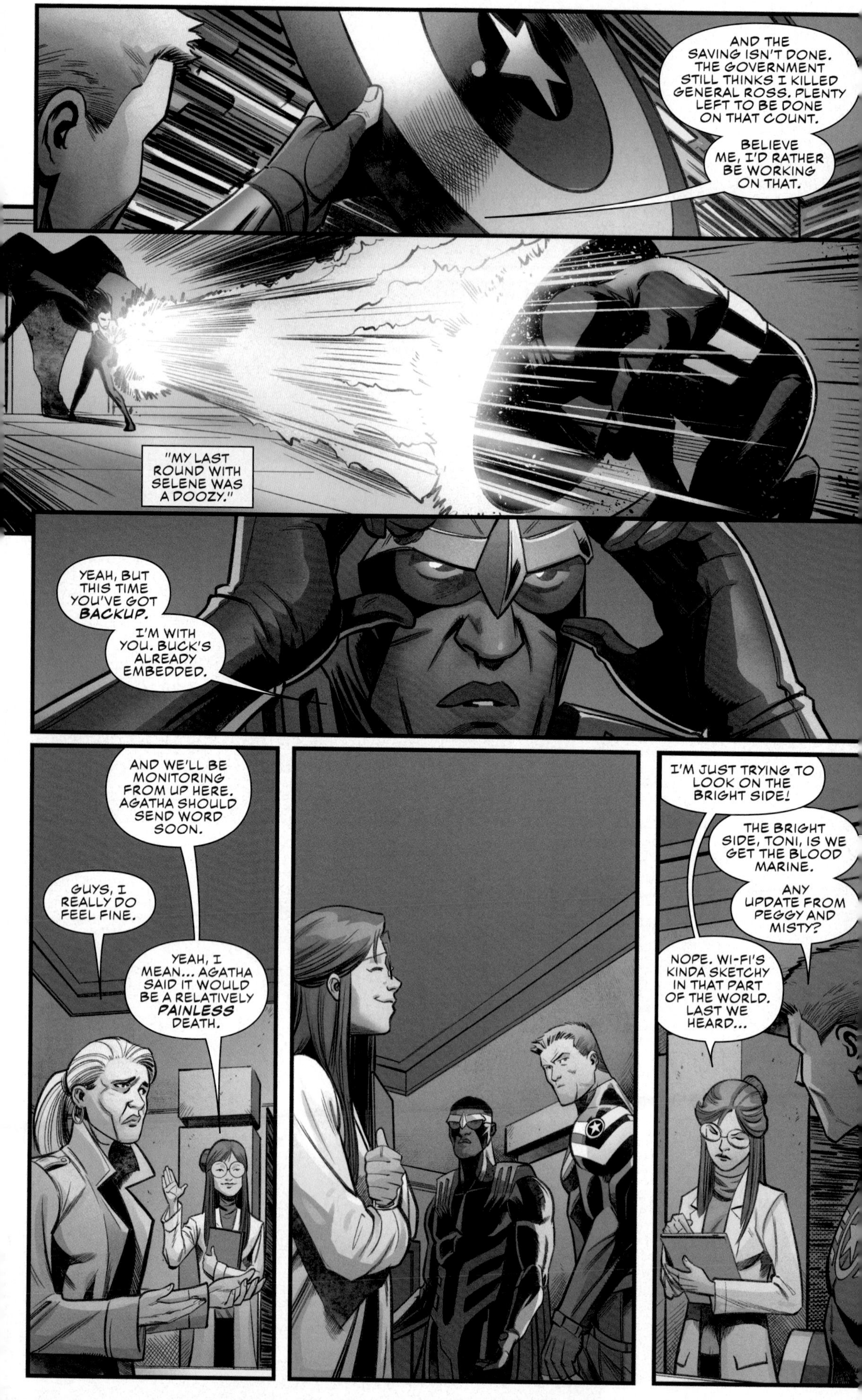
AND THE SAVING ISN'T DONE. THE GOVERNMENT STILL THINKS I KILLED GENERAL ROSS. PLENTY LEFT TO BE DONE ON THAT COUNT.
BELIEVE ME, I'D RATHER BE WORKING ON THAT.
"MY LAST ROUND WITH SELENE WAS A DOOZY."
YEAH, BUT THIS TIME YOU'VE GOT BACKUP.
I'M WITH YOU. BUCK'S ALREADY EMBEDDED.
AND WE'LL BE MONITORING FROM UP HERE. AGATHA SHOULD SEND WORD SOON.
GUYS, I REALLY DO FEEL FINE.
YEAH, I MEAN... AGATHA SAID IT WOULD BE A RELATIVELY PAINLESS DEATH.
I'M JUST TRYING TO LOOK ON THE BRIGHT SIDE!
THE BRIGHT SIDE, TONI, IS WE GET THE BLOOD MARINE.
ANY UPDATE FROM PEGGY AND MISTY?
NOPE. WI-FI'S KINDA SKETCHY IN THAT PART OF THE WORLD. LAST WE HEARD...

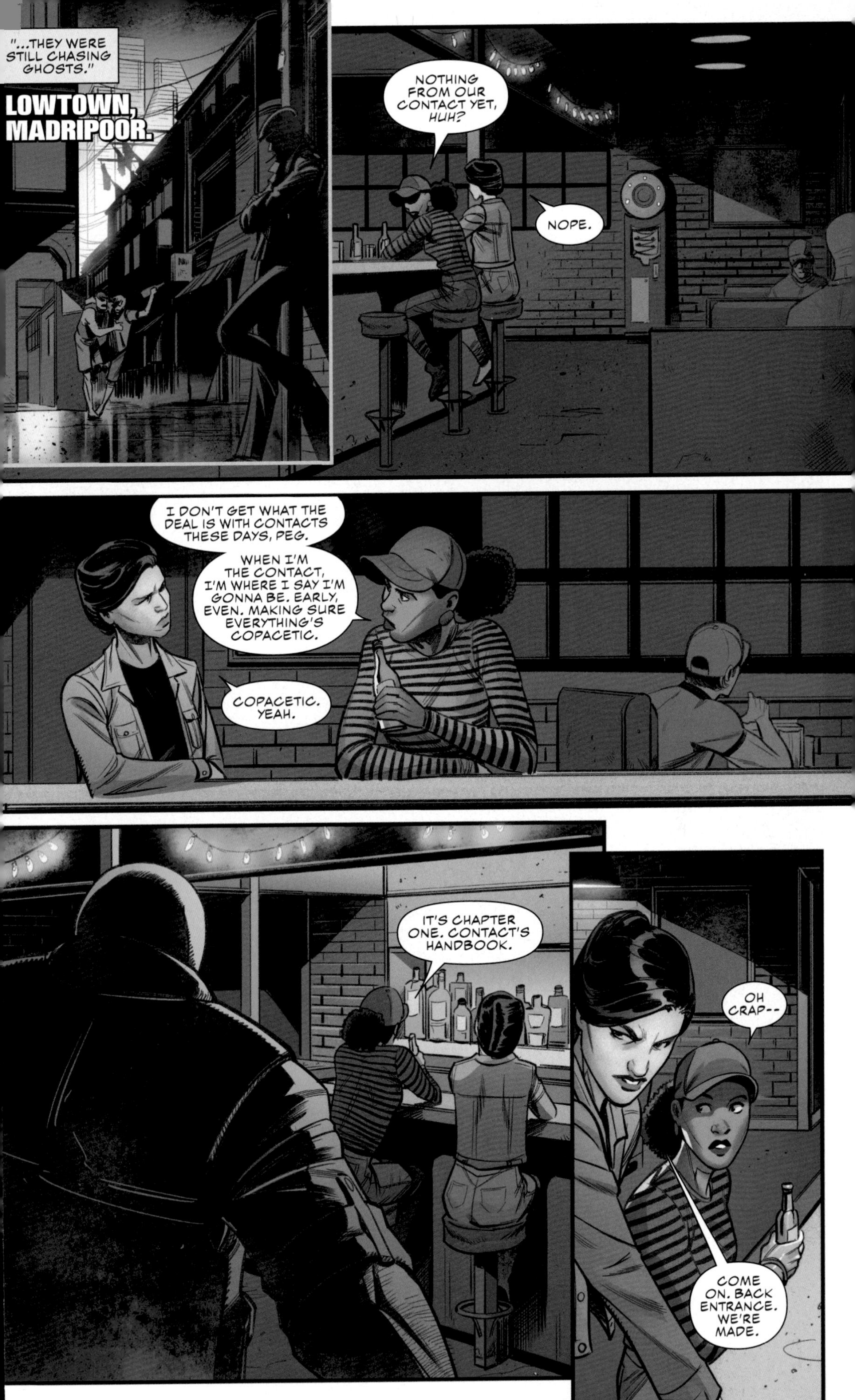
"...THEY WERE STILL CHASING GHOSTS."
LOWTOWN, MADRIPOOR.
NOTHING FROM OUR CONTACT YET, HUH?
NOPE.
I DON'T GET WHAT THE DEAL IS WITH CONTACTS THESE DAYS, PEG.
WHEN I'M THE CONTACT, I'M WHERE I SAY I'M GONNA BE. EARLY, EVEN. MAKING SURE EVERYTHING'S COPACETIC.
COPACETIC. YEAH.
IT'S CHAPTER ONE. CONTACT'S HANDBOOK.
OH CRAP--
COME ON. BACK ENTRANCE. WE'RE MADE.

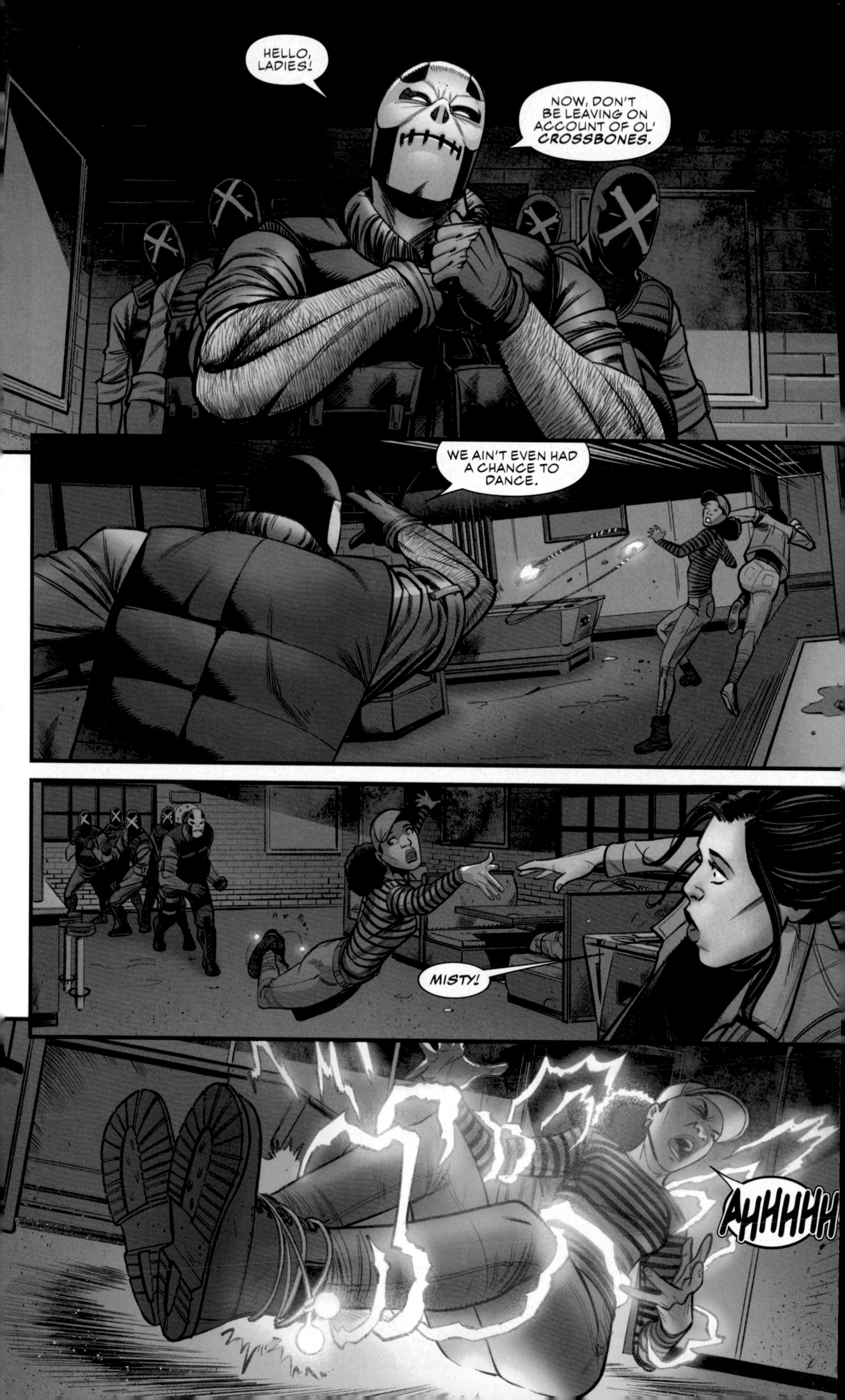
HELLO, LADIES!
NOW, DON'T BE LEAVING ON ACCOUNT OF OL' CROSSBONES.
WE AIN'T EVEN HAD A CHANCE TO DANCE.
MISTY!
AHHHHH

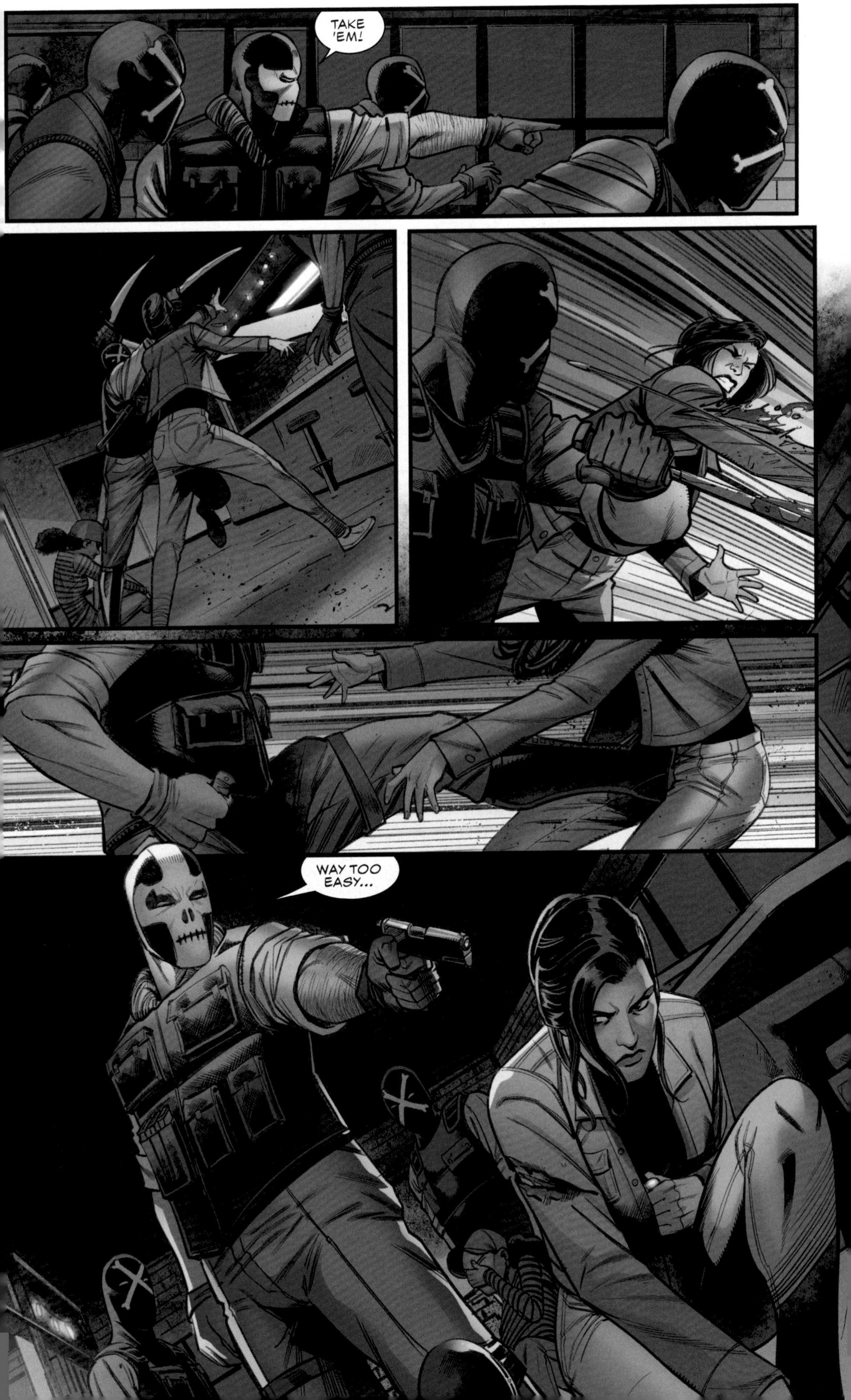
TAKE 'EM!
WAY TOO EASY...

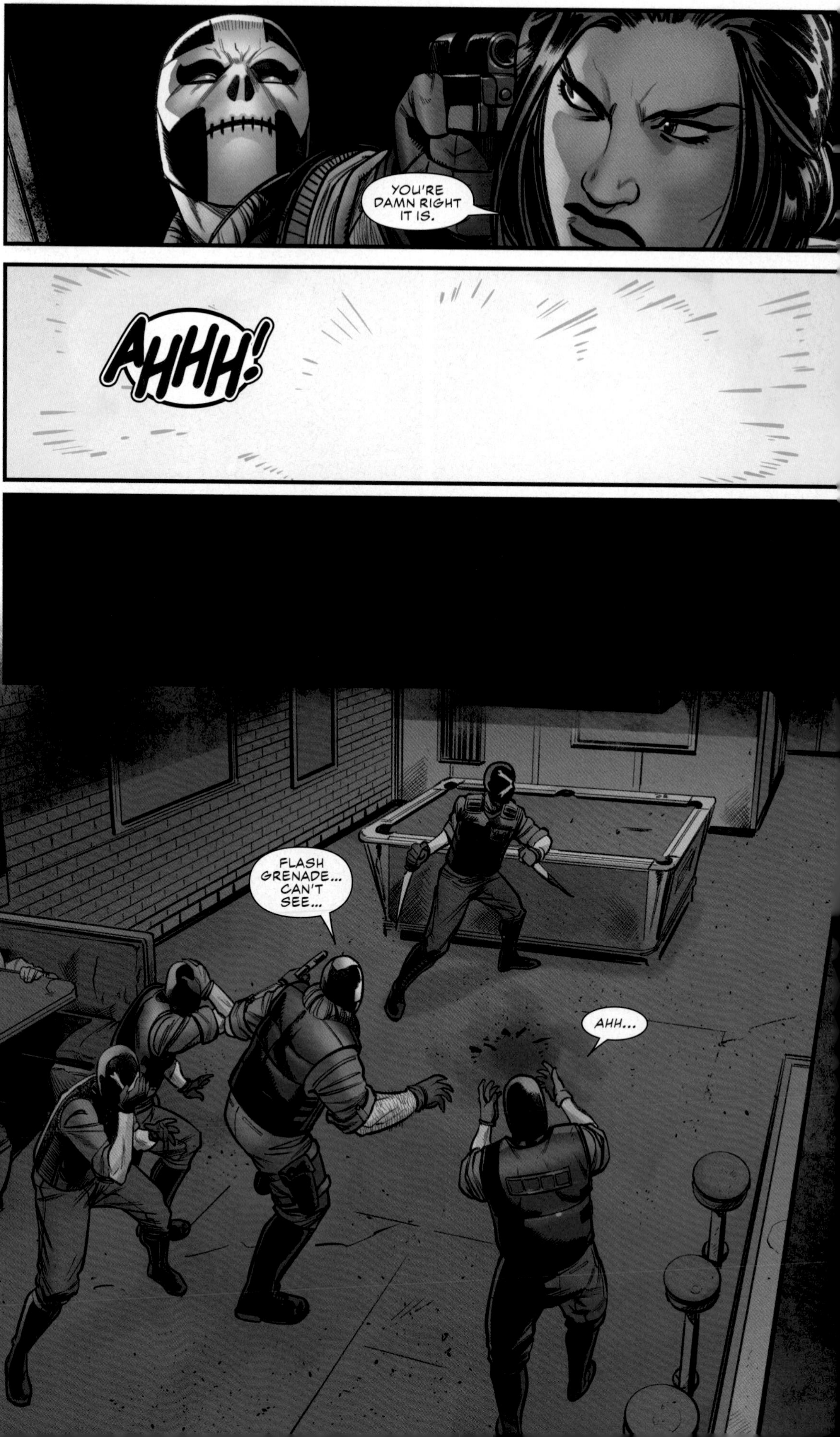
YOU'RE DAMN RIGHT IT IS.
AHHH!
FLASH GRENADE... CAN'T SEE...
AHH...

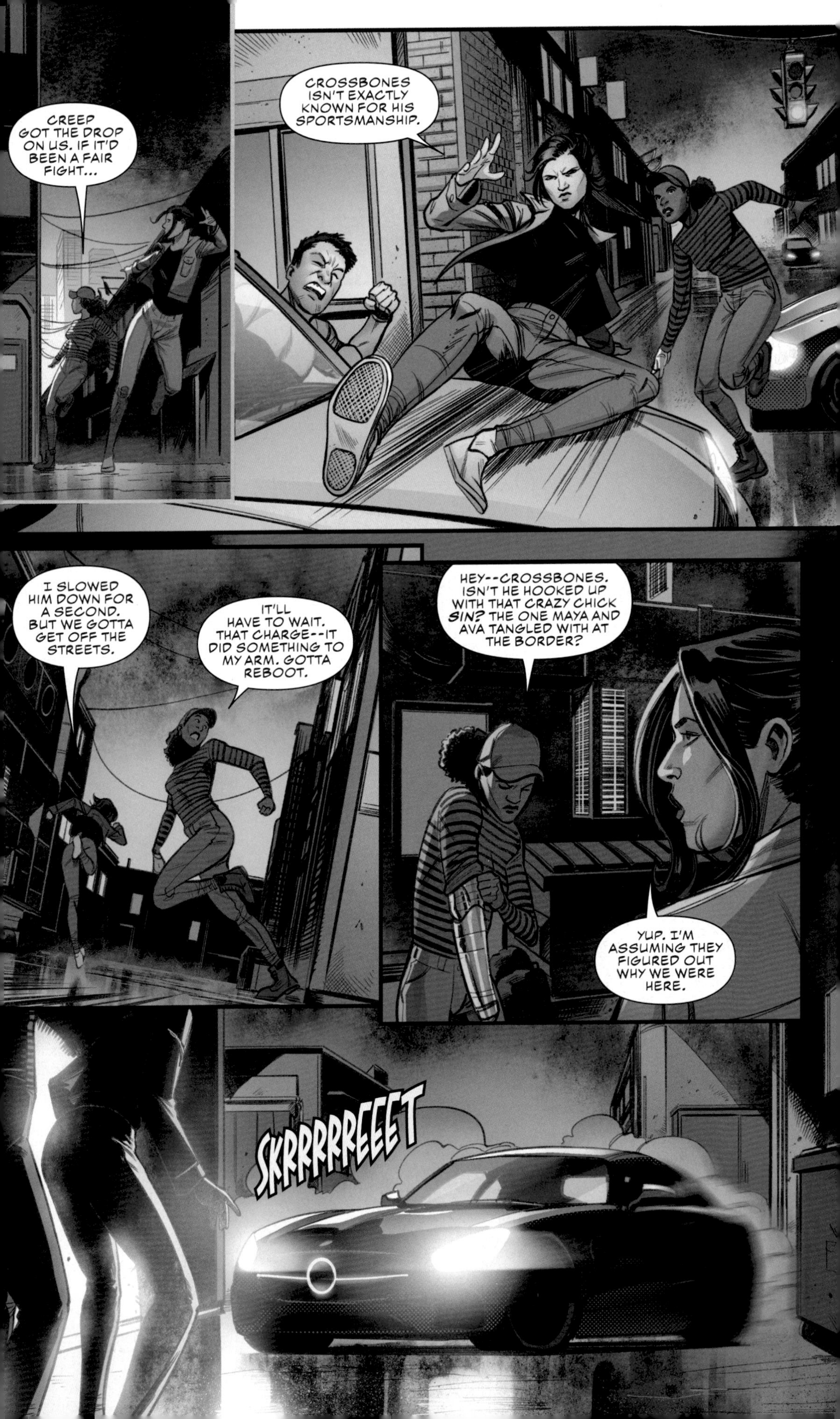
CREEP GOT THE DROP ON US. IF IT'D BEEN A FAIR FIGHT...
CROSSBONES ISN'T EXACTLY KNOWN FOR HIS SPORTSMANSHIP.
I SLOWED HIM DOWN FOR A SECOND. BUT WE GOTTA GET OFF THE STREETS.
IT'LL HAVE TO WAIT. THAT CHARGE--IT DID SOMETHING TO MY ARM. GOTTA REBOOT.
HEY--CROSSBONES. ISN'T HE HOOKED UP WITH THAT CRAZY CHICK SIN? THE ONE MAYA AND AVA TANGLED WITH AT THE BORDER?
YUP. I'M ASSUMING THEY FIGURED OUT WHY WE WERE HERE.
SKRRRRREEET

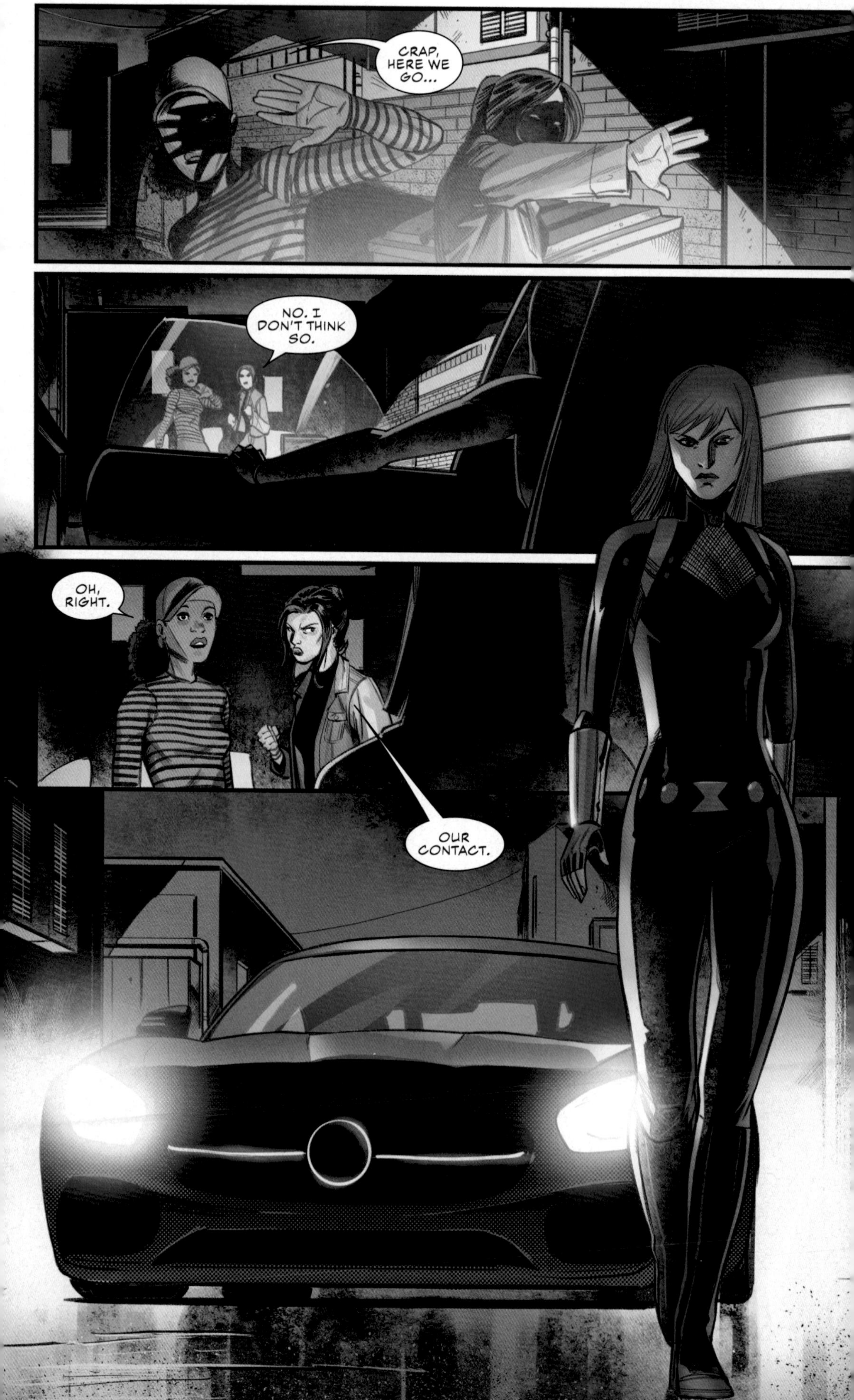
CRAP, HERE WE GO...
NO. I DON'T THINK SO.
OH, RIGHT.
OUR CONTACT.

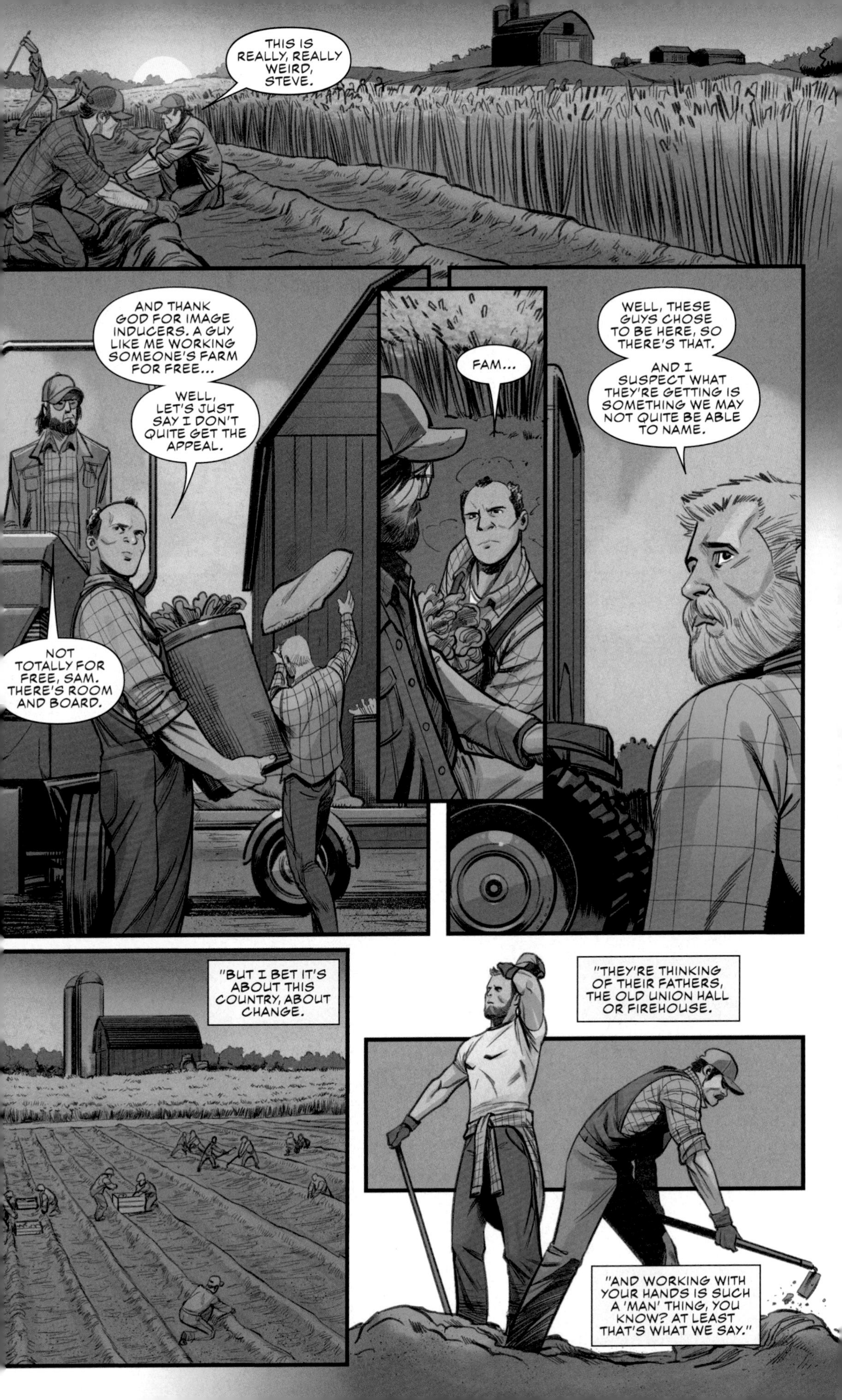
THIS IS REALLY, REALLY WEIRD, STEVE.
AND THANK GOD FOR IMAGE INDUCERS. A GUY LIKE ME WORKING SOMEONE'S FARM FOR FREE...
WELL, LET'S JUST SAY I DON'T QUITE GET THE APPEAL.
NOT TOTALLY FOR FREE, SAM. THERE'S ROOM AND BOARD.
FAM...
WELL, THESE GUYS CHOSE TO BE HERE, SO THERE'S THAT.
AND I SUSPECT WHAT THEY'RE GETTING IS SOMETHING WE MAY NOT QUITE BE ABLE TO NAME.
"BUT I BET IT'S ABOUT THIS COUNTRY, ABOUT CHANGE.
"THEY'RE THINKING OF THEIR FATHERS, THE OLD UNION HALL OR FIREHOUSE.
"AND WORKING WITH YOUR HANDS IS SUCH A 'MAN' THING, YOU KNOW? AT LEAST THAT'S WHAT WE SAY."

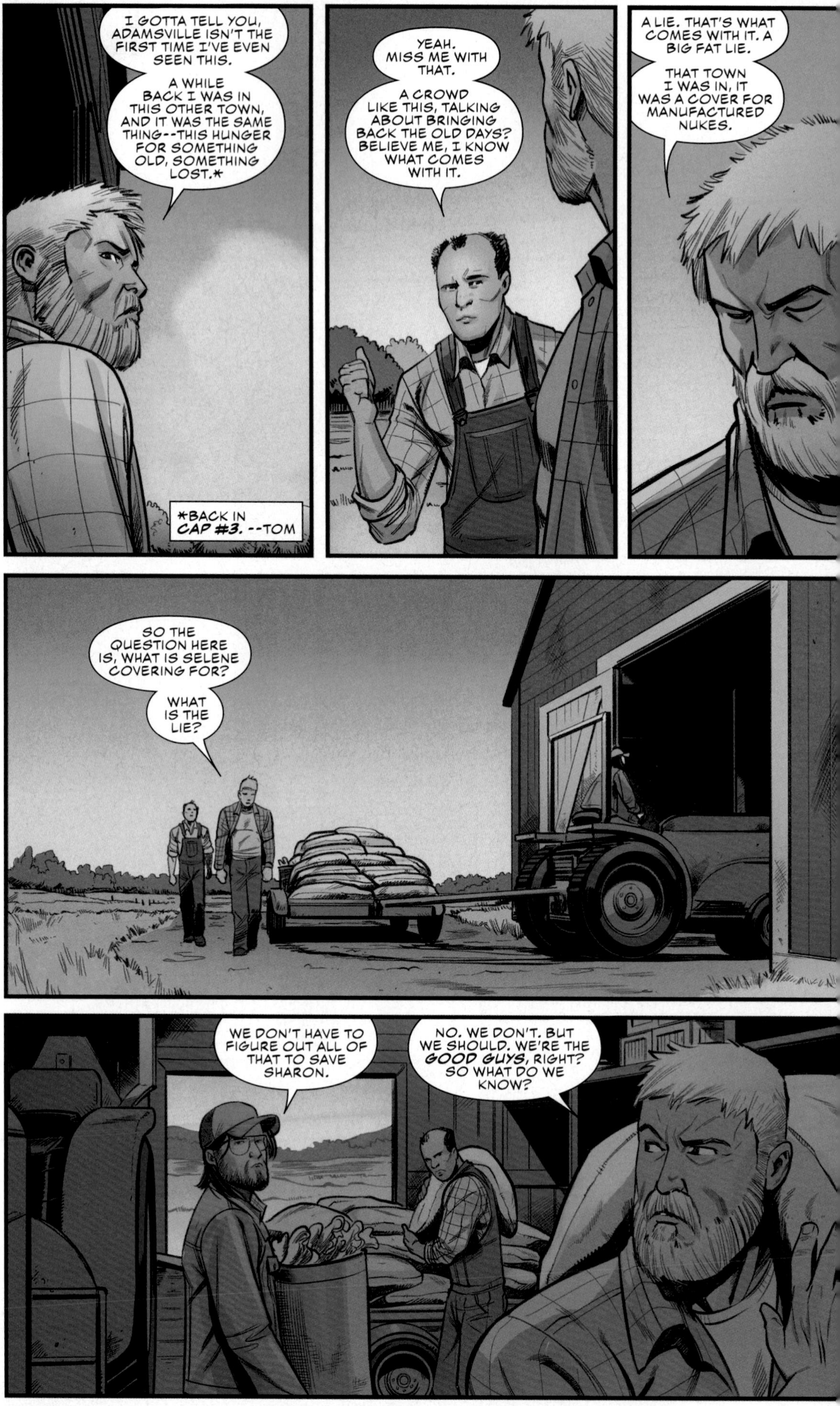
I GOTTA TELL YOU, ADAMSVILLE ISN'T THE FIRST TIME I'VE EVEN SEEN THIS.
A WHILE BACK I WAS IN THIS OTHER TOWN, AND IT WAS THE SAME THING--THIS HUNGER FOR SOMETHING OLD, SOMETHING LOST.*
*BACK IN CAP #3. --TOM
YEAH. MISS ME WITH THAT.
A CROWD LIKE THIS, TALKING ABOUT BRINGING BACK THE OLD DAYS? BELIEVE ME, I KNOW WHAT COMES WITH IT.
A LIE. THAT'S WHAT COMES WITH IT. A BIG FAT LIE.
THAT TOWN I WAS IN, IT WAS A COVER FOR MANUFACTURED NUKES.
SO THE QUESTION HERE IS, WHAT IS SELENE COVERING FOR?
WHAT IS THE LIE?
WE DON'T HAVE TO FIGURE OUT ALL OF THAT TO SAVE SHARON.
NO. WE DON'T. BUT WE SHOULD. WE'RE THE GOOD GUYS, RIGHT? SO WHAT DO WE KNOW?

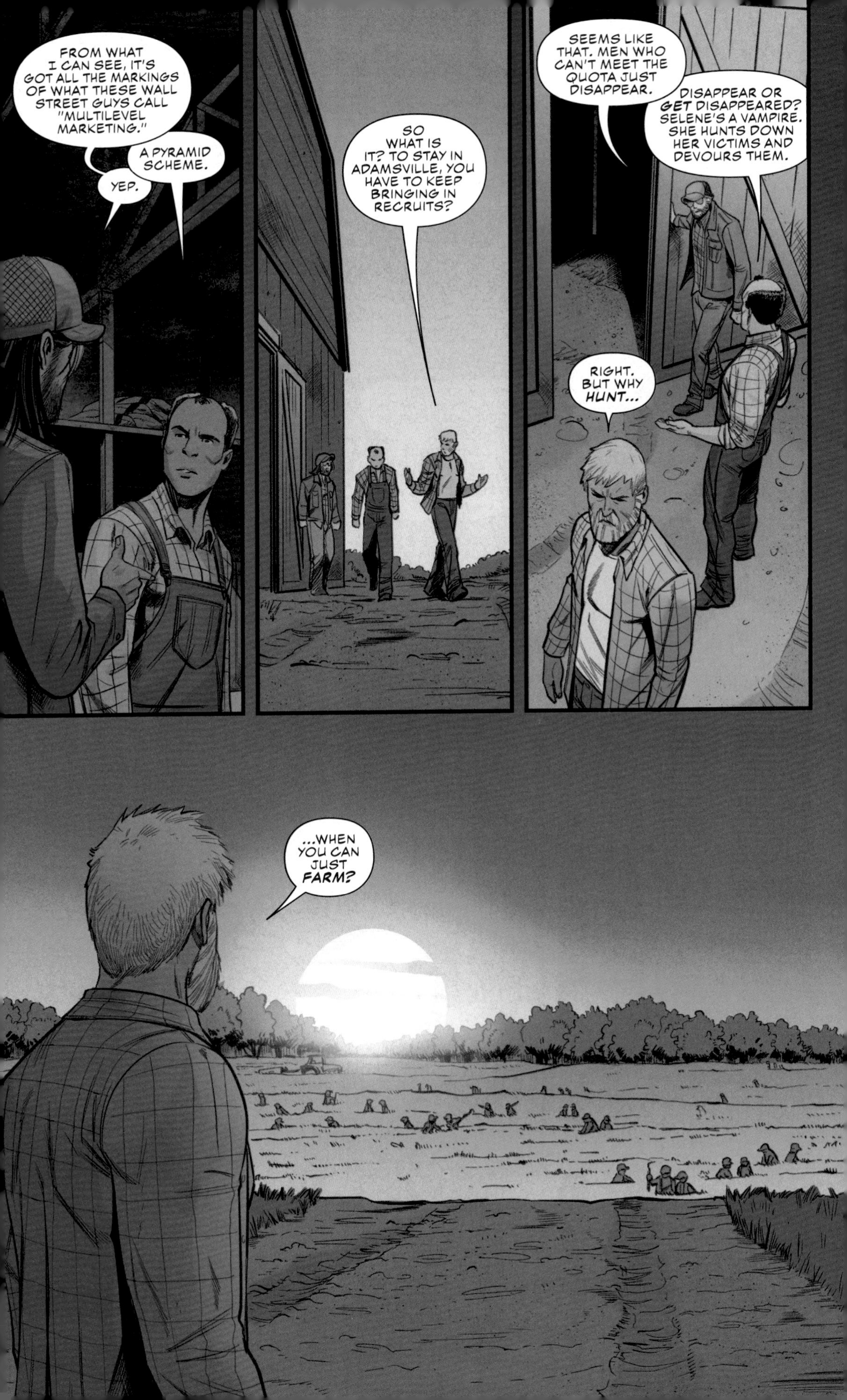
FROM WHAT I CAN SEE, IT'S GOT ALL THE MARKINGS OF WHAT THESE WALL STREET GUYS CALL "MULTILEVEL MARKETING."
A PYRAMID SCHEME.
YEP.
SO WHAT IS IT? TO STAY IN ADAMSVILLE, YOU HAVE TO KEEP BRINGING IN RECRUITS?
SEEMS LIKE THAT. MEN WHO CAN'T MEET THE QUOTA JUST DISAPPEAR.
DISAPPEAR OR **GET** DISAPPEARED? SELENE'S A VAMPIRE. SHE HUNTS DOWN HER VICTIMS AND DEVOURS THEM.
RIGHT. BUT WHY ***HUNT...***
...WHEN YOU CAN JUST ***FARM?***

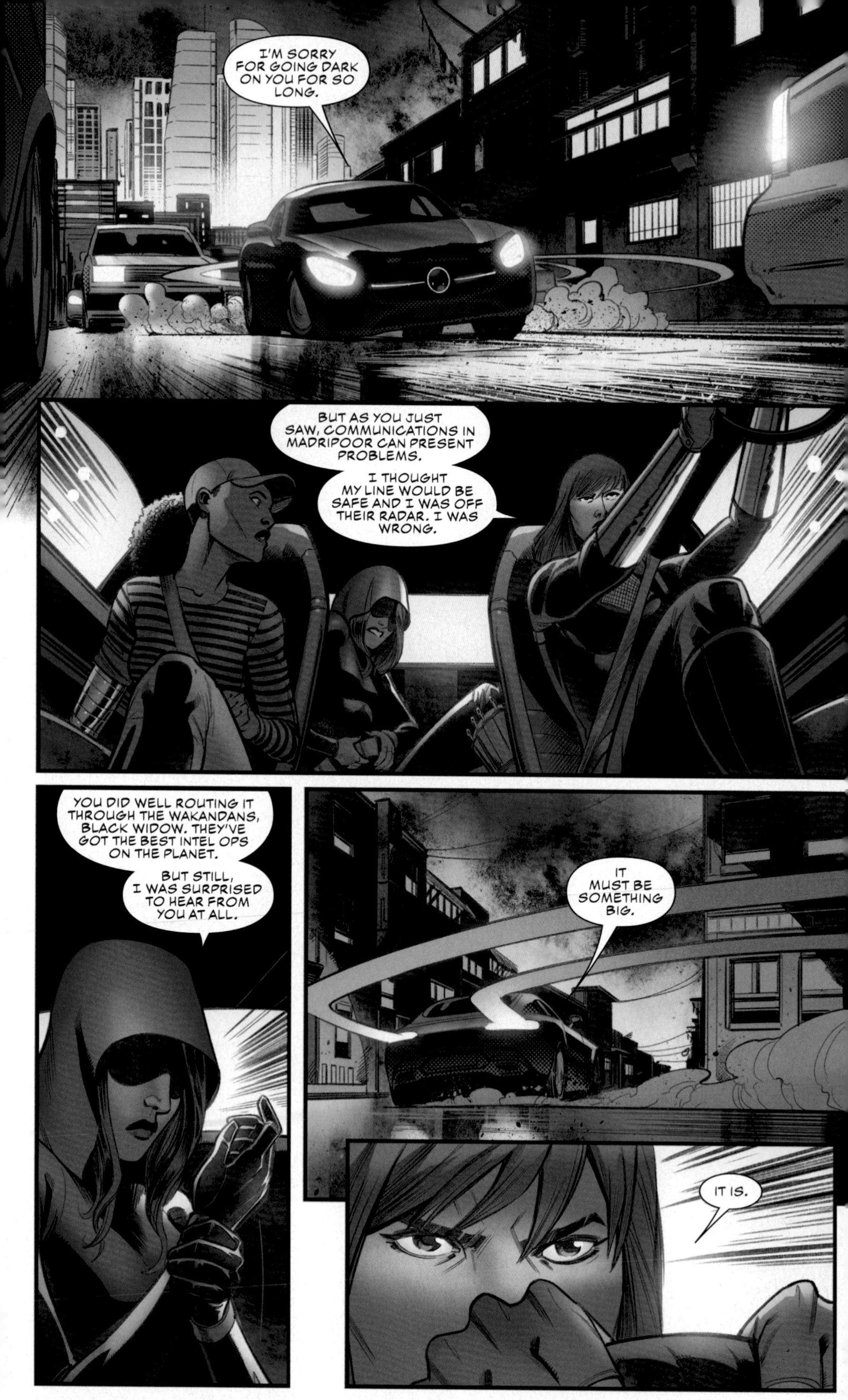
I'M SORRY FOR GOING DARK ON YOU FOR SO LONG.
BUT AS YOU JUST SAW, COMMUNICATIONS IN MADRIPOOR CAN PRESENT PROBLEMS.
I THOUGHT MY LINE WOULD BE SAFE AND I WAS OFF THEIR RADAR. I WAS WRONG.
YOU DID WELL ROUTING IT THROUGH THE WAKANDANS, BLACK WIDOW. THEY'VE GOT THE BEST INTEL OPS ON THE PLANET.
BUT STILL, I WAS SURPRISED TO HEAR FROM YOU AT ALL.
IT MUST BE SOMETHING BIG.
IT IS.

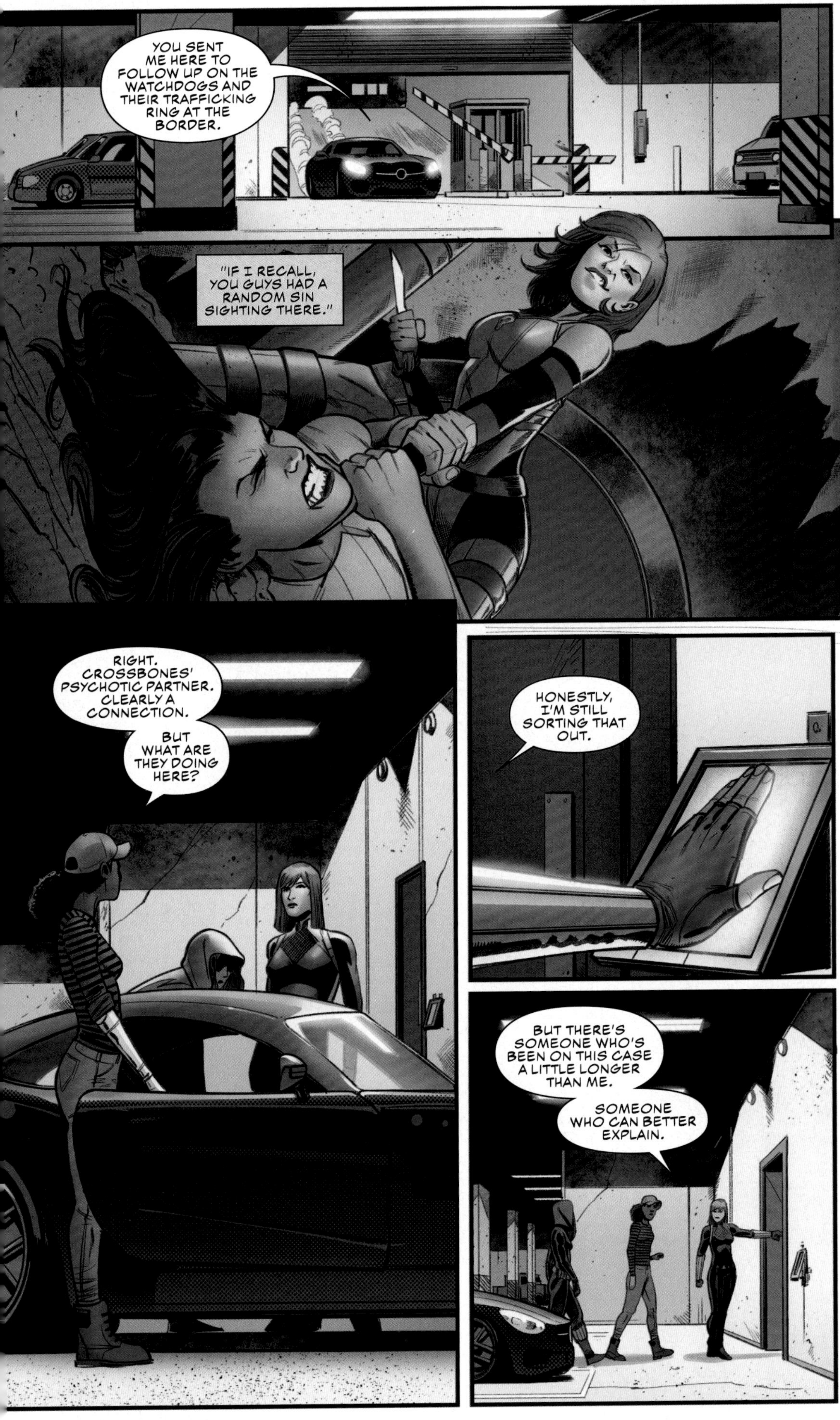
YOU SENT ME HERE TO FOLLOW UP ON THE WATCHDOGS AND THEIR TRAFFICKING RING AT THE BORDER.
"IF I RECALL, YOU GUYS HAD A RANDOM SIN SIGHTING THERE."
RIGHT. CROSSBONES' PSYCHOTIC PARTNER. CLEARLY A CONNECTION.
BUT WHAT ARE THEY DOING HERE?
HONESTLY, I'M STILL SORTING THAT OUT.
BUT THERE'S SOMEONE WHO'S BEEN ON THIS CASE A LITTLE LONGER THAN ME.
SOMEONE WHO CAN BETTER EXPLAIN.

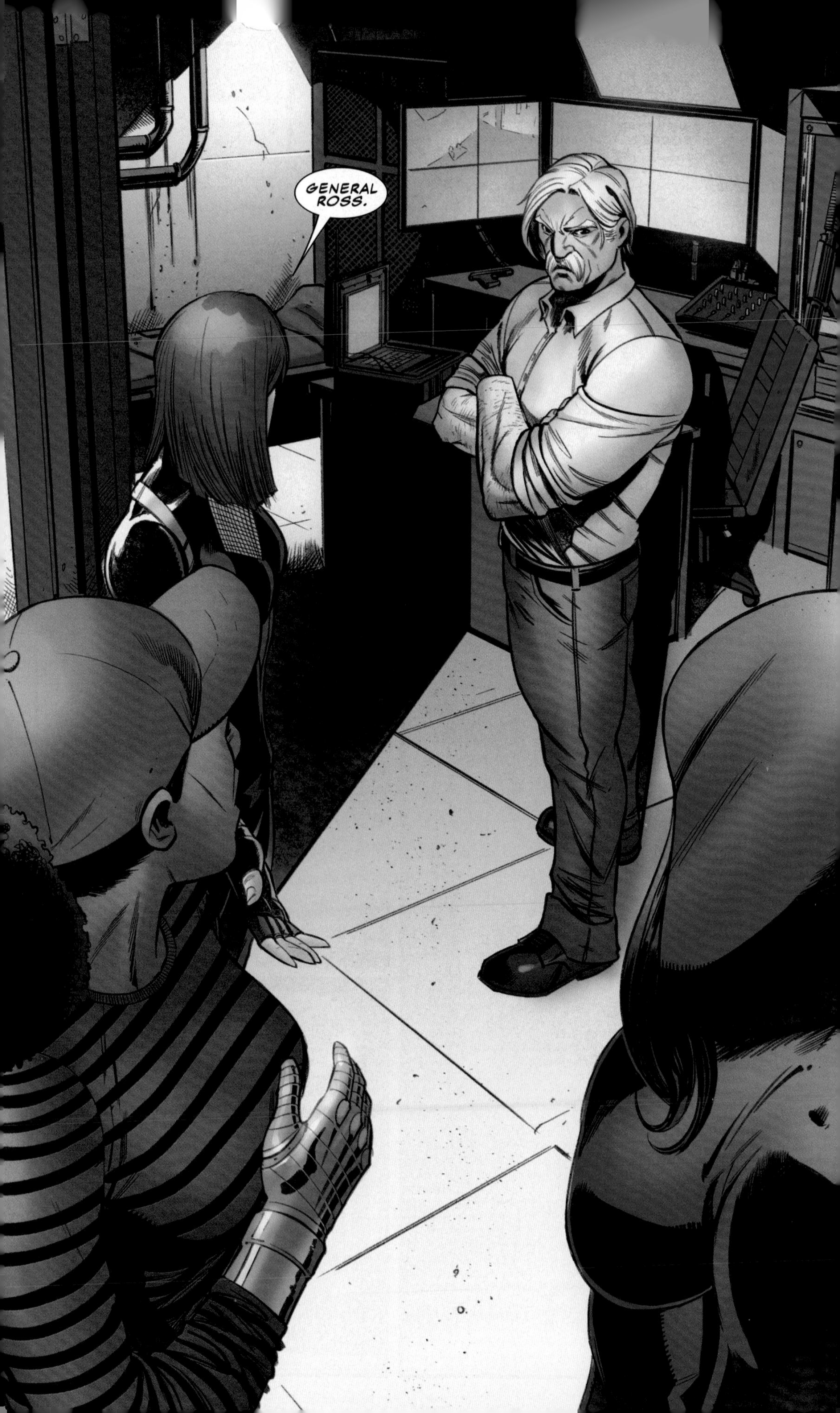
GENERAL ROSS.

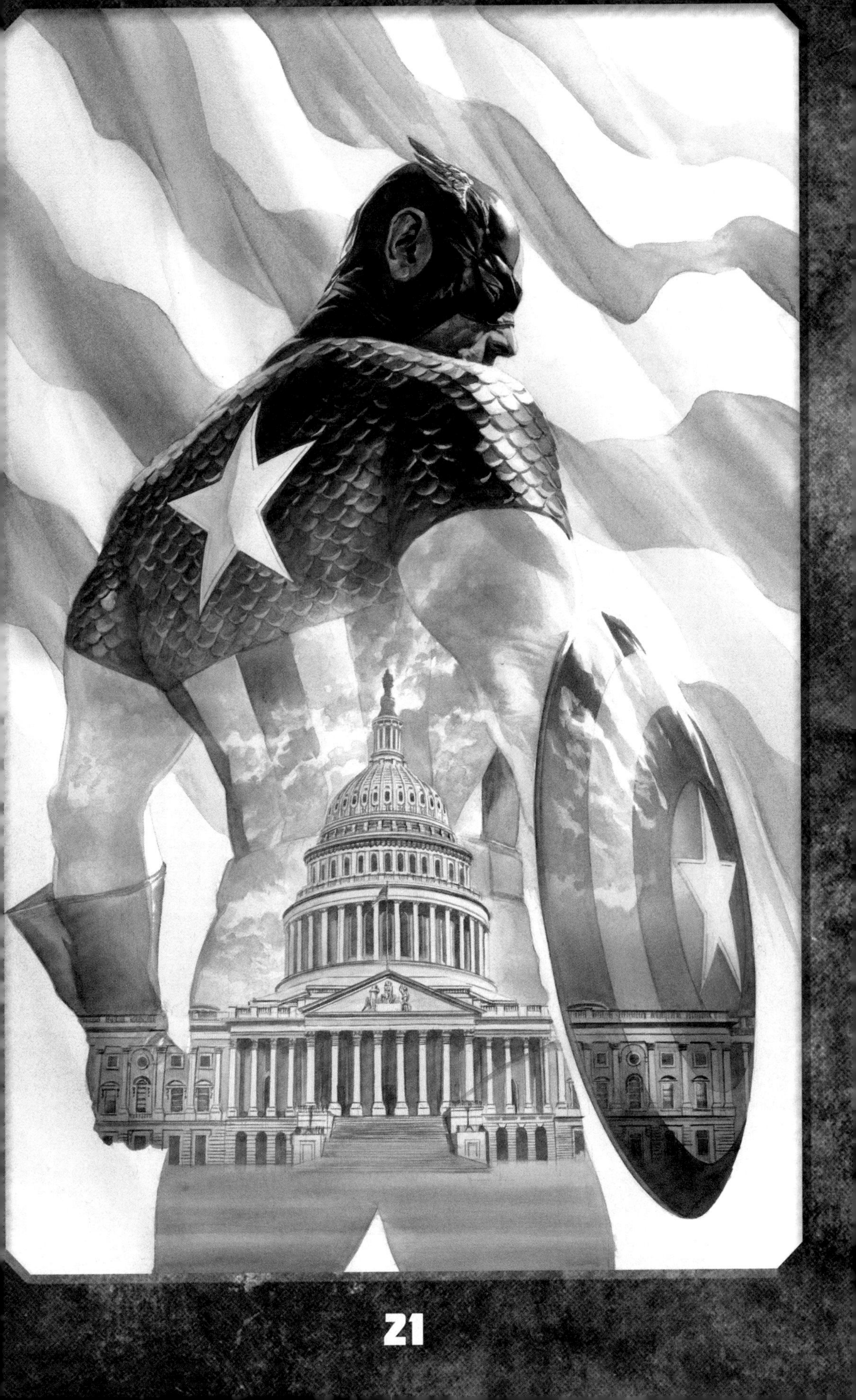

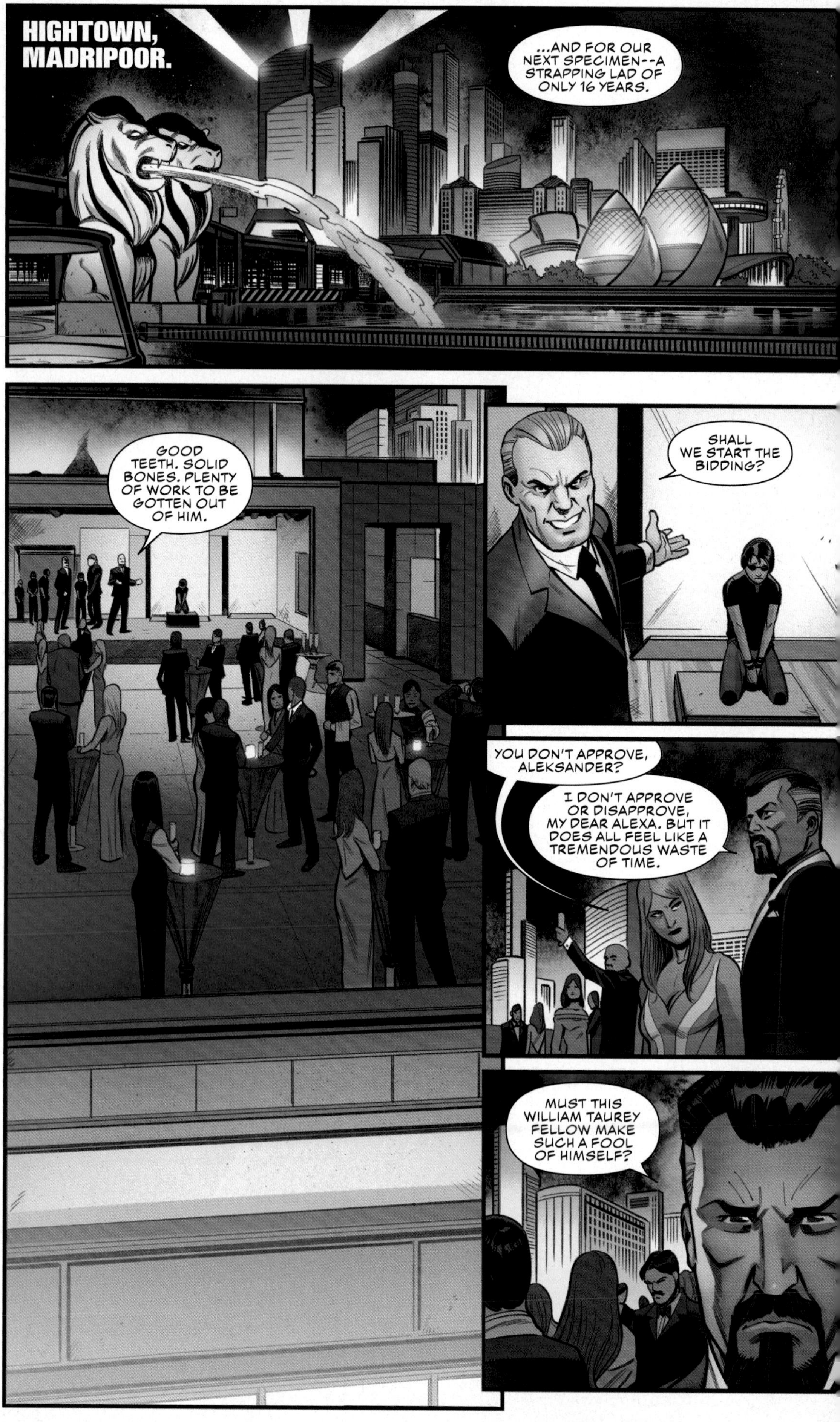
HIGHTOWN, MADRIPOOR.
...AND FOR OUR NEXT SPECIMEN--A STRAPPING LAD OF ONLY 16 YEARS.
GOOD TEETH. SOLID BONES. PLENTY OF WORK TO BE GOTTEN OUT OF HIM.
SHALL WE START THE BIDDING?
YOU DON'T APPROVE, ALEKSANDER?
I DON'T APPROVE OR DISAPPROVE, MY DEAR ALEXA. BUT IT DOES ALL FEEL LIKE A TREMENDOUS WASTE OF TIME.
MUST THIS WILLIAM TAUREY FELLOW MAKE SUCH A FOOL OF HIMSELF?

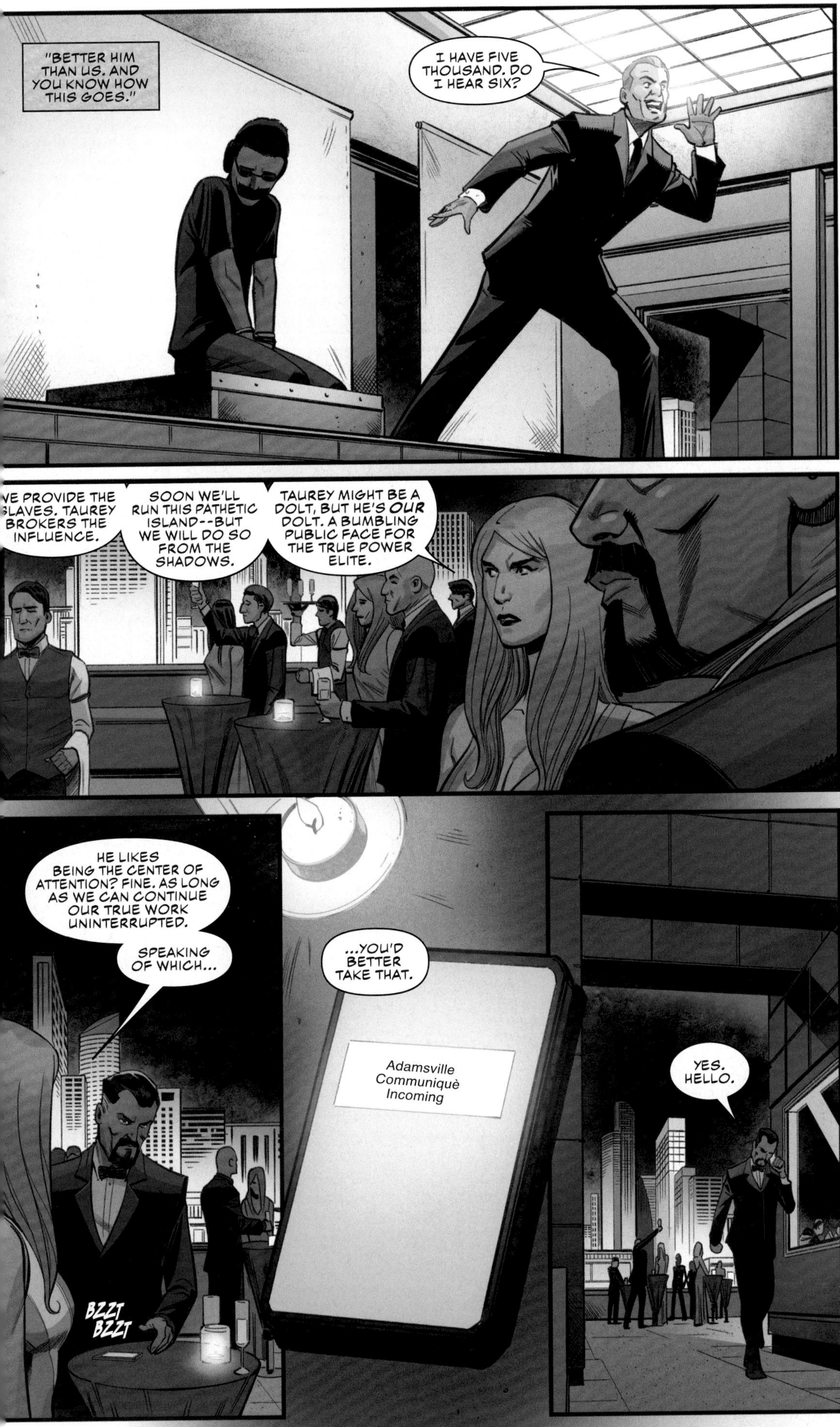
"BETTER HIM THAN US. AND YOU KNOW HOW THIS GOES."
I HAVE FIVE THOUSAND. DO I HEAR SIX?
WE PROVIDE THE SLAVES. TAUREY BROKERS THE INFLUENCE.
SOON WE'LL RUN THIS PATHETIC ISLAND--BUT WE WILL DO SO FROM THE SHADOWS.
TAUREY MIGHT BE A DOLT, BUT HE'S *OUR* DOLT. A BUMBLING PUBLIC FACE FOR THE TRUE POWER ELITE.
HE LIKES BEING THE CENTER OF ATTENTION? FINE. AS LONG AS WE CAN CONTINUE OUR TRUE WORK UNINTERRUPTED.
SPEAKING OF WHICH...
BZZT BZZT
...YOU'D BETTER TAKE THAT.
Adamsville Communiquè Incoming
YES. HELLO.

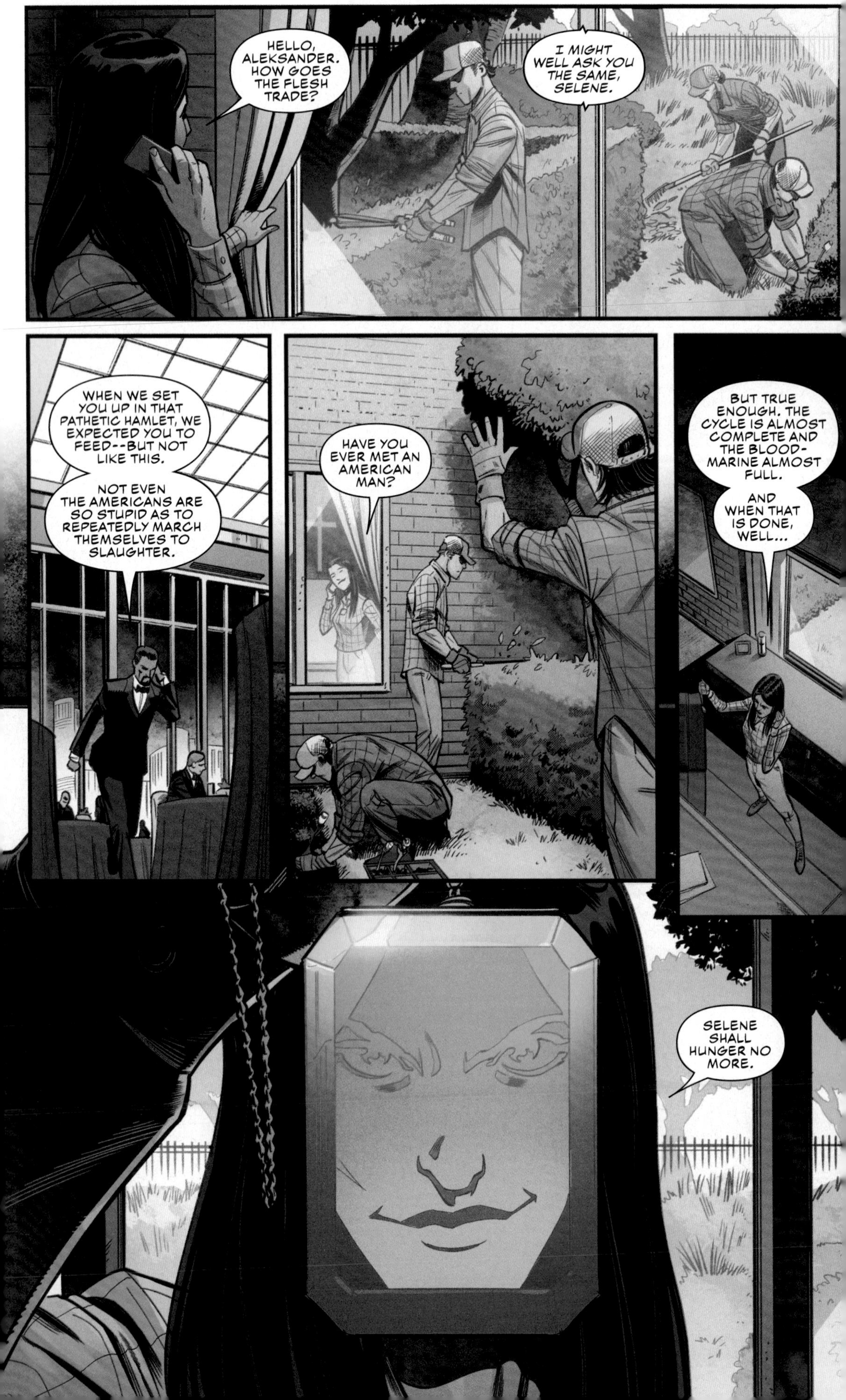

HELLO, ALEKSANDER. HOW GOES THE FLESH TRADE?
I MIGHT WELL ASK YOU THE SAME, SELENE.
WHEN WE SET YOU UP IN THAT PATHETIC HAMLET, WE EXPECTED YOU TO FEED--BUT NOT LIKE THIS.
NOT EVEN THE AMERICANS ARE SO STUPID AS TO REPEATEDLY MARCH THEMSELVES TO SLAUGHTER.
HAVE YOU EVER MET AN AMERICAN MAN?
BUT TRUE ENOUGH. THE CYCLE IS ALMOST COMPLETE AND THE BLOOD-MARINE ALMOST FULL.
AND WHEN THAT IS DONE, WELL...
SELENE SHALL HUNGER NO MORE.

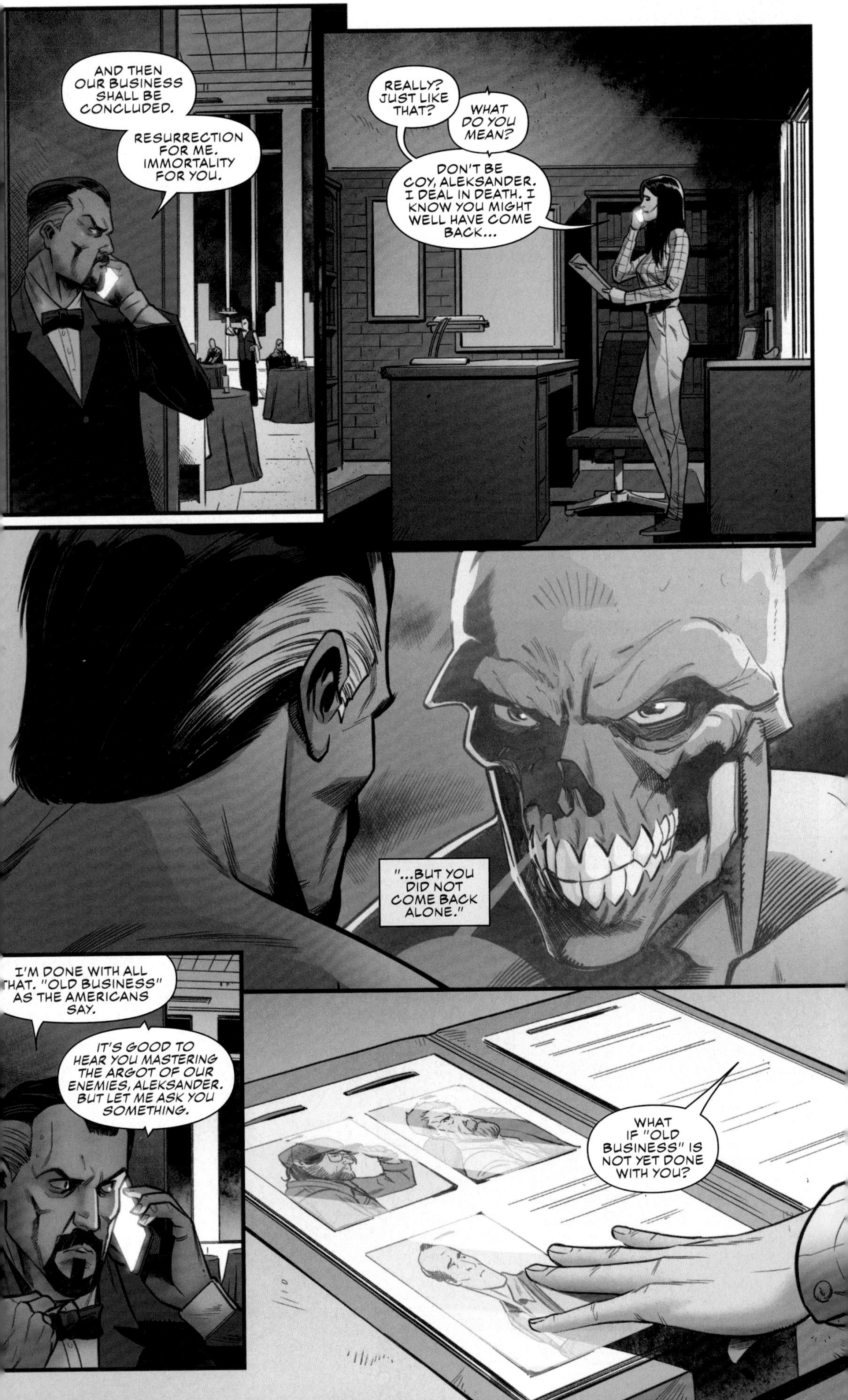
AND THEN OUR BUSINESS SHALL BE CONCLUDED.
RESURRECTION FOR ME. IMMORTALITY FOR YOU.
REALLY? JUST LIKE THAT?
WHAT DO YOU MEAN?
DON'T BE COY, ALEKSANDER. I DEAL IN DEATH. I KNOW YOU MIGHT WELL HAVE COME BACK...
"...BUT YOU DID NOT COME BACK ALONE."
I'M DONE WITH ALL THAT. "OLD BUSINESS" AS THE AMERICANS SAY.
IT'S GOOD TO HEAR YOU MASTERING THE ARGOT OF OUR ENEMIES, ALEKSANDER. BUT LET ME ASK YOU SOMETHING.
WHAT IF "OLD BUSINESS" IS NOT YET DONE WITH YOU?

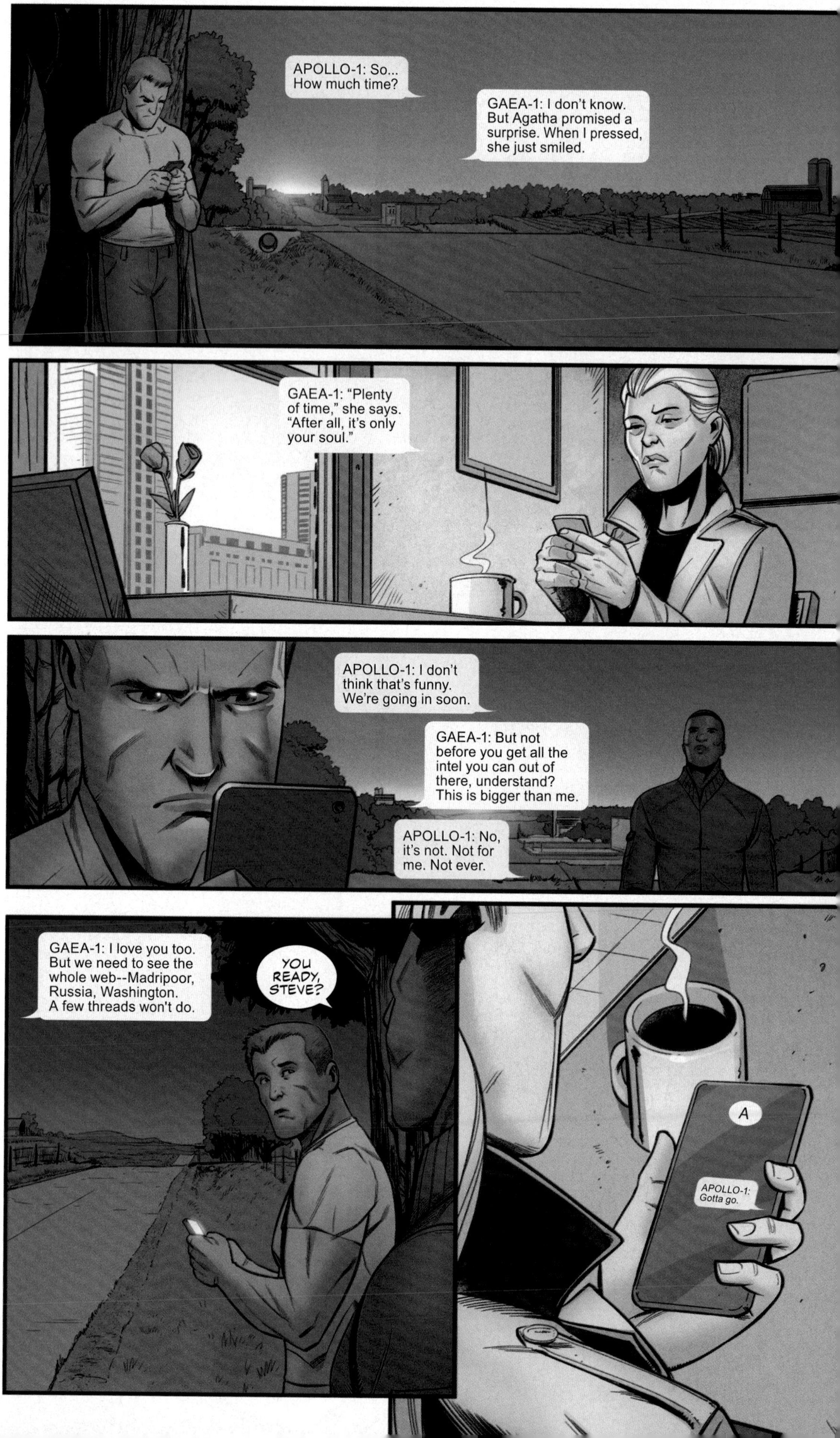
APOLLO-1: So... How much time?
GAEA-1: I don't know. But Agatha promised a surprise. When I pressed, she just smiled.
GAEA-1: "Plenty of time," she says. "After all, it's only your soul."
APOLLO-1: I don't think that's funny. We're going in soon.
GAEA-1: But not before you get all the intel you can out of there, understand? This is bigger than me.
APOLLO-1: No, it's not. Not for me. Not ever.
GAEA-1: I love you too. But we need to see the whole web--Madripoor, Russia, Washington. A few threads won't do.
YOU READY, STEVE?
A
APOLLO-1: Gotta go.

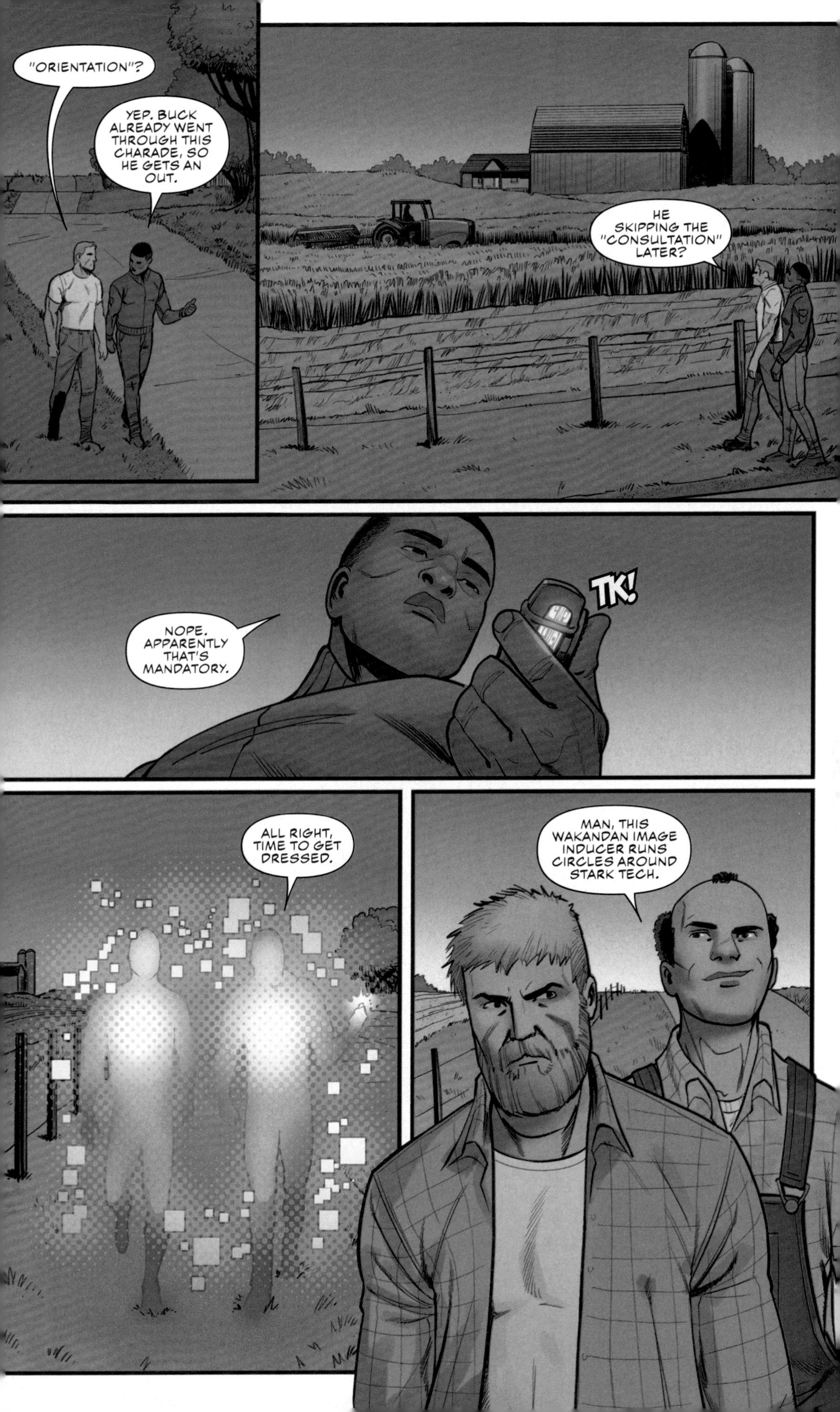
"ORIENTATION"?
YEP. BUCK ALREADY WENT THROUGH THIS CHARADE, SO HE GETS AN OUT.
HE SKIPPING THE "CONSULTATION" LATER?
TK!
NOPE. APPARENTLY THAT'S MANDATORY.
ALL RIGHT, TIME TO GET DRESSED.
MAN, THIS WAKANDAN IMAGE INDUCER RUNS CIRCLES AROUND STARK TECH.

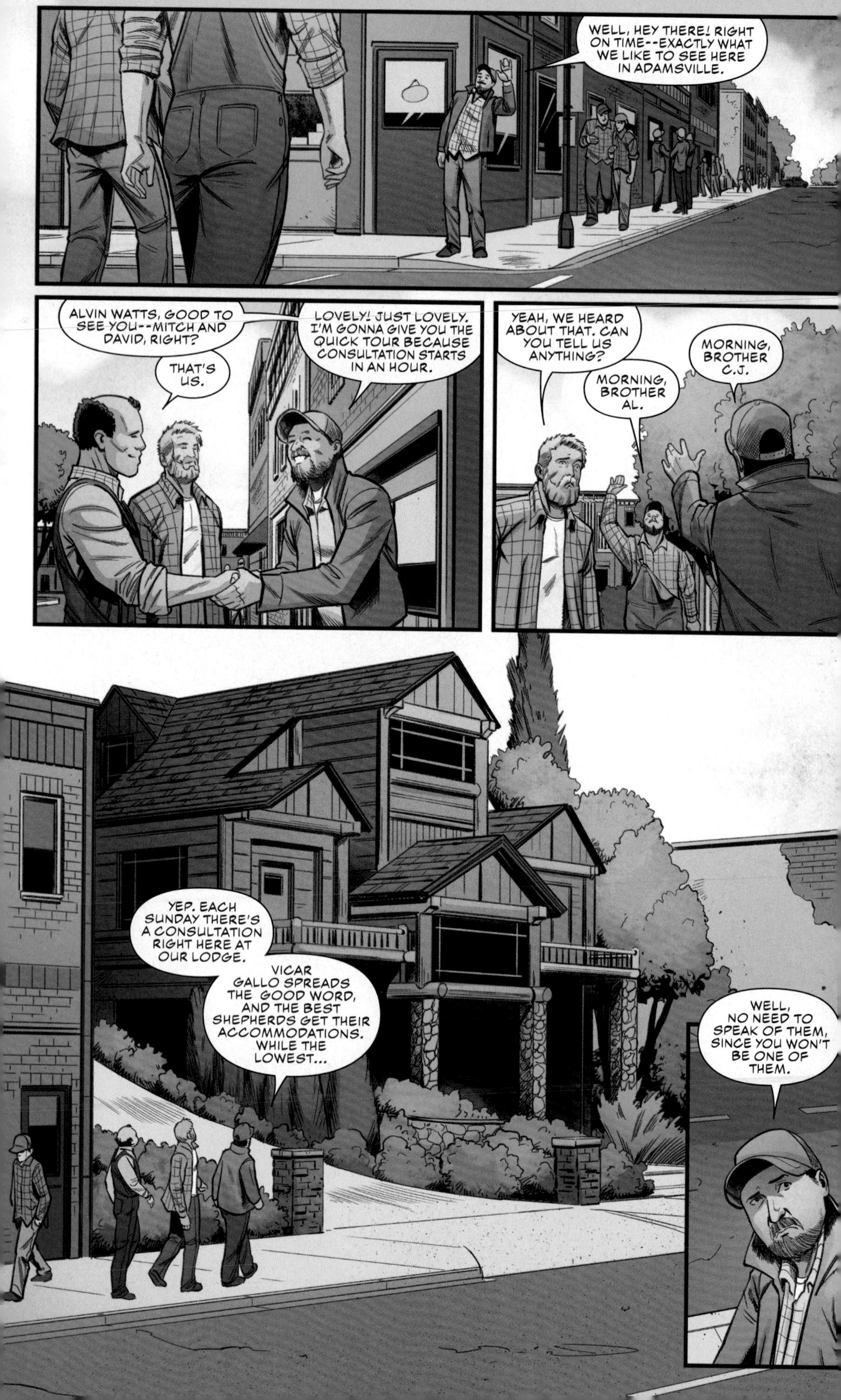
WELL, HEY THERE! RIGHT ON TIME--EXACTLY WHAT WE LIKE TO SEE HERE IN ADAMSVILLE.
ALVIN WATTS, GOOD TO SEE YOU--MITCH AND DAVID, RIGHT?
THAT'S US.
LOVELY! JUST LOVELY. I'M GONNA GIVE YOU THE QUICK TOUR BECAUSE CONSULTATION STARTS IN AN HOUR.
YEAH, WE HEARD ABOUT THAT. CAN YOU TELL US ANYTHING?
MORNING, BROTHER AL.
MORNING, BROTHER C.J.
YEP. EACH SUNDAY THERE'S A CONSULTATION RIGHT HERE AT OUR LODGE.
VICAR GALLO SPREADS THE GOOD WORD, AND THE BEST SHEPHERDS GET THEIR ACCOMMODATIONS. WHILE THE LOWEST...
WELL, NO NEED TO SPEAK OF THEM, SINCE YOU WON'T BE ONE OF THEM.

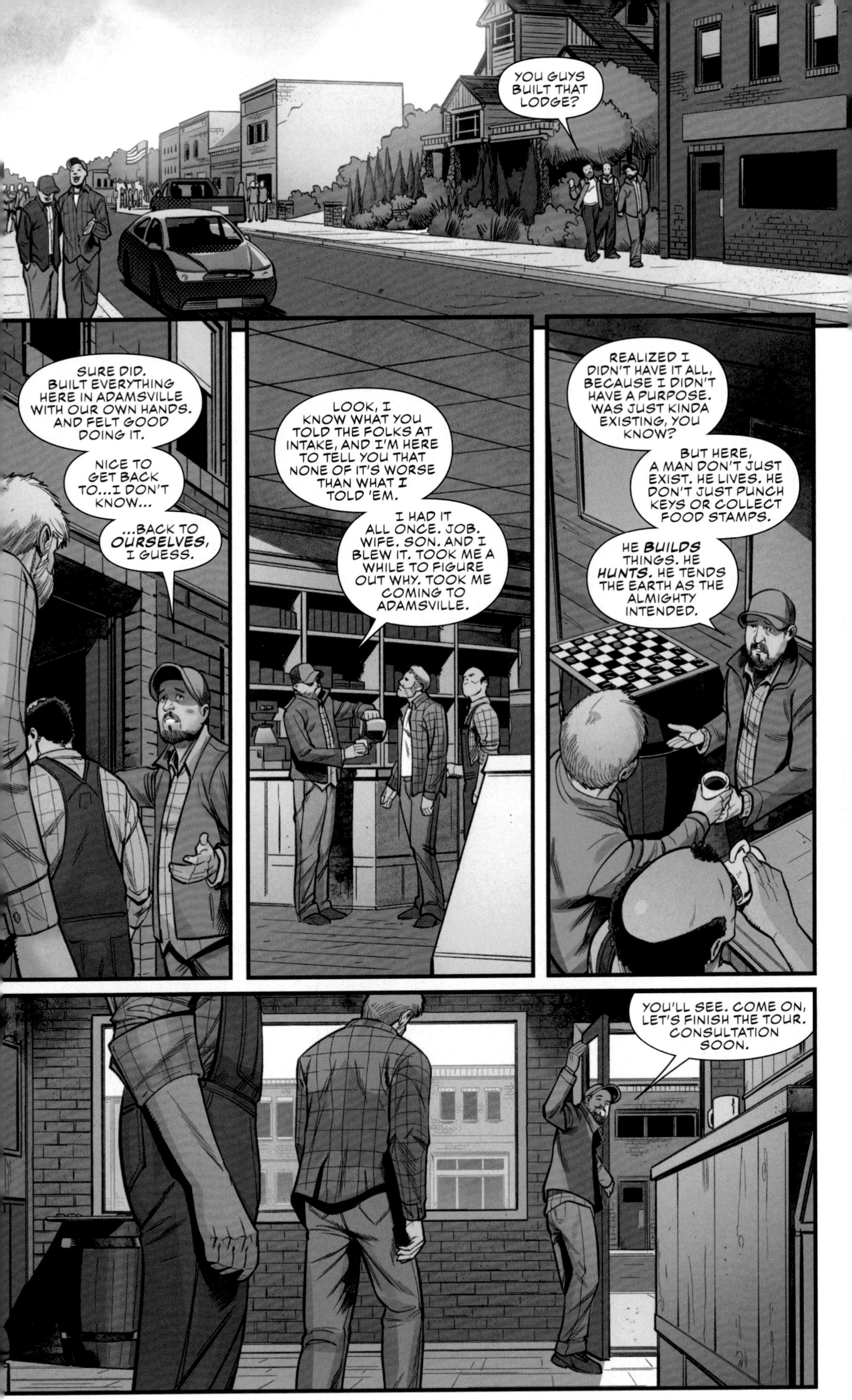
YOU GUYS BUILT THAT LODGE?
SURE DID. BUILT EVERYTHING HERE IN ADAMSVILLE WITH OUR OWN HANDS. AND FELT GOOD DOING IT.
NICE TO GET BACK TO...I DON'T KNOW...
...BACK TO OURSELVES, I GUESS.
LOOK, I KNOW WHAT YOU TOLD THE FOLKS AT INTAKE, AND I'M HERE TO TELL YOU THAT NONE OF IT'S WORSE THAN WHAT I TOLD 'EM.
I HAD IT ALL ONCE. JOB. WIFE. SON. AND I BLEW IT. TOOK ME A WHILE TO FIGURE OUT WHY. TOOK ME COMING TO ADAMSVILLE.
REALIZED I DIDN'T HAVE IT ALL, BECAUSE I DIDN'T HAVE A PURPOSE. WAS JUST KINDA EXISTING, YOU KNOW?
BUT HERE, A MAN DON'T JUST EXIST. HE LIVES. HE DON'T JUST PUNCH KEYS OR COLLECT FOOD STAMPS.
HE BUILDS THINGS. HE HUNTS. HE TENDS THE EARTH AS THE ALMIGHTY INTENDED.
YOU'LL SEE. COME ON, LET'S FINISH THE TOUR. CONSULTATION SOON.

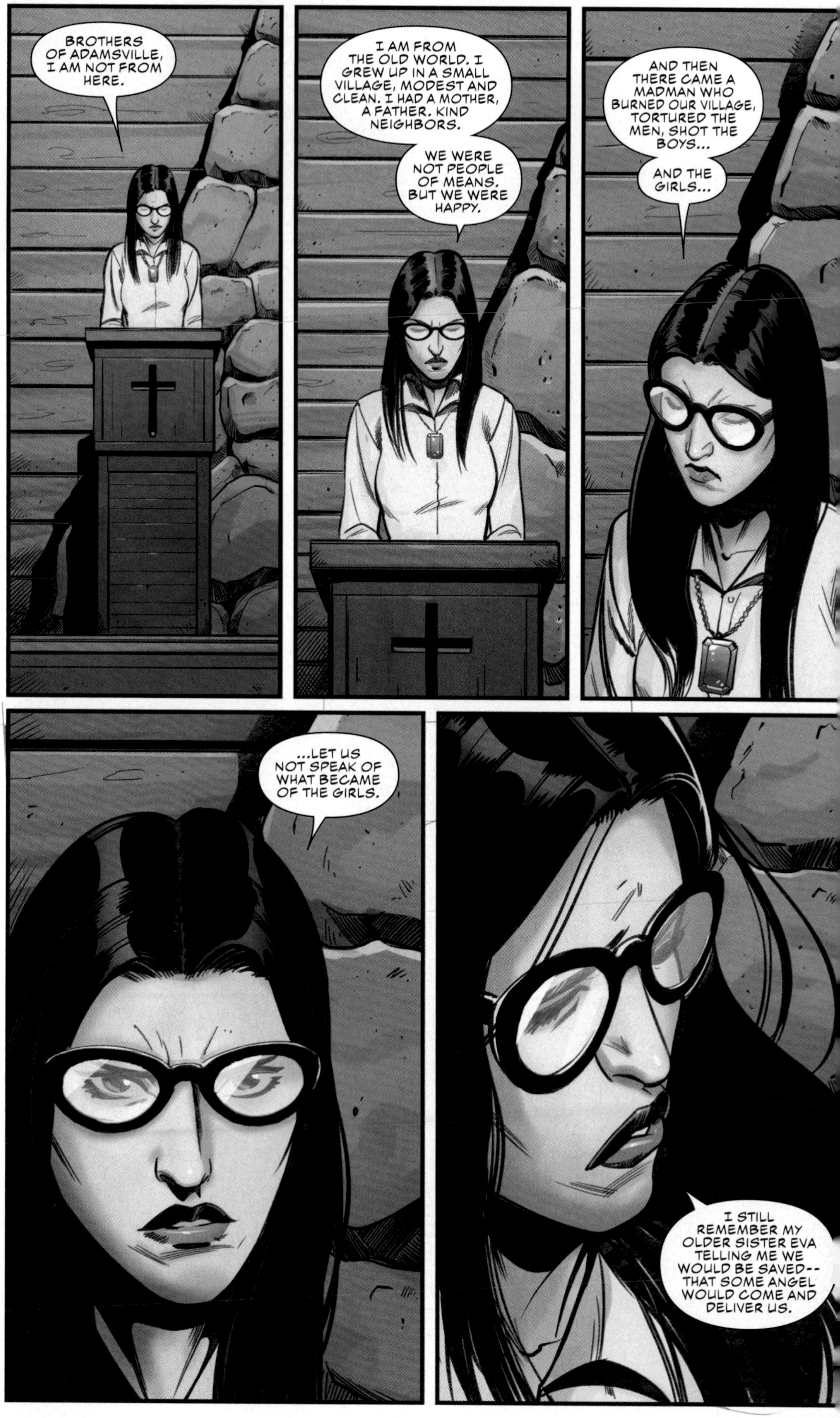
BROTHERS OF ADAMSVILLE, I AM NOT FROM HERE.
I AM FROM THE OLD WORLD. I GREW UP IN A SMALL VILLAGE, MODEST AND CLEAN. I HAD A MOTHER, A FATHER. KIND NEIGHBORS.
WE WERE NOT PEOPLE OF MEANS. BUT WE WERE HAPPY.
AND THEN THERE CAME A MADMAN WHO BURNED OUR VILLAGE, TORTURED THE MEN, SHOT THE BOYS...
AND THE GIRLS...
...LET US NOT SPEAK OF WHAT BECAME OF THE GIRLS.
I STILL REMEMBER MY OLDER SISTER EVA TELLING ME WE WOULD BE SAVED-- THAT SOME ANGEL WOULD COME AND DELIVER US.

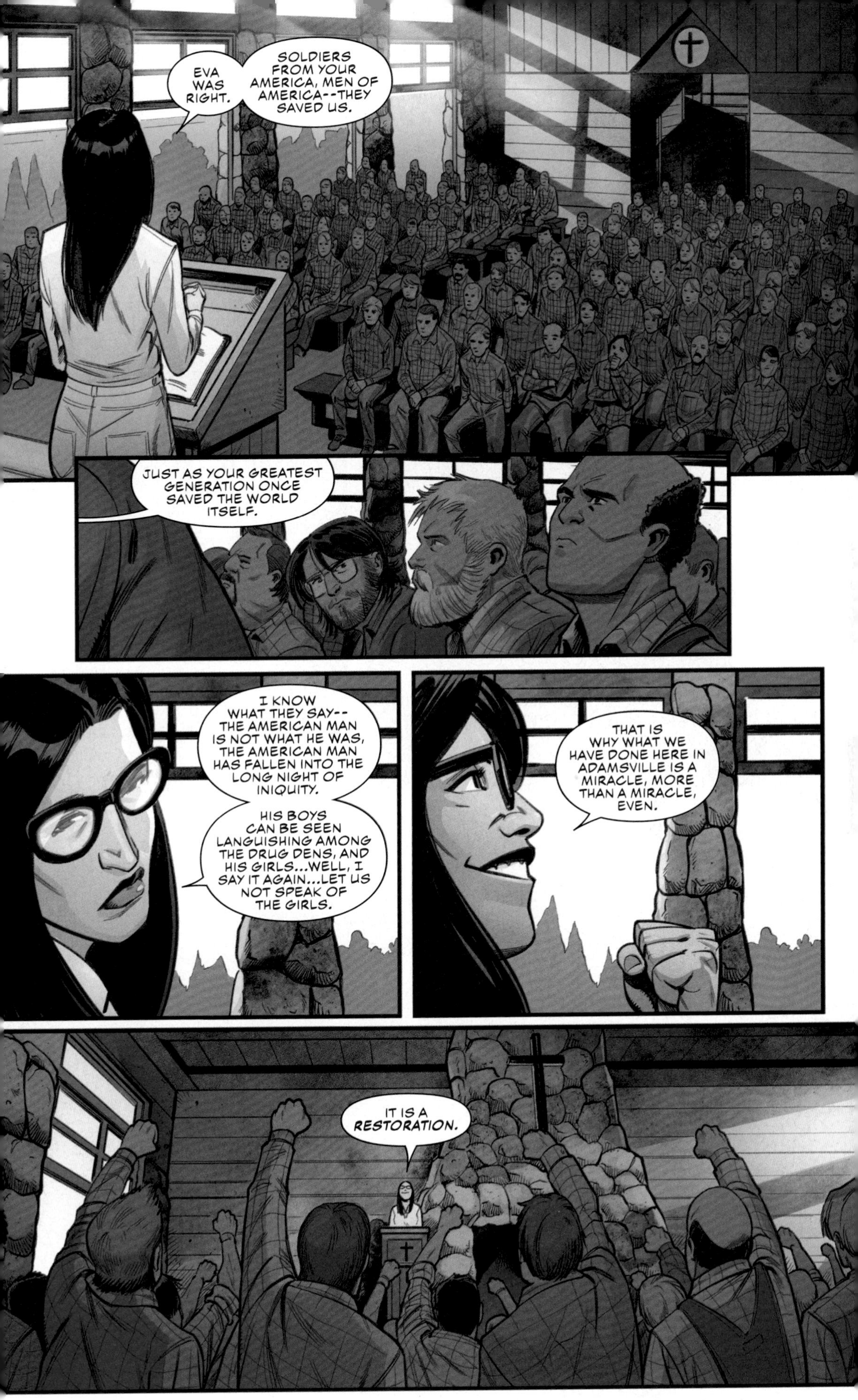
EVA WAS RIGHT.
SOLDIERS FROM YOUR AMERICA, MEN OF AMERICA--THEY SAVED US.
JUST AS YOUR GREATEST GENERATION ONCE SAVED THE WORLD ITSELF.
I KNOW WHAT THEY SAY--THE AMERICAN MAN IS NOT WHAT HE WAS, THE AMERICAN MAN HAS FALLEN INTO THE LONG NIGHT OF INIQUITY.
HIS BOYS CAN BE SEEN LANGUISHING AMONG THE DRUG DENS, AND HIS GIRLS...WELL, I SAY IT AGAIN...LET US NOT SPEAK OF THE GIRLS.
THAT IS WHY WHAT WE HAVE DONE HERE IN ADAMSVILLE IS A MIRACLE, MORE THAN A MIRACLE, EVEN.
IT IS A *RESTORATION.*

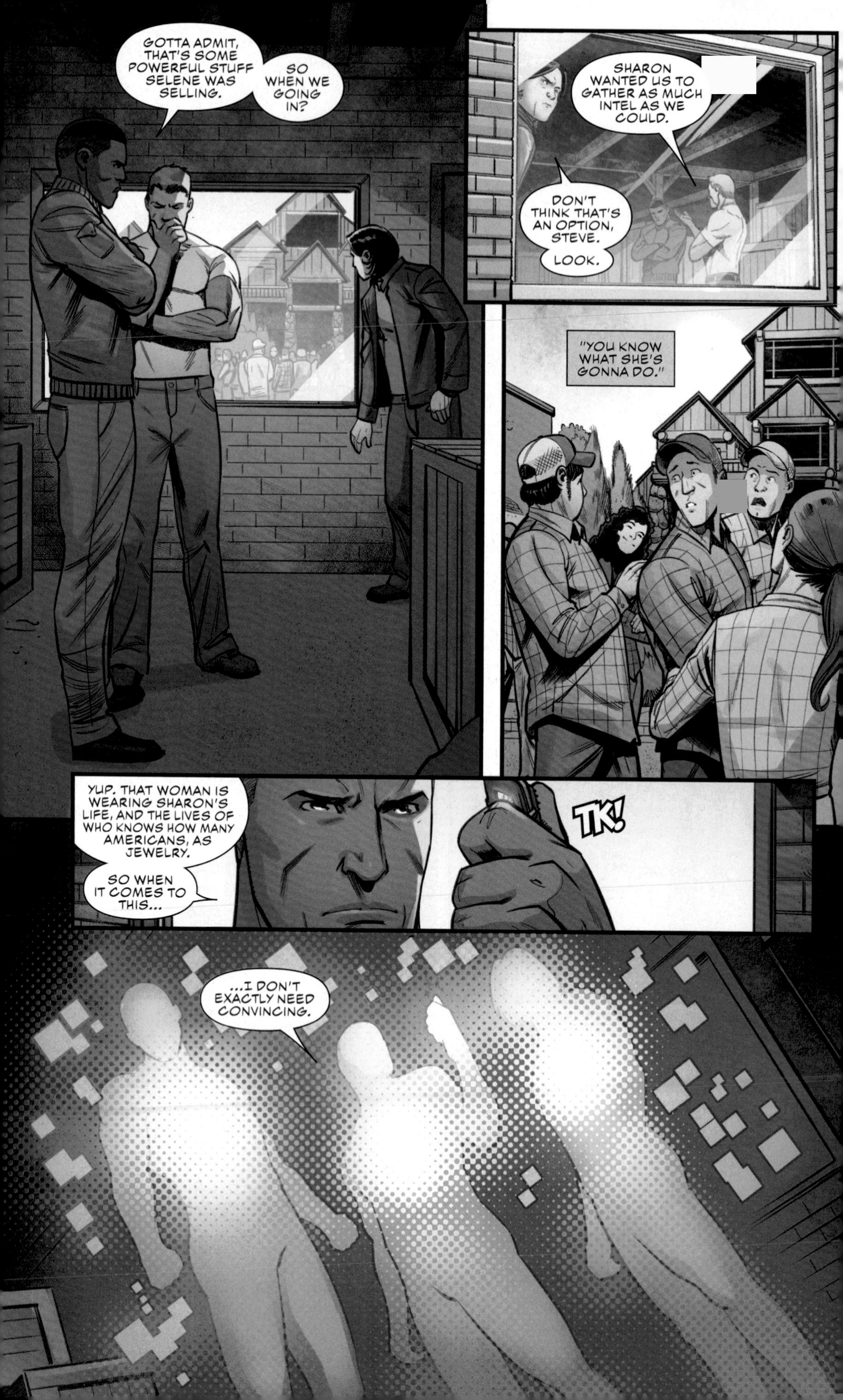
GOTTA ADMIT, THAT'S SOME POWERFUL STUFF SELENE WAS SELLING.
SO WHEN WE GOING IN?
SHARON WANTED US TO GATHER AS MUCH INTEL AS WE COULD.
DON'T THINK THAT'S AN OPTION, STEVE.
LOOK.
"YOU KNOW WHAT SHE'S GONNA DO."
YUP. THAT WOMAN IS WEARING SHARON'S LIFE, AND THE LIVES OF WHO KNOWS HOW MANY AMERICANS, AS JEWELRY.
SO WHEN IT COMES TO THIS...
TK!
...I DON'T EXACTLY NEED CONVINCING.

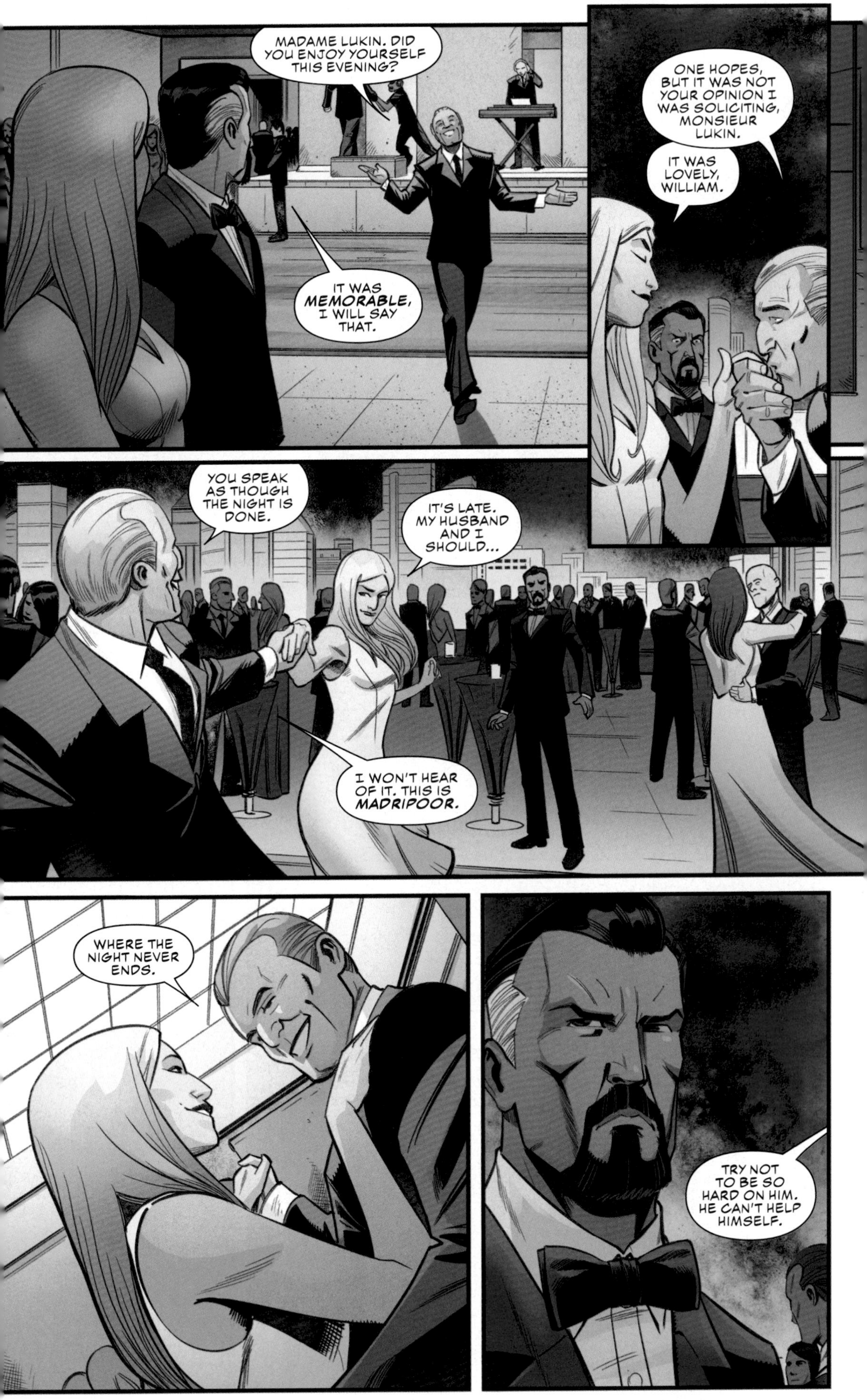
MADAME LUKIN. DID YOU ENJOY YOURSELF THIS EVENING?
IT WAS *MEMORABLE*, I WILL SAY THAT.
ONE HOPES, BUT IT WAS NOT YOUR OPINION I WAS SOLICITING, MONSIEUR LUKIN.
IT WAS LOVELY, WILLIAM.
YOU SPEAK AS THOUGH THE NIGHT IS DONE.
IT'S LATE. MY HUSBAND AND I SHOULD...
I WON'T HEAR OF IT. THIS IS *MADRIPOOR*.
WHERE THE NIGHT NEVER ENDS.
TRY NOT TO BE SO HARD ON HIM. HE CAN'T HELP HIMSELF.

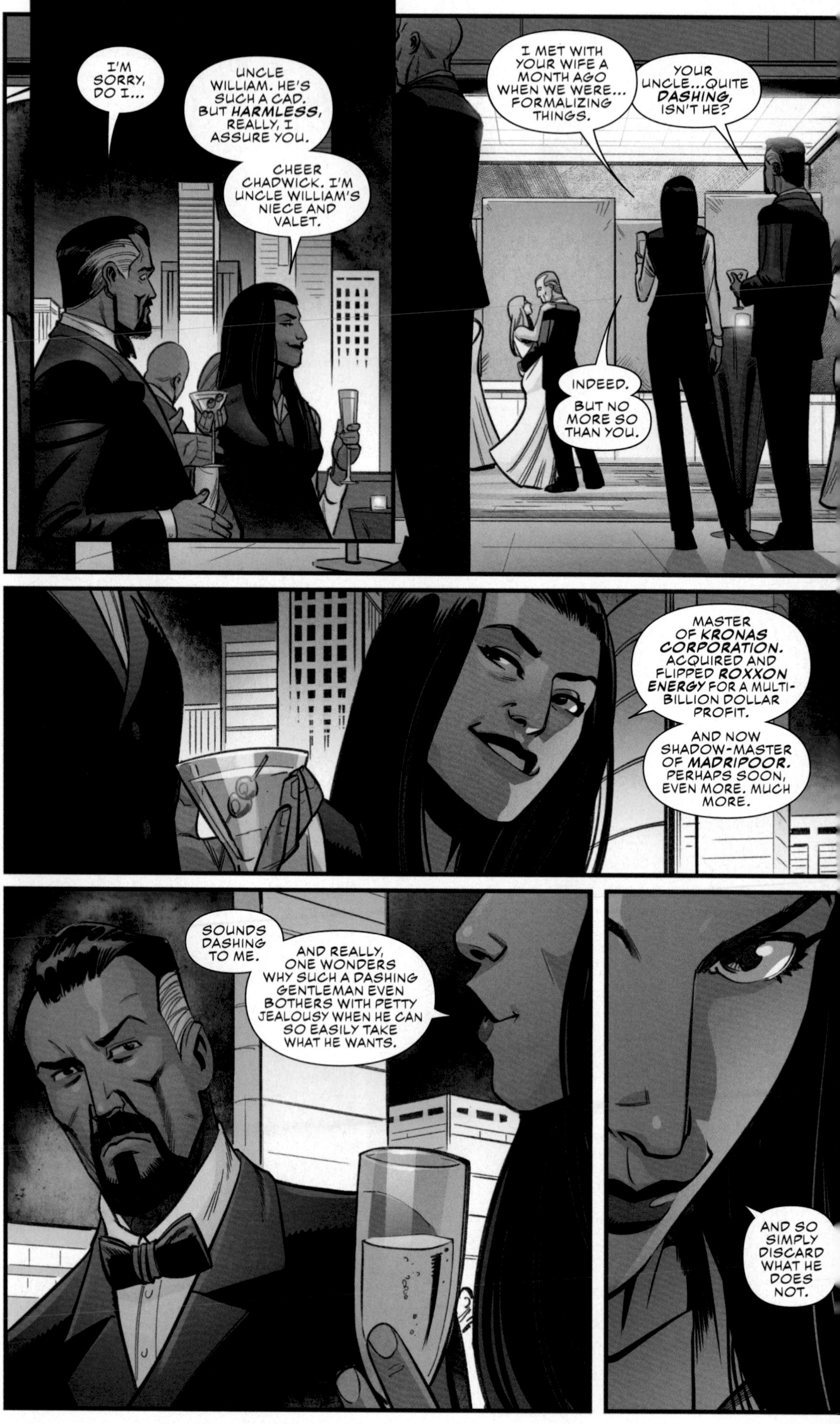
I'M SORRY, DO I...
UNCLE WILLIAM. HE'S SUCH A CAD. BUT HARMLESS, REALLY, I ASSURE YOU.
CHEER CHADWICK. I'M UNCLE WILLIAM'S NIECE AND VALET.
I MET WITH YOUR WIFE A MONTH AGO WHEN WE WERE... FORMALIZING THINGS.
YOUR UNCLE...QUITE DASHING, ISN'T HE?
INDEED.
BUT NO MORE SO THAN YOU.
MASTER OF KRONAS CORPORATION. ACQUIRED AND FLIPPED ROXXON ENERGY FOR A MULTI-BILLION DOLLAR PROFIT.
AND NOW SHADOW-MASTER OF MADRIPOOR. PERHAPS SOON, EVEN MORE. MUCH MORE.
SOUNDS DASHING TO ME.
AND REALLY, ONE WONDERS WHY SUCH A DASHING GENTLEMAN EVEN BOTHERS WITH PETTY JEALOUSY WHEN HE CAN SO EASILY TAKE WHAT HE WANTS.
AND SO SIMPLY DISCARD WHAT HE DOES NOT.

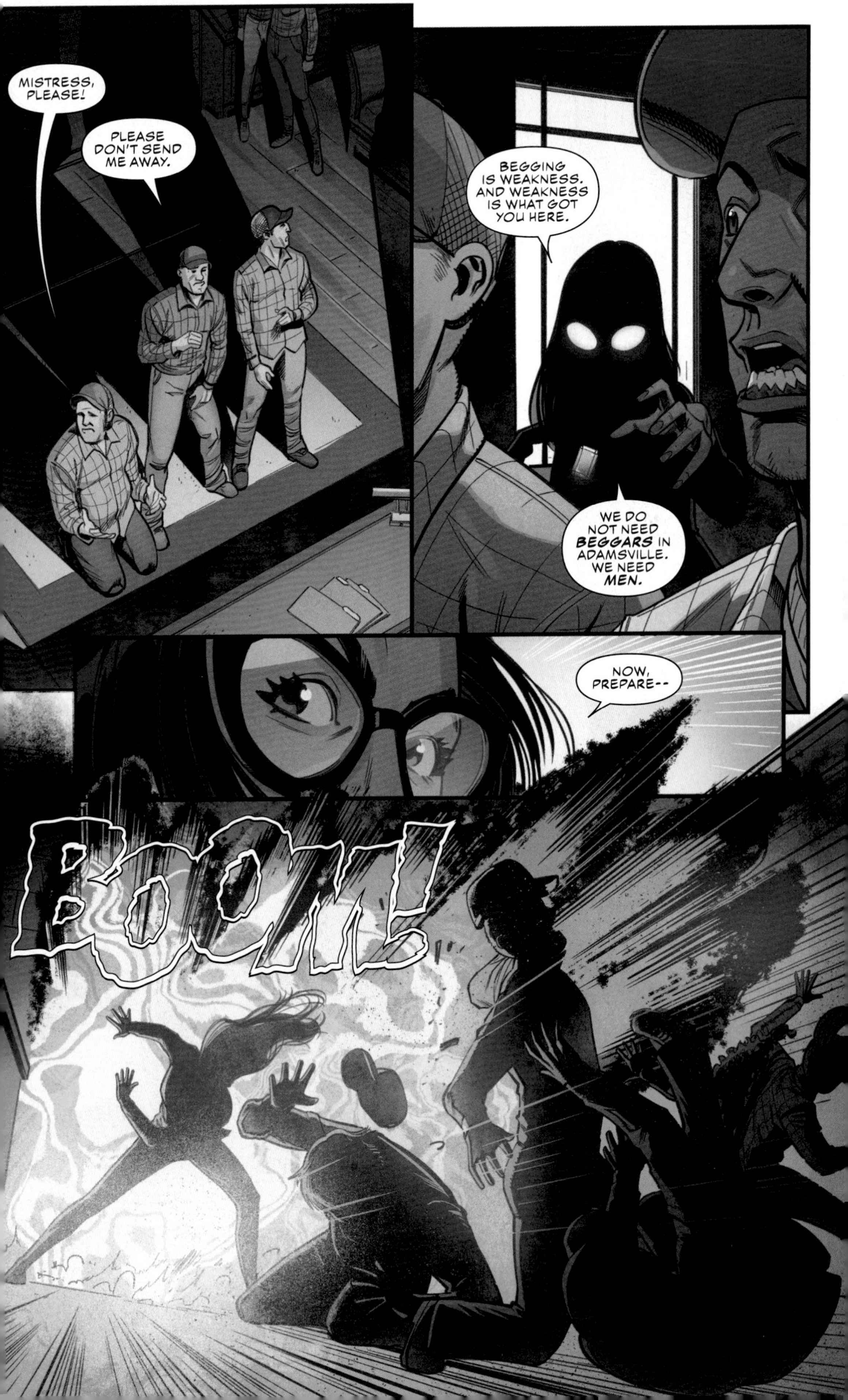
MISTRESS, PLEASE!
PLEASE DON'T SEND ME AWAY.
BEGGING IS WEAKNESS. AND WEAKNESS IS WHAT GOT YOU HERE.
WE DO NOT NEED **BEGGARS** IN ADAMSVILLE. WE NEED **MEN.**
NOW, PREPARE--
BOOM!

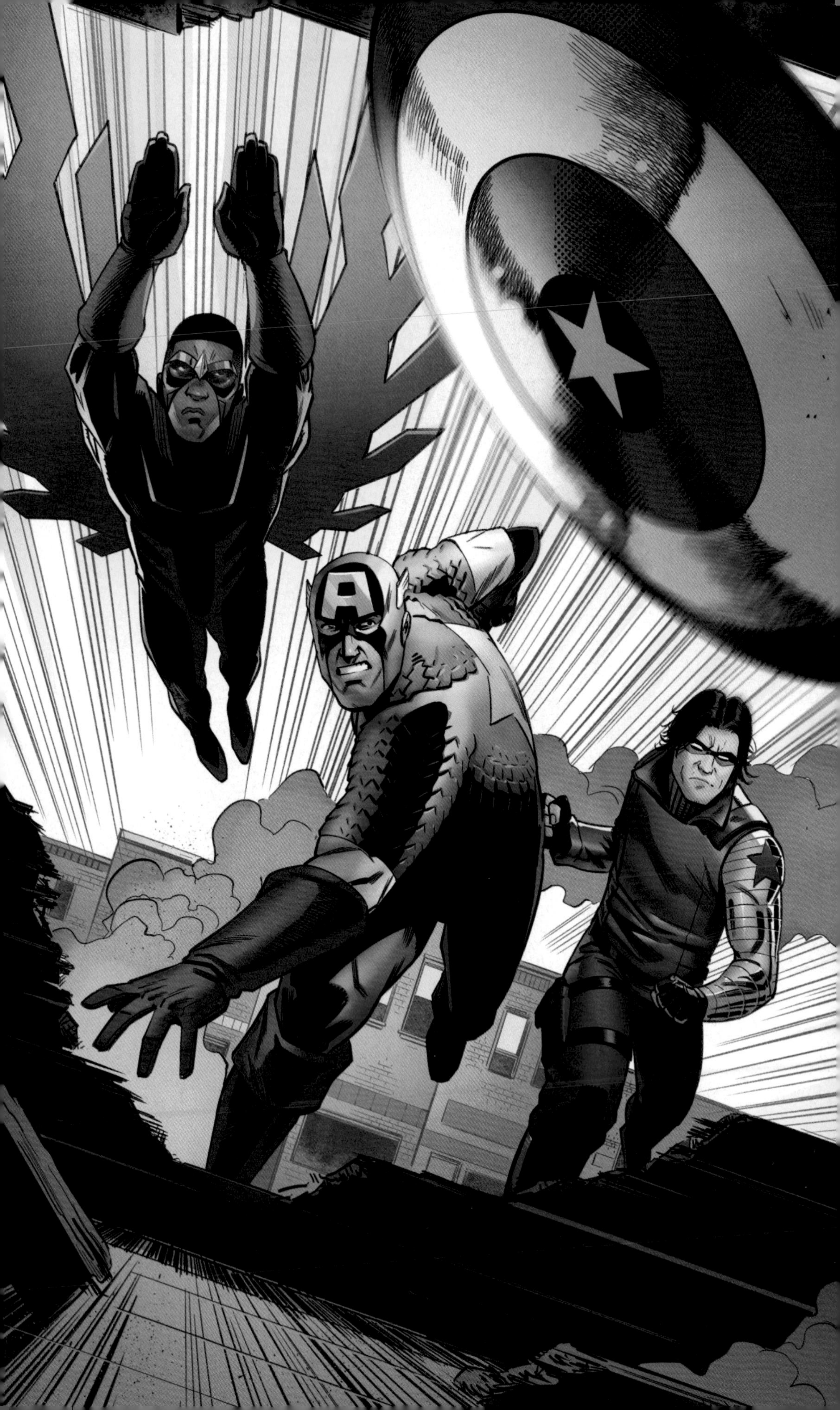

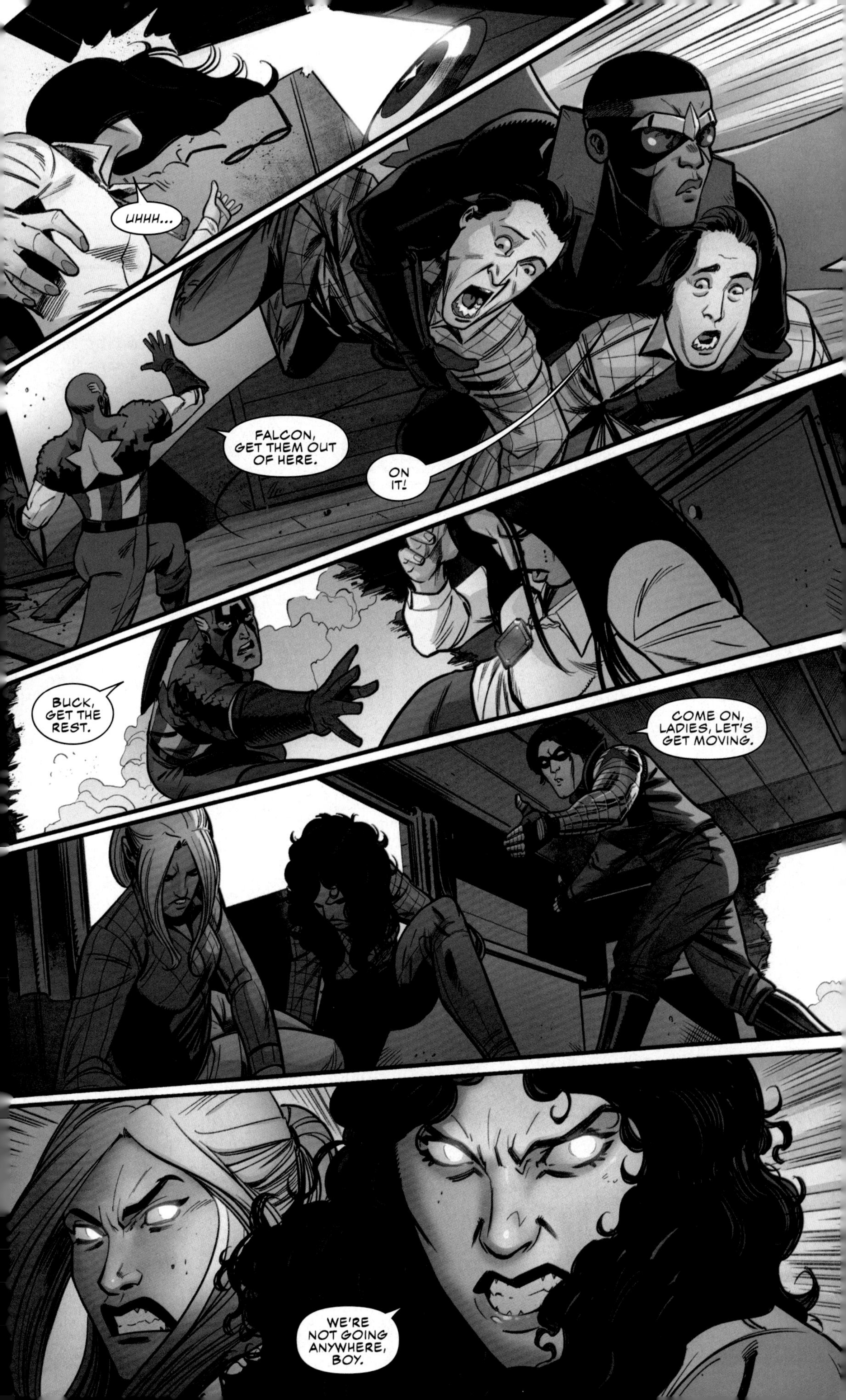
UHHH...
FALCON, GET THEM OUT OF HERE.
ON IT!
BUCK, GET THE REST.
COME ON, LADIES, LET'S GET MOVING.
WE'RE NOT GOING ANYWHERE, BOY.

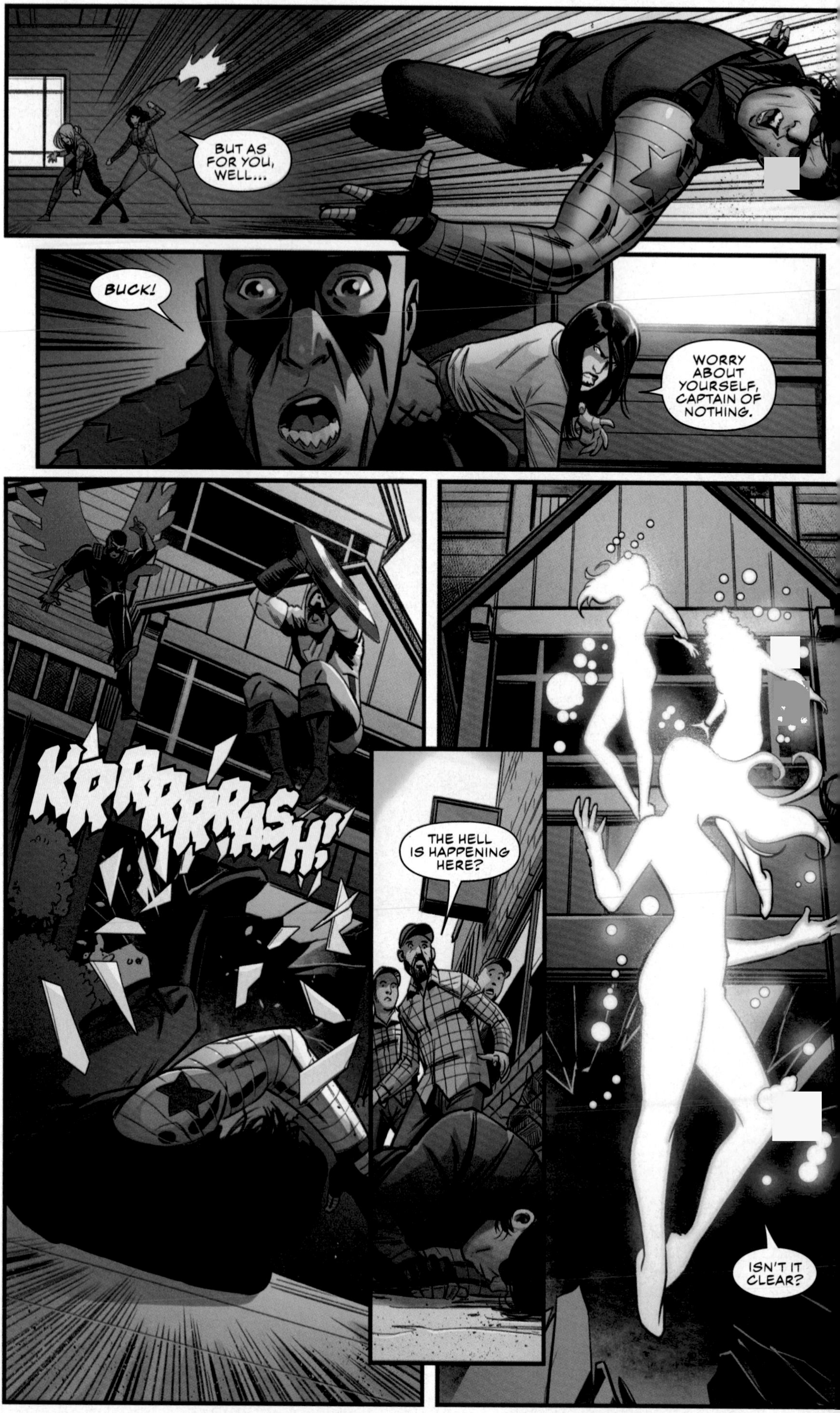
BUT AS FOR YOU, WELL...
BUCK!
WORRY ABOUT YOURSELF, CAPTAIN OF NOTHING.
KRRRRRASH!
THE HELL IS HAPPENING HERE?
ISN'T IT CLEAR?

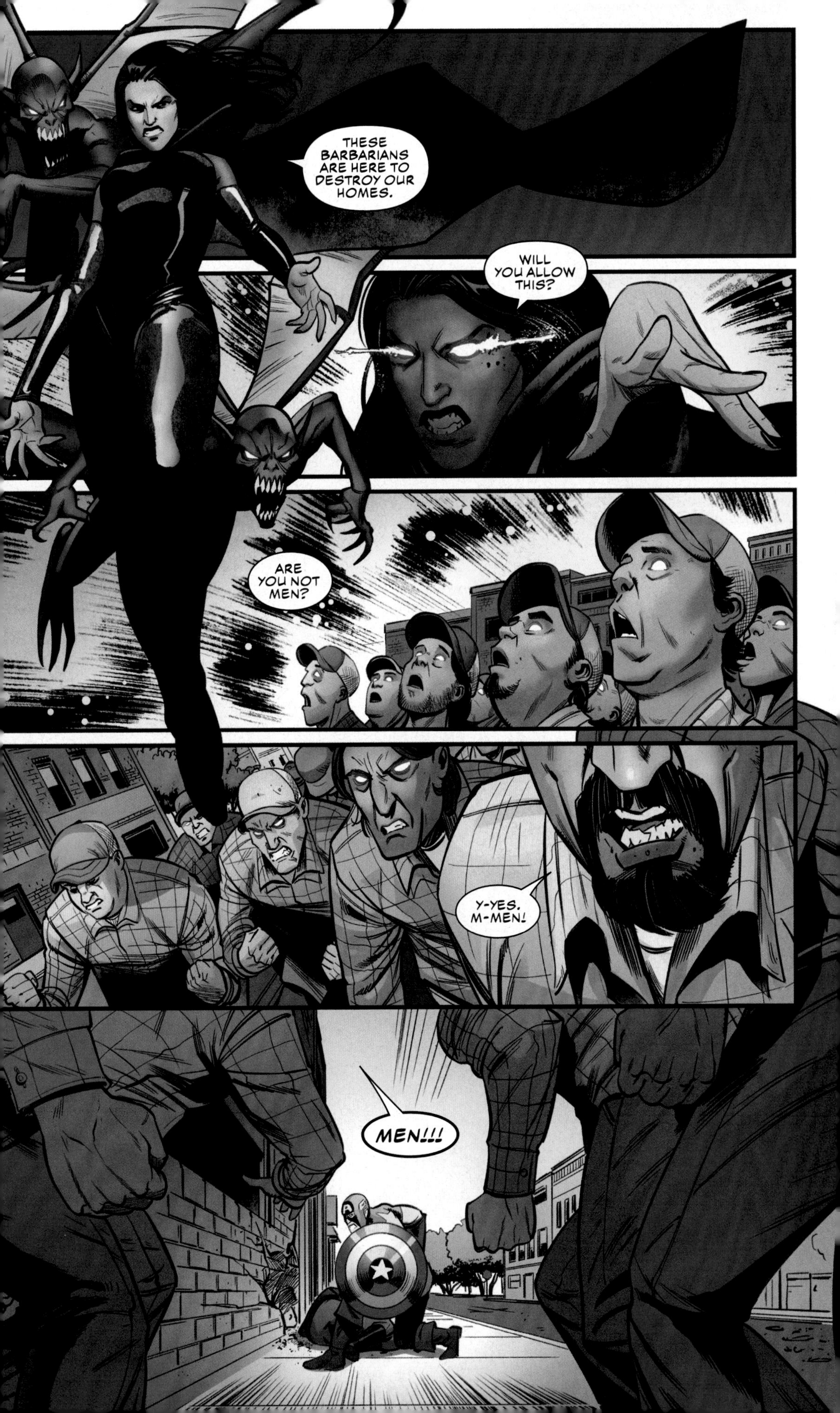
THESE BARBARIANS ARE HERE TO DESTROY OUR HOMES.
WILL YOU ALLOW THIS?
ARE YOU NOT MEN?
Y-YES. M-MEN!
MEN!!!

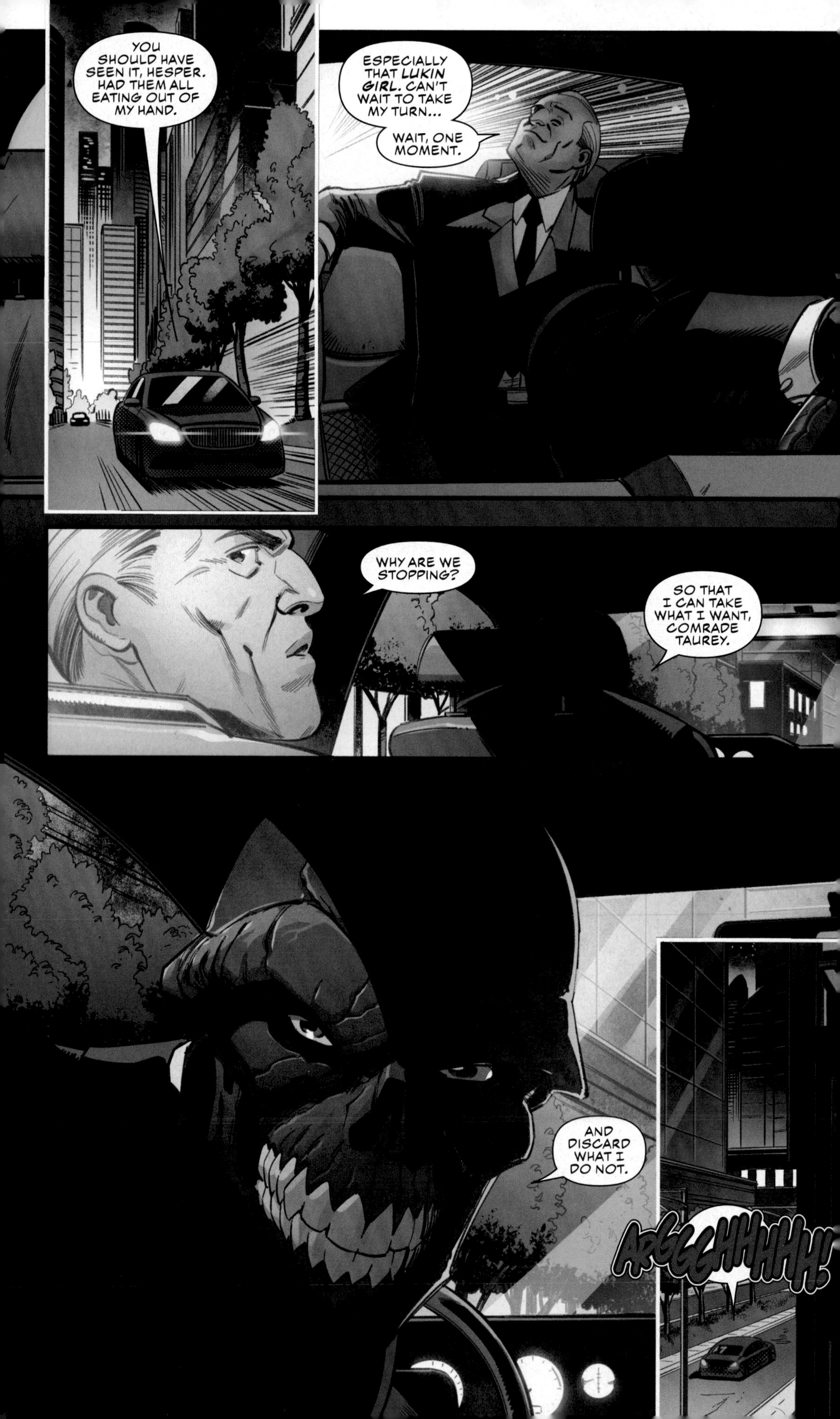
YOU SHOULD HAVE SEEN IT, HESPER. HAD THEM ALL EATING OUT OF MY HAND.
ESPECIALLY THAT LUKIN GIRL. CAN'T WAIT TO TAKE MY TURN...
WAIT, ONE MOMENT.
WHY ARE WE STOPPING?
SO THAT I CAN TAKE WHAT I WANT, COMRADE TAUREY.
AND DISCARD WHAT I DO NOT.
ARGGGHHHHHH!

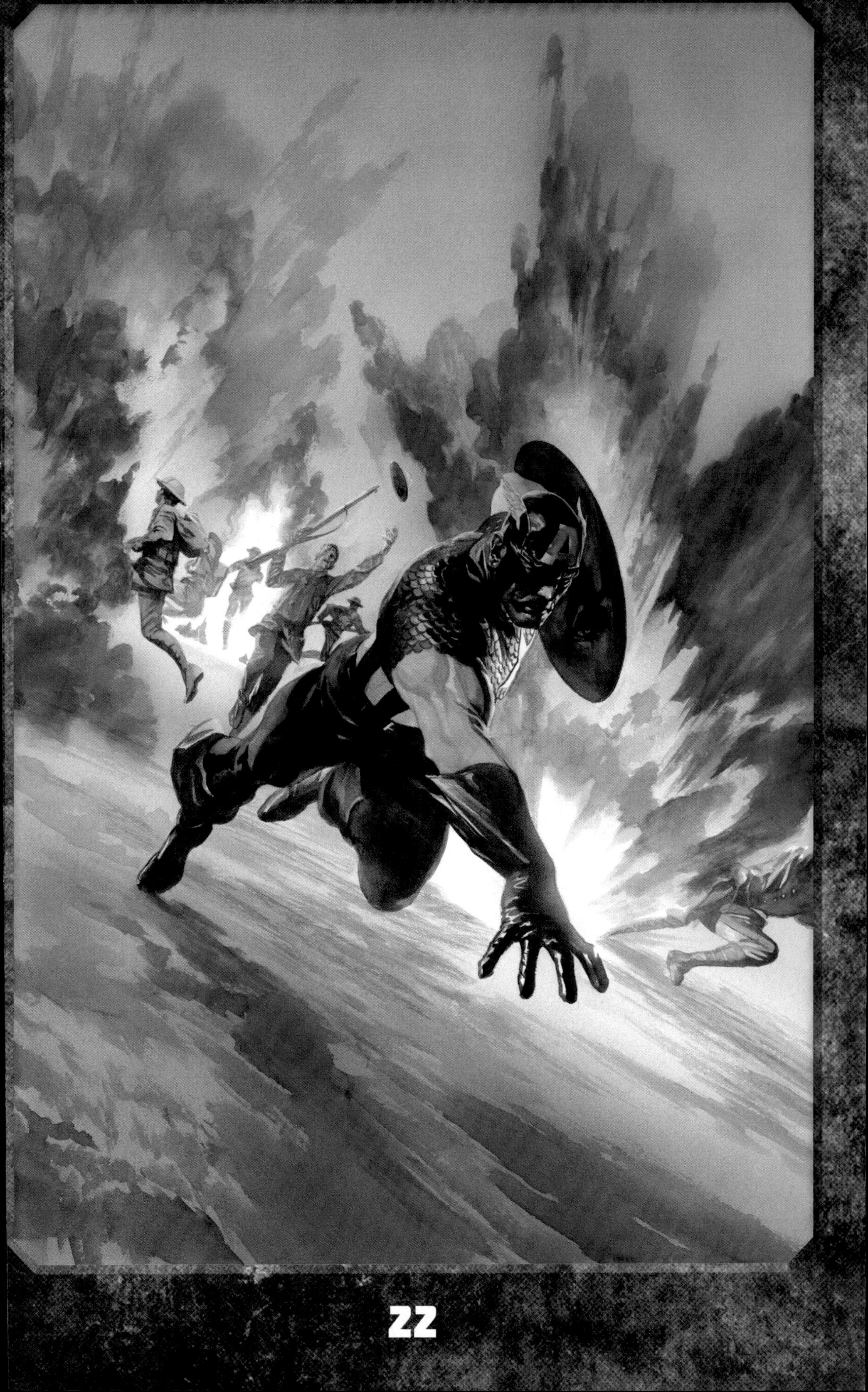

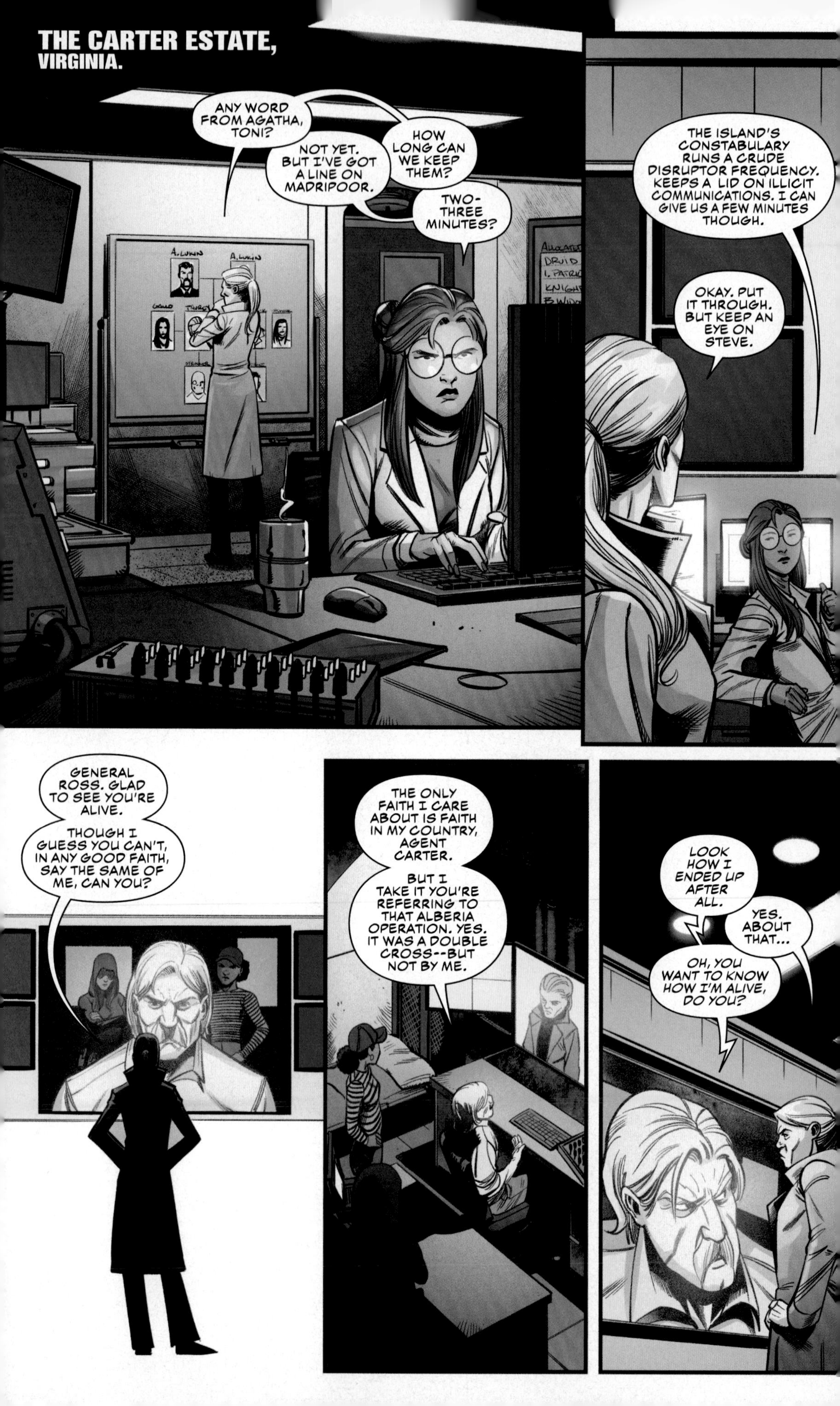

THE CARTER ESTATE, VIRGINIA.
ANY WORD FROM AGATHA, TONI?
NOT YET. BUT I'VE GOT A LINE ON MADRIPOOR.
HOW LONG CAN WE KEEP THEM?
TWO-THREE MINUTES?
THE ISLAND'S CONSTABULARY RUNS A CRUDE DISRUPTOR FREQUENCY. KEEPS A LID ON ILLICIT COMMUNICATIONS. I CAN GIVE US A FEW MINUTES THOUGH.
OKAY. PUT IT THROUGH. BUT KEEP AN EYE ON STEVE.
GENERAL ROSS. GLAD TO SEE YOU'RE ALIVE.
THOUGH I GUESS YOU CAN'T, IN ANY GOOD FAITH, SAY THE SAME OF ME, CAN YOU?
THE ONLY FAITH I CARE ABOUT IS FAITH IN MY COUNTRY, AGENT CARTER.
BUT I TAKE IT YOU'RE REFERRING TO THAT ALBERIA OPERATION. YES. IT WAS A DOUBLE CROSS--BUT NOT BY ME.
LOOK HOW I ENDED UP AFTER ALL.
YES. ABOUT THAT...
OH, YOU WANT TO KNOW HOW I'M ALIVE, DO YOU?

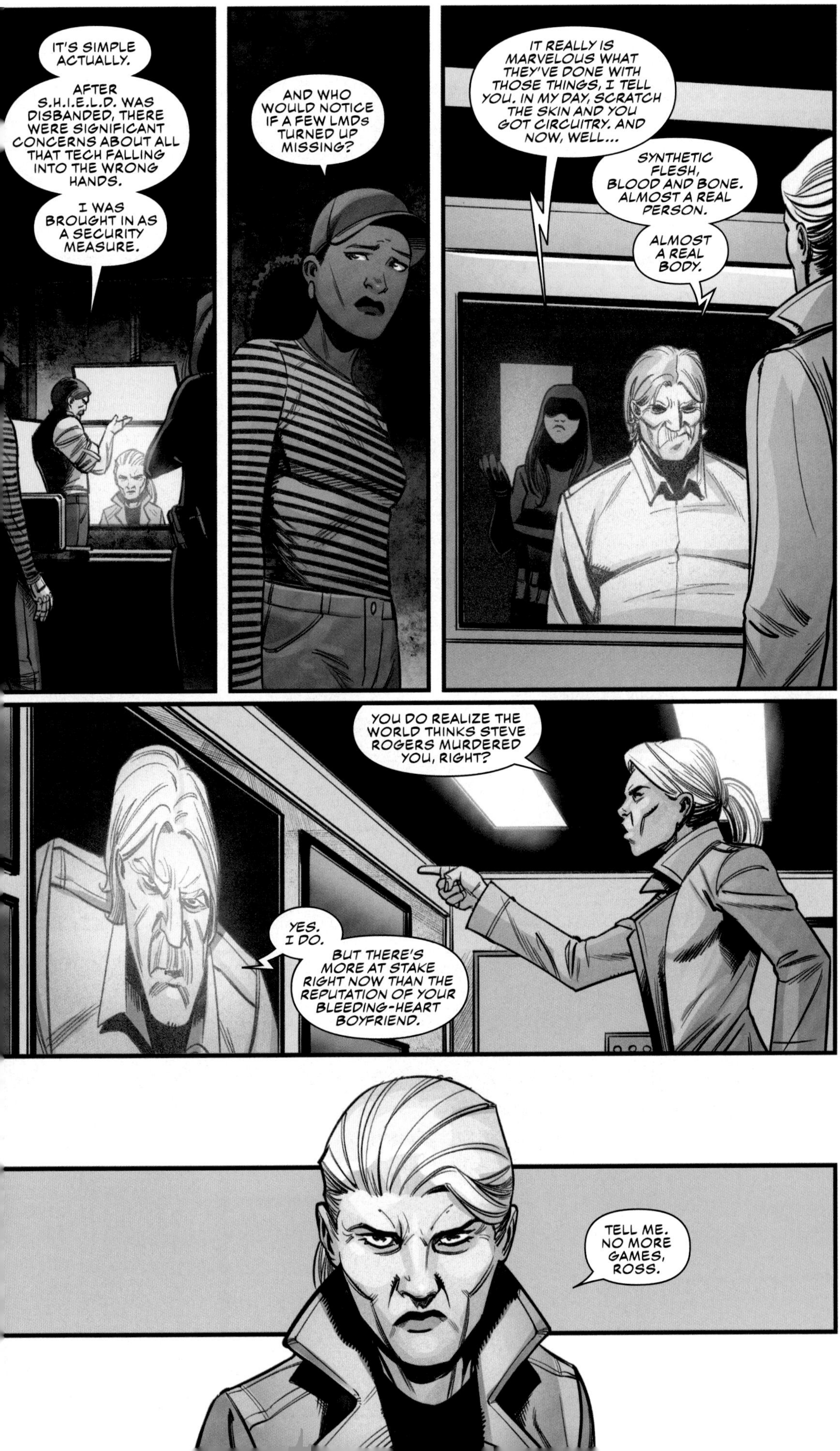
IT'S SIMPLE ACTUALLY.
AFTER S.H.I.E.L.D. WAS DISBANDED, THERE WERE SIGNIFICANT CONCERNS ABOUT ALL THAT TECH FALLING INTO THE WRONG HANDS.
I WAS BROUGHT IN AS A SECURITY MEASURE.
AND WHO WOULD NOTICE IF A FEW LMDs TURNED UP MISSING?
IT REALLY IS MARVELOUS WHAT THEY'VE DONE WITH THOSE THINGS, I TELL YOU. IN MY DAY, SCRATCH THE SKIN AND YOU GOT CIRCUITRY. AND NOW, WELL...
SYNTHETIC FLESH, BLOOD AND BONE. ALMOST A REAL PERSON.
ALMOST A REAL BODY.
YOU DO REALIZE THE WORLD THINKS STEVE ROGERS MURDERED YOU, RIGHT?
YES. I DO.
BUT THERE'S MORE AT STAKE RIGHT NOW THAN THE REPUTATION OF YOUR BLEEDING-HEART BOYFRIEND.
TELL ME. NO MORE GAMES, ROSS.

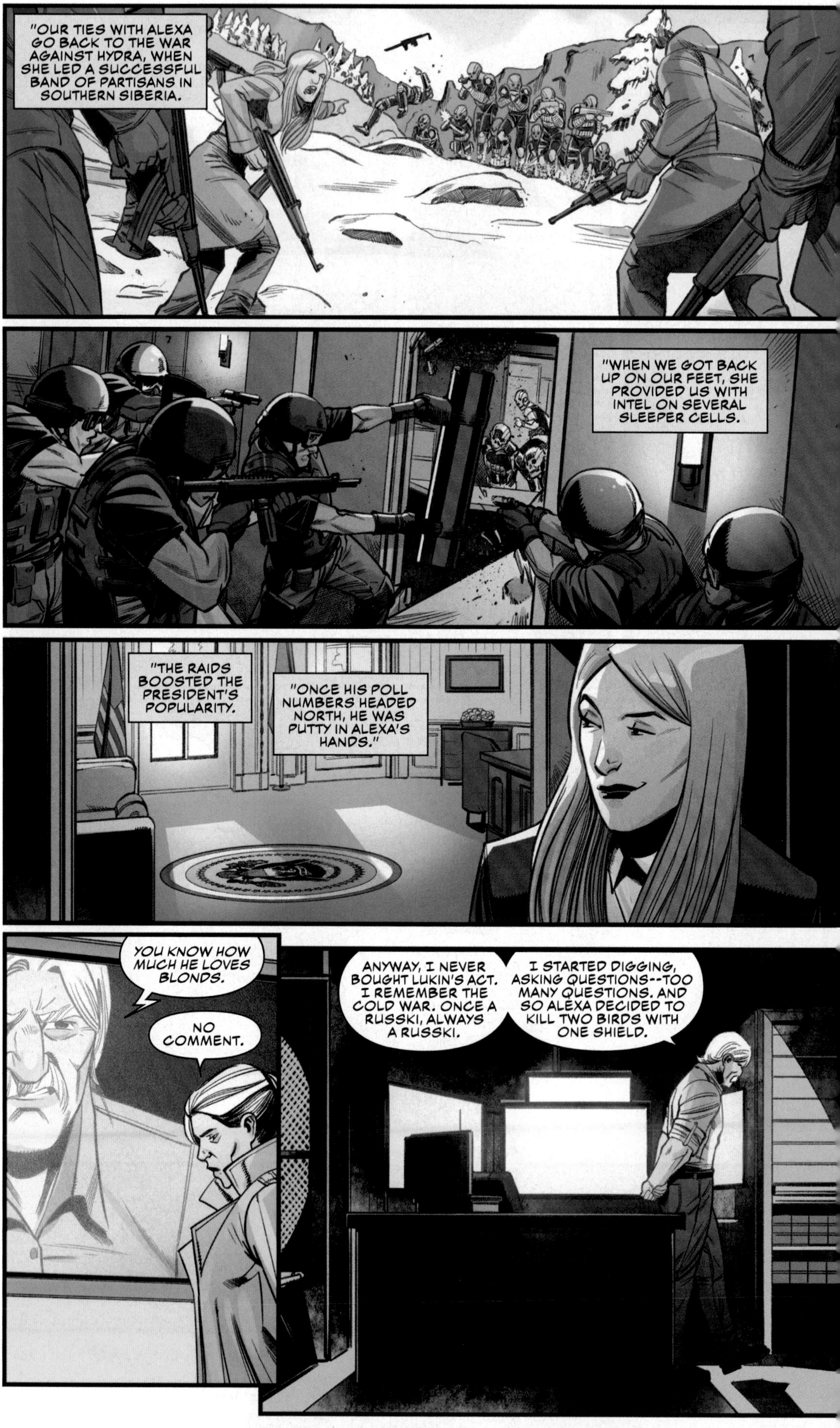
"OUR TIES WITH ALEXA GO BACK TO THE WAR AGAINST HYDRA, WHEN SHE LED A SUCCESSFUL BAND OF PARTISANS IN SOUTHERN SIBERIA.
"WHEN WE GOT BACK UP ON OUR FEET, SHE PROVIDED US WITH INTEL ON SEVERAL SLEEPER CELLS.
"THE RAIDS BOOSTED THE PRESIDENT'S POPULARITY.
"ONCE HIS POLL NUMBERS HEADED NORTH, HE WAS PUTTY IN ALEXA'S HANDS."
YOU KNOW HOW MUCH HE LOVES BLONDS.
NO COMMENT.
ANYWAY, I NEVER BOUGHT LUKIN'S ACT. I REMEMBER THE COLD WAR. ONCE A RUSSKI, ALWAYS A RUSSKI.
I STARTED DIGGING, ASKING QUESTIONS--TOO MANY QUESTIONS. AND SO ALEXA DECIDED TO KILL TWO BIRDS WITH ONE SHIELD.

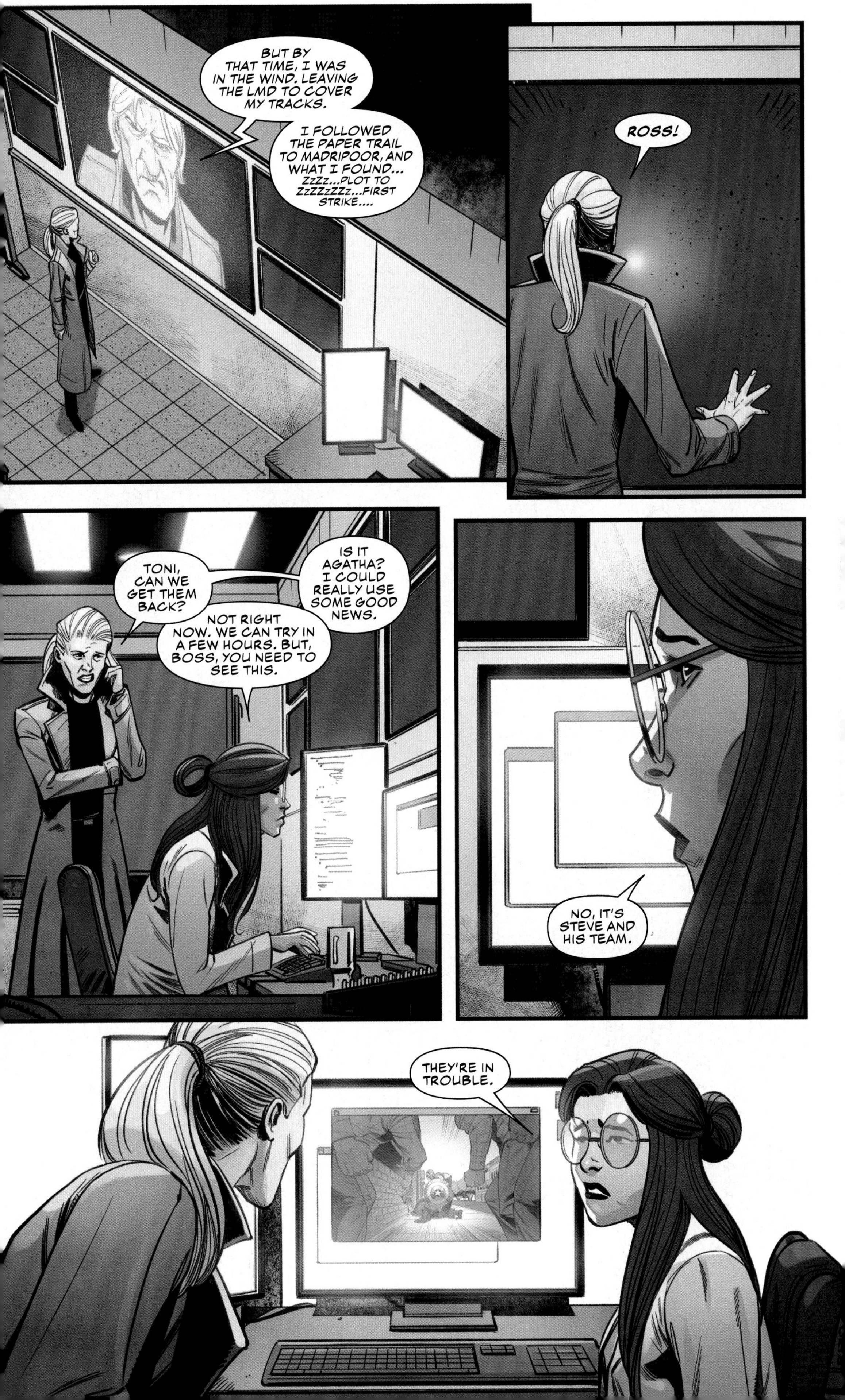
BUT BY THAT TIME, I WAS IN THE WIND. LEAVING THE LMD TO COVER MY TRACKS.
I FOLLOWED THE PAPER TRAIL TO MADRIPOOR, AND WHAT I FOUND... ZzZz...PLOT TO ZzZZzZZz...FIRST STRIKE....
ROSS!
TONI, CAN WE GET THEM BACK?
IS IT AGATHA? I COULD REALLY USE SOME GOOD NEWS.
NOT RIGHT NOW. WE CAN TRY IN A FEW HOURS. BUT, BOSS, YOU NEED TO SEE THIS.
NO, IT'S STEVE AND HIS TEAM.
THEY'RE IN TROUBLE.

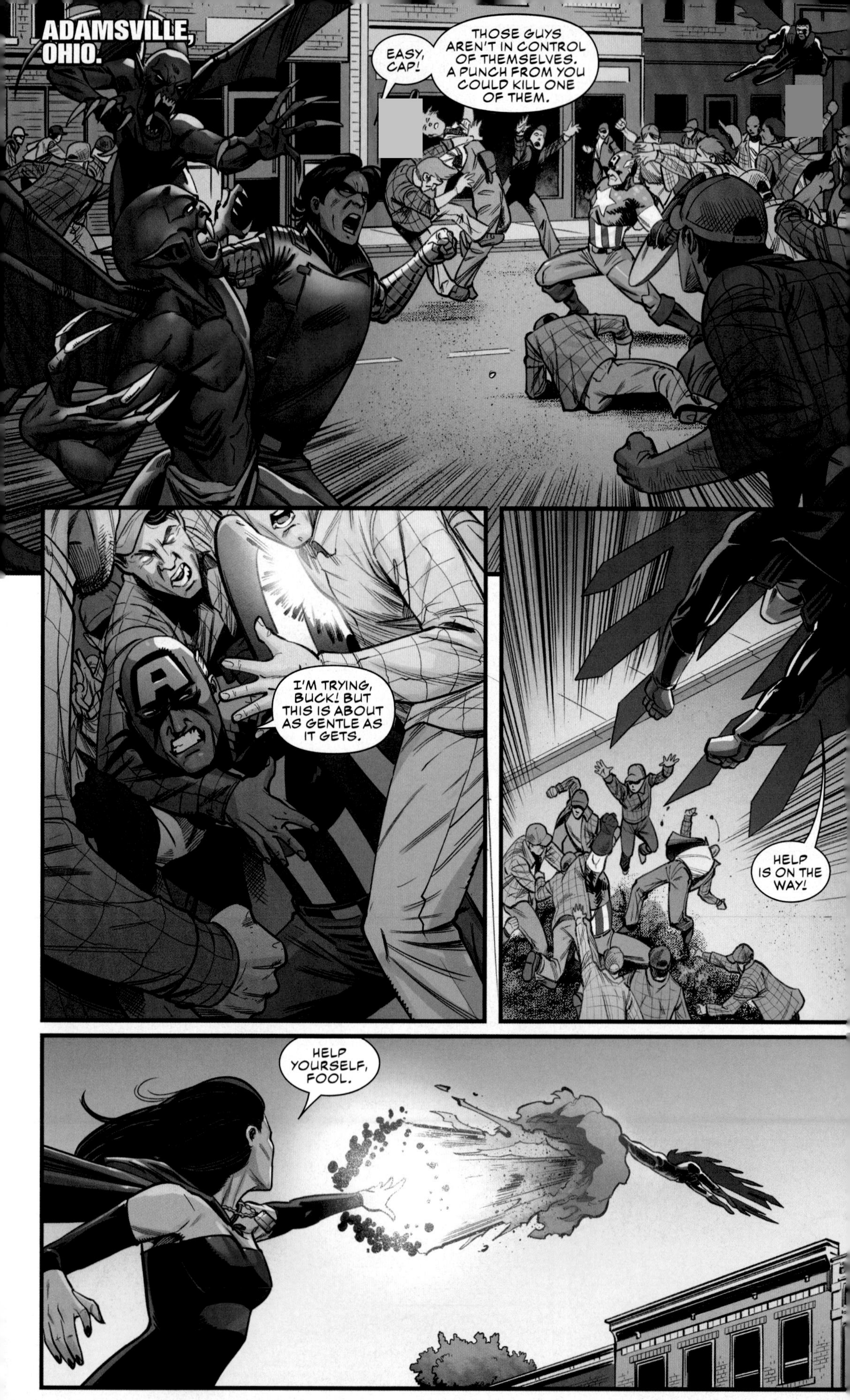
ADAMSVILLE, OHIO.
EASY, CAP!
THOSE GUYS AREN'T IN CONTROL OF THEMSELVES. A PUNCH FROM YOU COULD KILL ONE OF THEM.
I'M TRYING, BUCK! BUT THIS IS ABOUT AS GENTLE AS IT GETS.
HELP IS ON THE WAY!
HELP YOURSELF, FOOL.

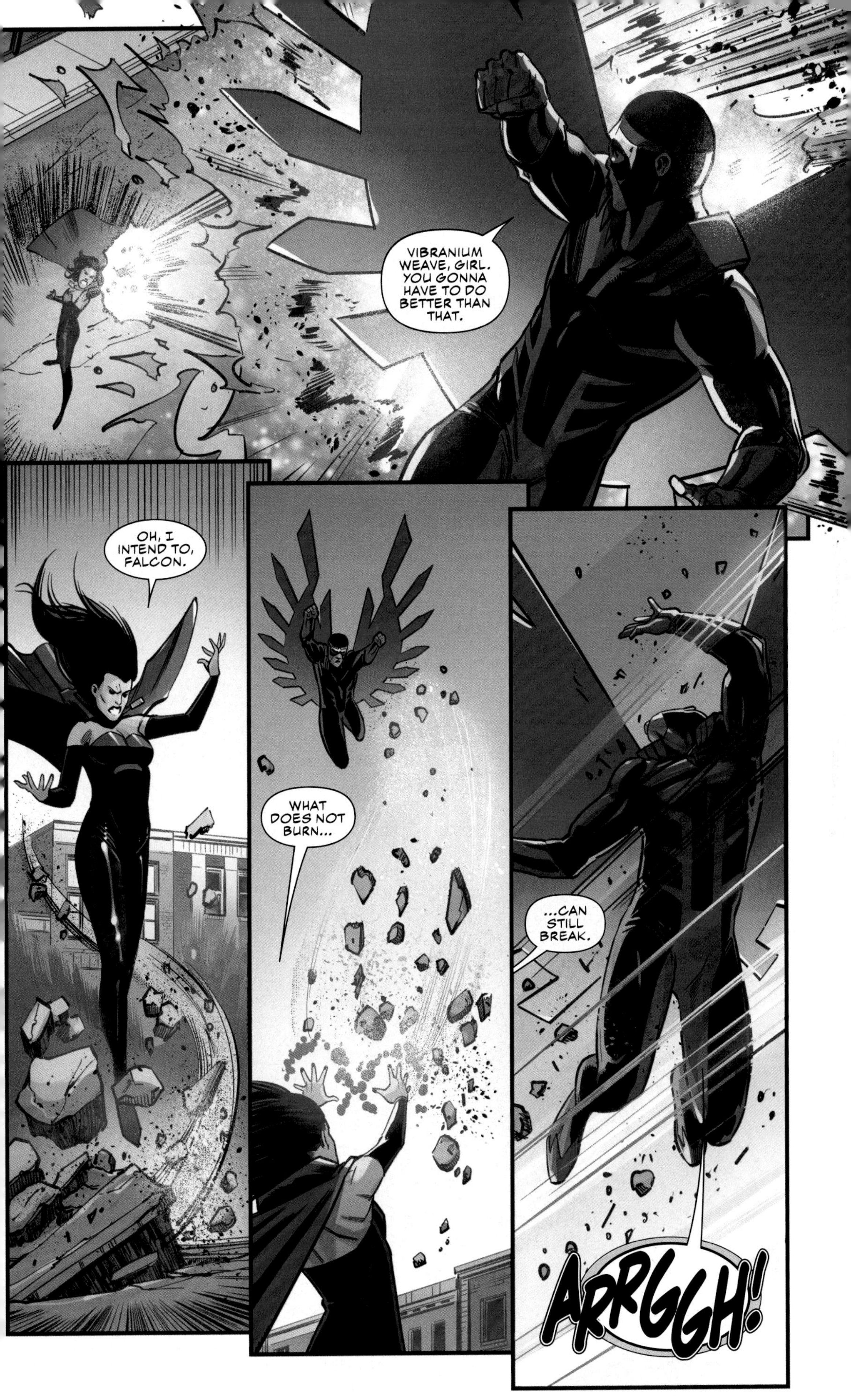
VIBRANIUM WEAVE, GIRL. YOU GONNA HAVE TO DO BETTER THAN THAT.
OH, I INTEND TO, FALCON.
WHAT DOES NOT BURN...
...CAN STILL BREAK.
ARRGGH!

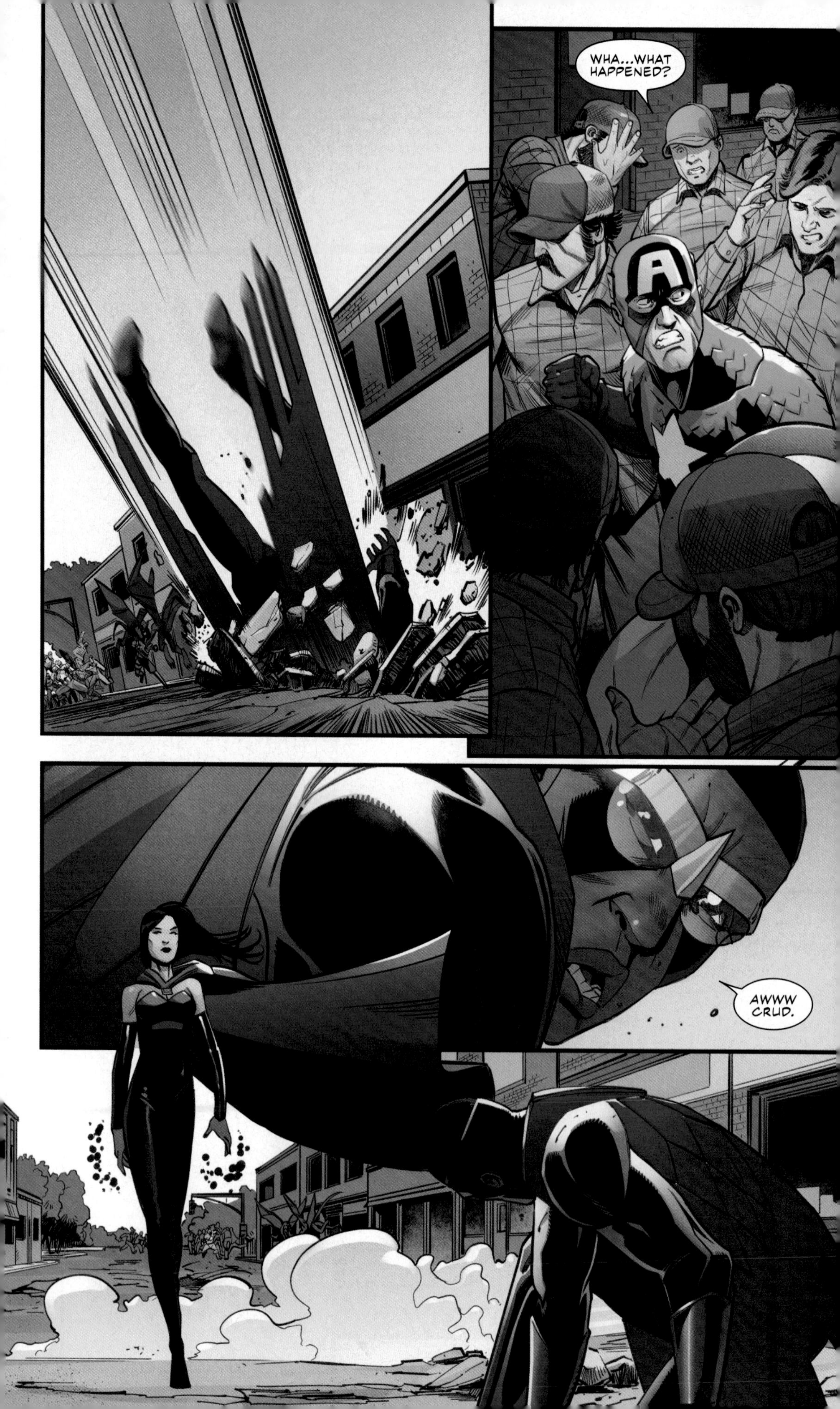
WHA...WHAT HAPPENED?
AWWW CRUD.

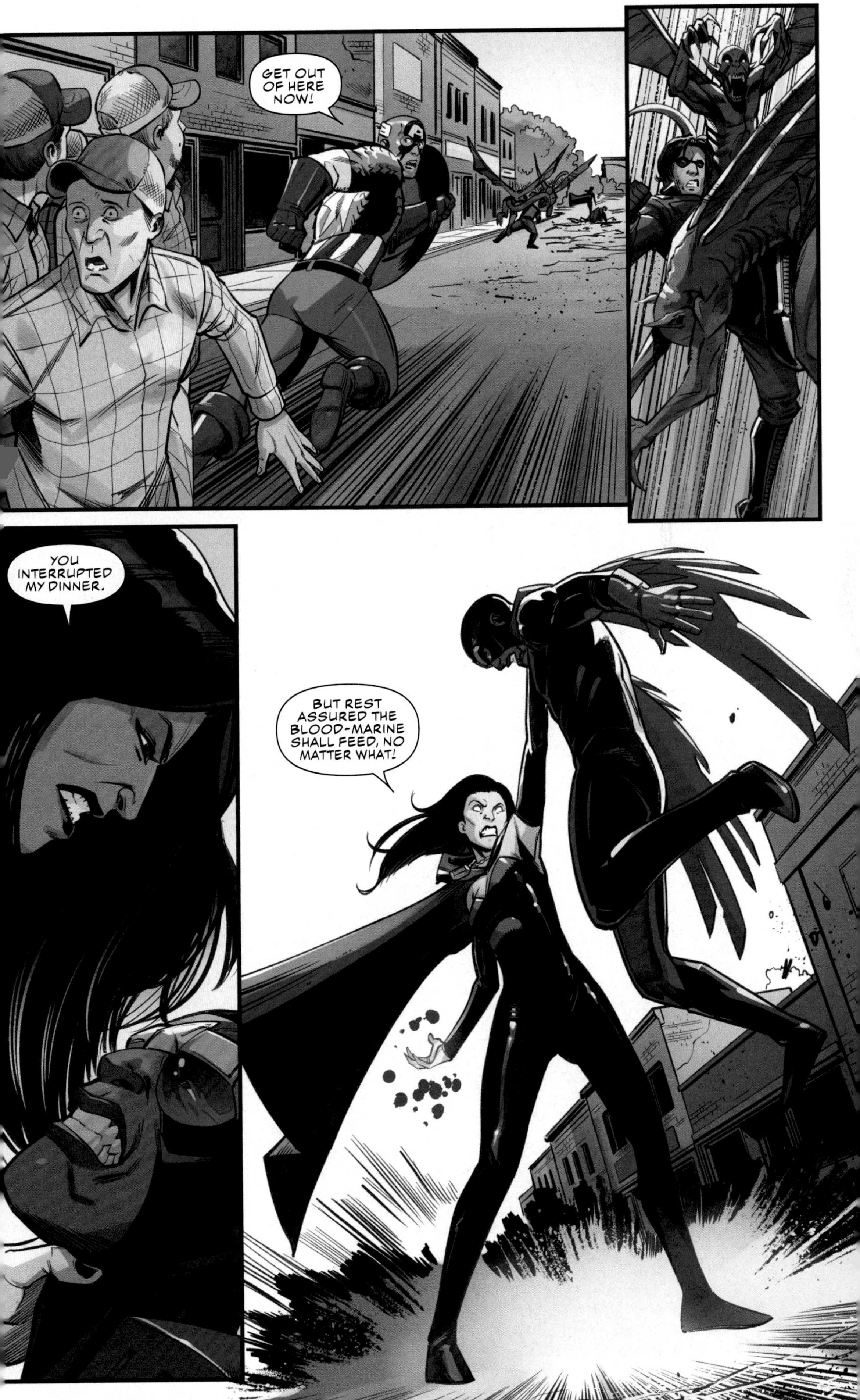
GET OUT OF HERE NOW!
YOU INTERRUPTED MY DINNER.
BUT REST ASSURED THE BLOOD-MARINE SHALL FEED, NO MATTER WHAT!

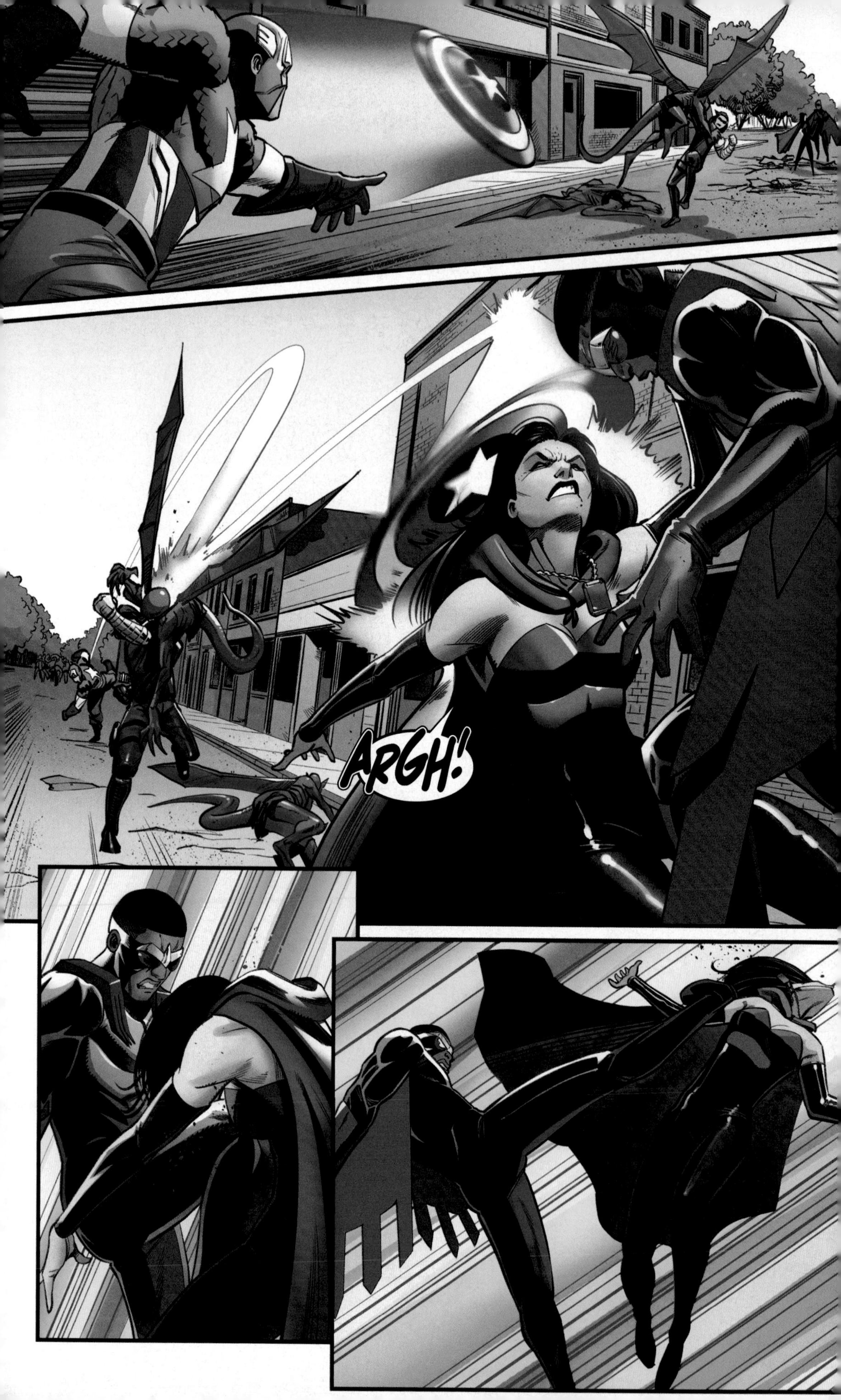
ARGH!

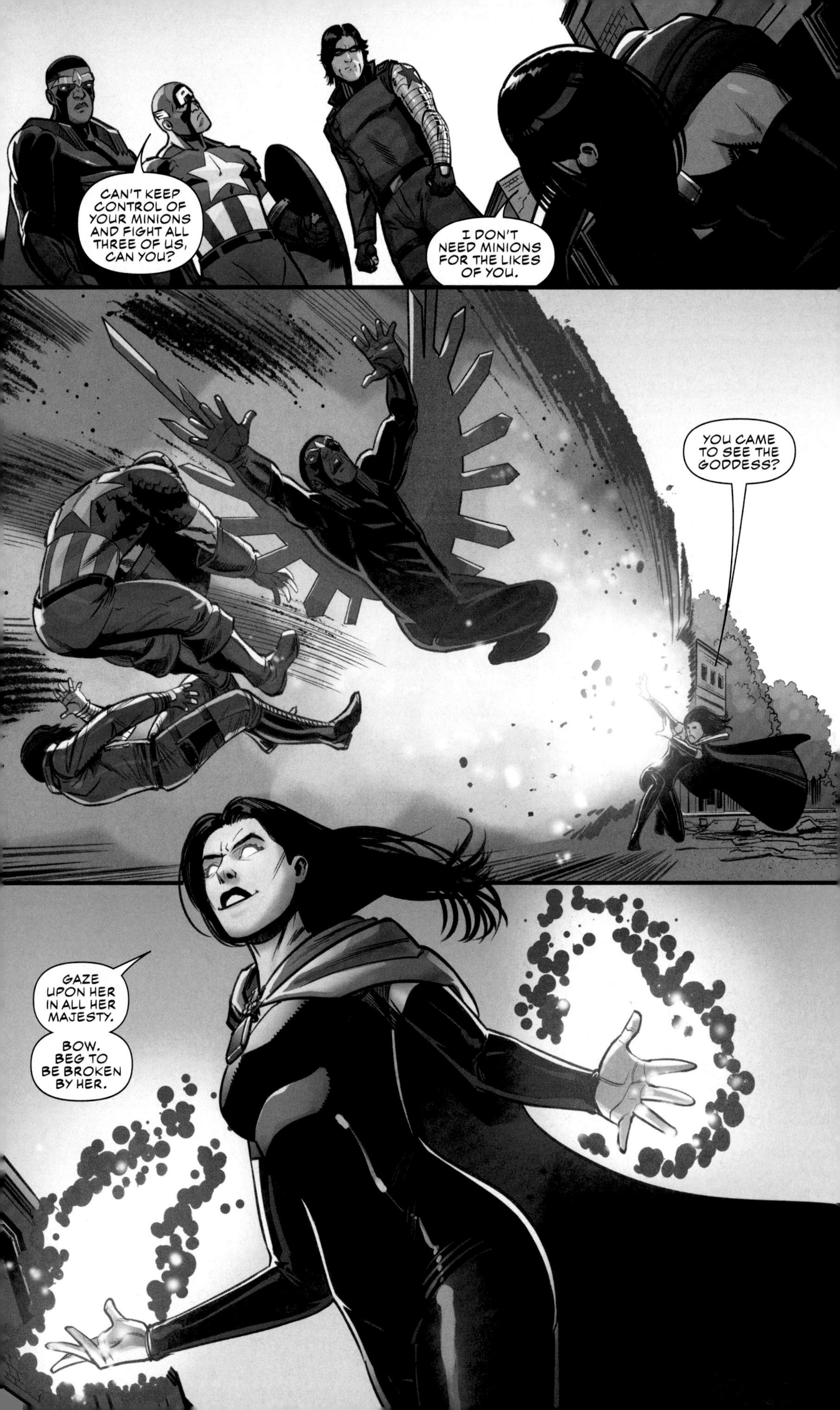
CAN'T KEEP CONTROL OF YOUR MINIONS AND FIGHT ALL THREE OF US, CAN YOU?
I DON'T NEED MINIONS FOR THE LIKES OF YOU.
YOU CAME TO SEE THE GODDESS?
GAZE UPON HER IN ALL HER MAJESTY.
BOW. BEG TO BE BROKEN BY HER.

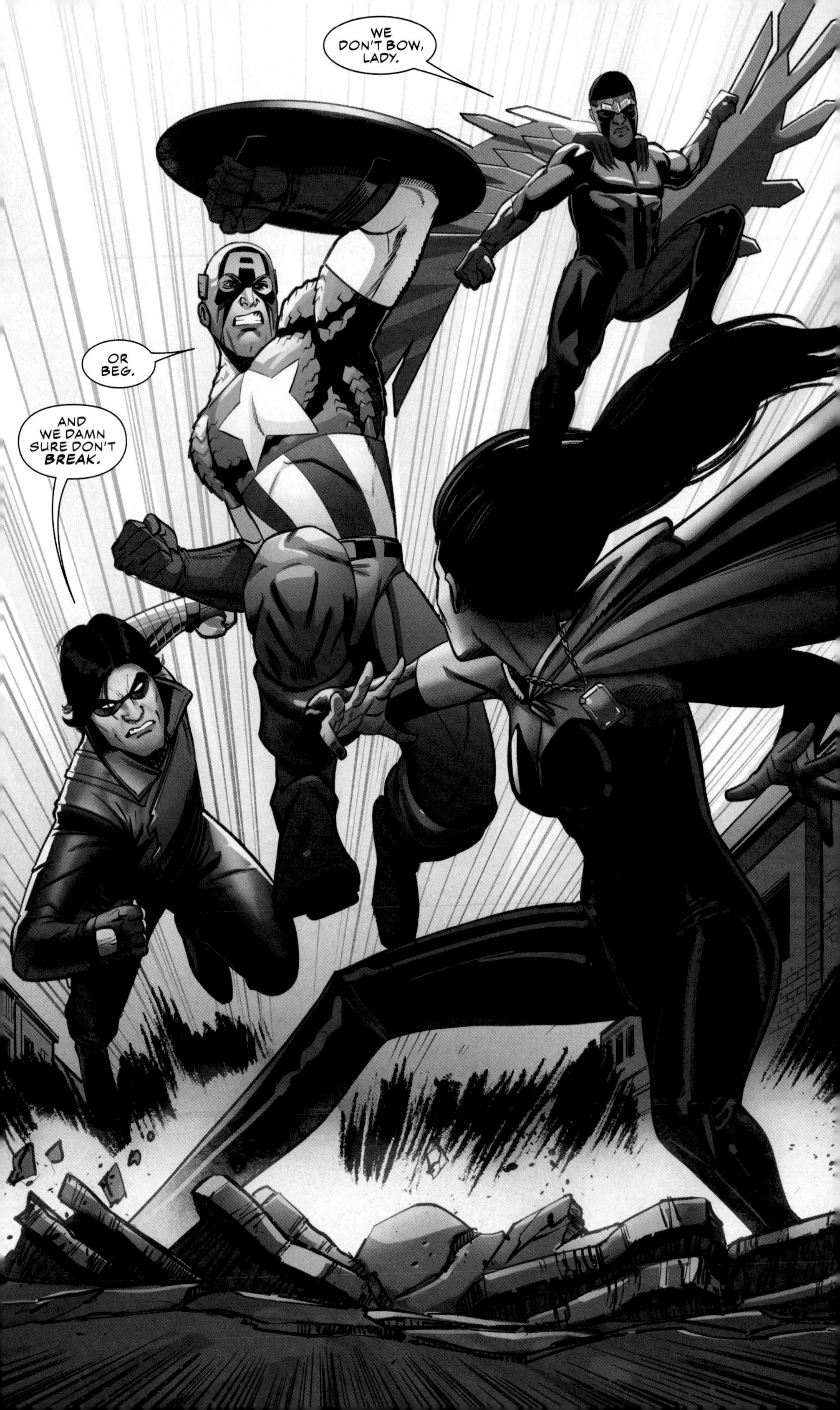
WE DON'T BOW, LADY.
OR BEG.
AND WE DAMN SURE DON'T **BREAK.**

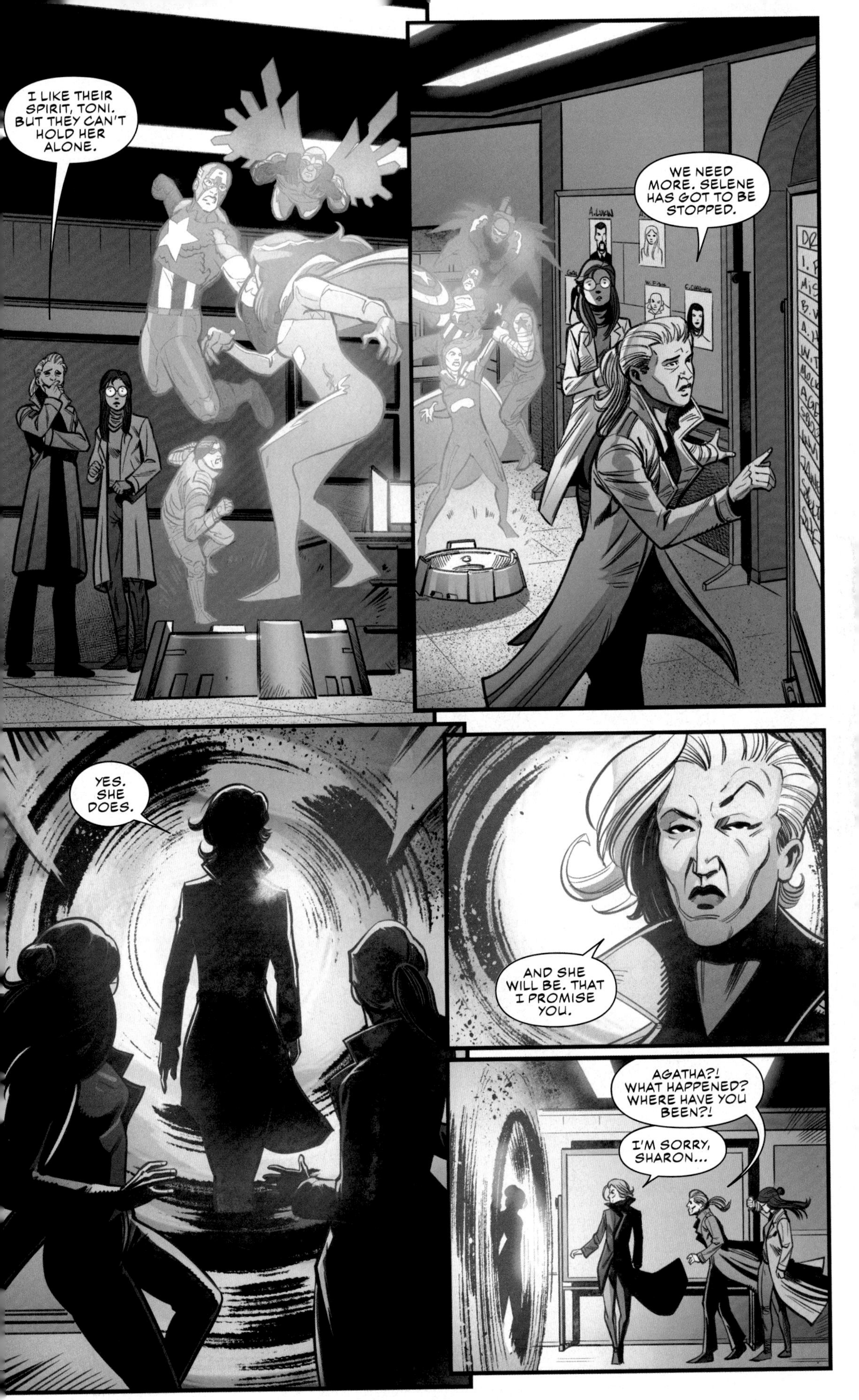
I LIKE THEIR SPIRIT, TONI. BUT THEY CAN'T HOLD HER ALONE.
WE NEED MORE. SELENE HAS GOT TO BE STOPPED.
YES. SHE DOES.
AND SHE WILL BE. THAT I PROMISE YOU.
AGATHA?! WHAT HAPPENED? WHERE HAVE YOU BEEN?!
I'M SORRY, SHARON...

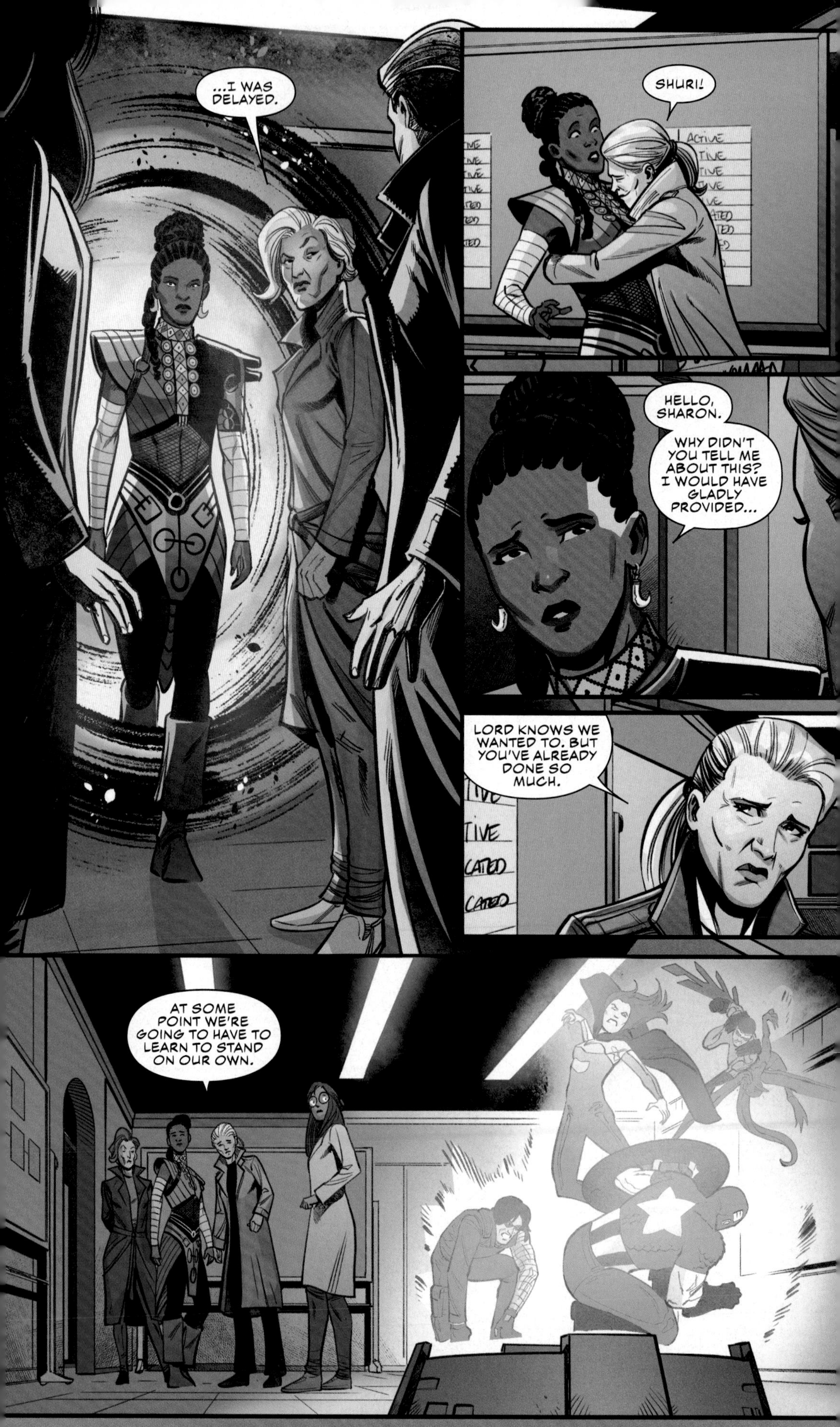
...I WAS DELAYED.
SHURI!
HELLO, SHARON.
WHY DIDN'T YOU TELL ME ABOUT THIS? I WOULD HAVE GLADLY PROVIDED...
LORD KNOWS WE WANTED TO. BUT YOU'VE ALREADY DONE SO MUCH.
AT SOME POINT WE'RE GOING TO HAVE TO LEARN TO STAND ON OUR OWN.

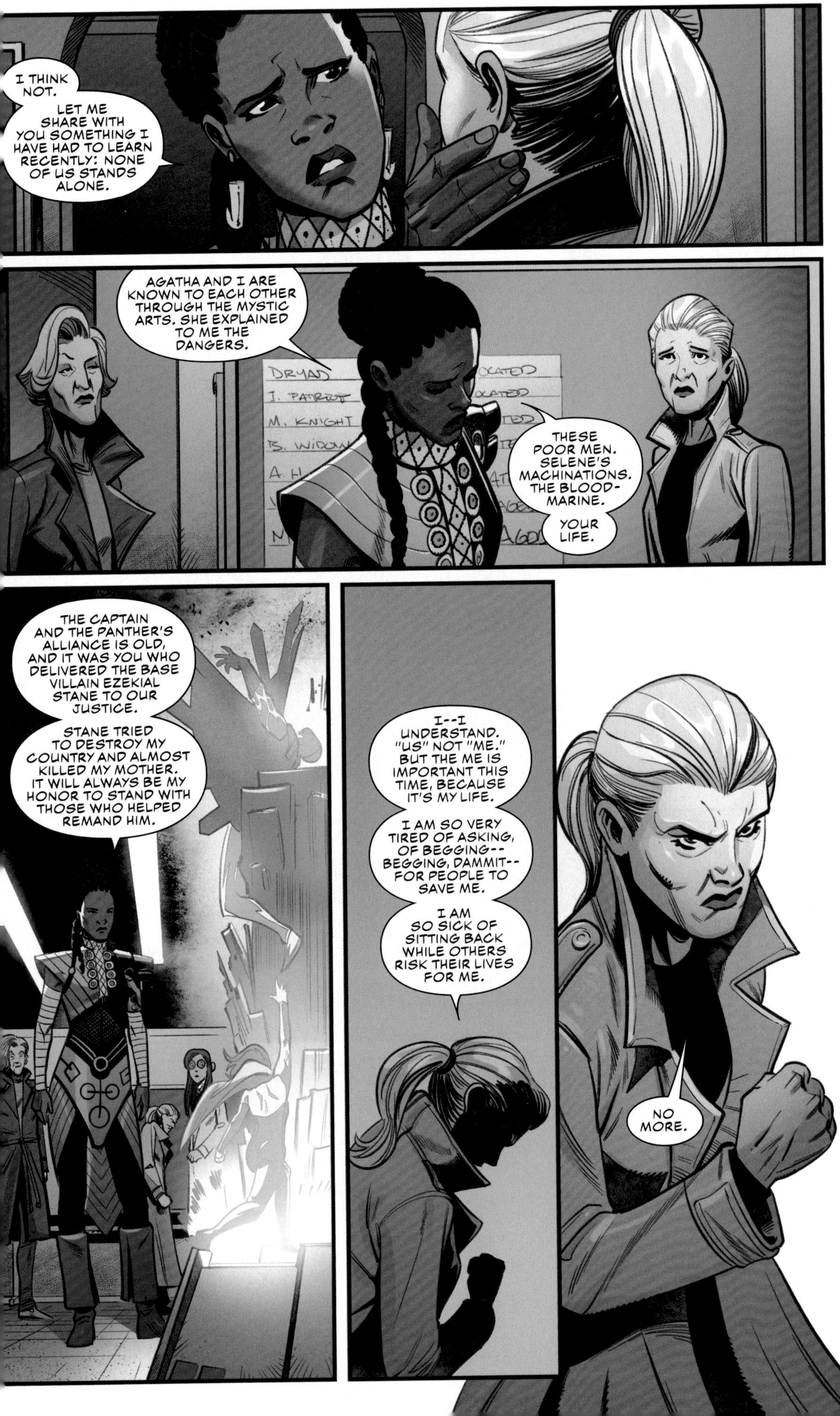

I THINK NOT.
LET ME SHARE WITH YOU SOMETHING I HAVE HAD TO LEARN RECENTLY: NONE OF US STANDS ALONE.
AGATHA AND I ARE KNOWN TO EACH OTHER THROUGH THE MYSTIC ARTS. SHE EXPLAINED TO ME THE DANGERS.
THESE POOR MEN. SELENE'S MACHINATIONS. THE BLOOD-MARINE.
YOUR LIFE.
THE CAPTAIN AND THE PANTHER'S ALLIANCE IS OLD, AND IT WAS YOU WHO DELIVERED THE BASE VILLAIN EZEKIAL STANE TO OUR JUSTICE.
STANE TRIED TO DESTROY MY COUNTRY AND ALMOST KILLED MY MOTHER. IT WILL ALWAYS BE MY HONOR TO STAND WITH THOSE WHO HELPED REMAND HIM.
I--I UNDERSTAND. "US" NOT "ME." BUT THE ME IS IMPORTANT THIS TIME, BECAUSE IT'S MY LIFE.
I AM SO VERY TIRED OF ASKING, OF BEGGING--BEGGING, DAMMIT--FOR PEOPLE TO SAVE ME.
I AM SO SICK OF SITTING BACK WHILE OTHERS RISK THEIR LIVES FOR ME.
NO MORE.

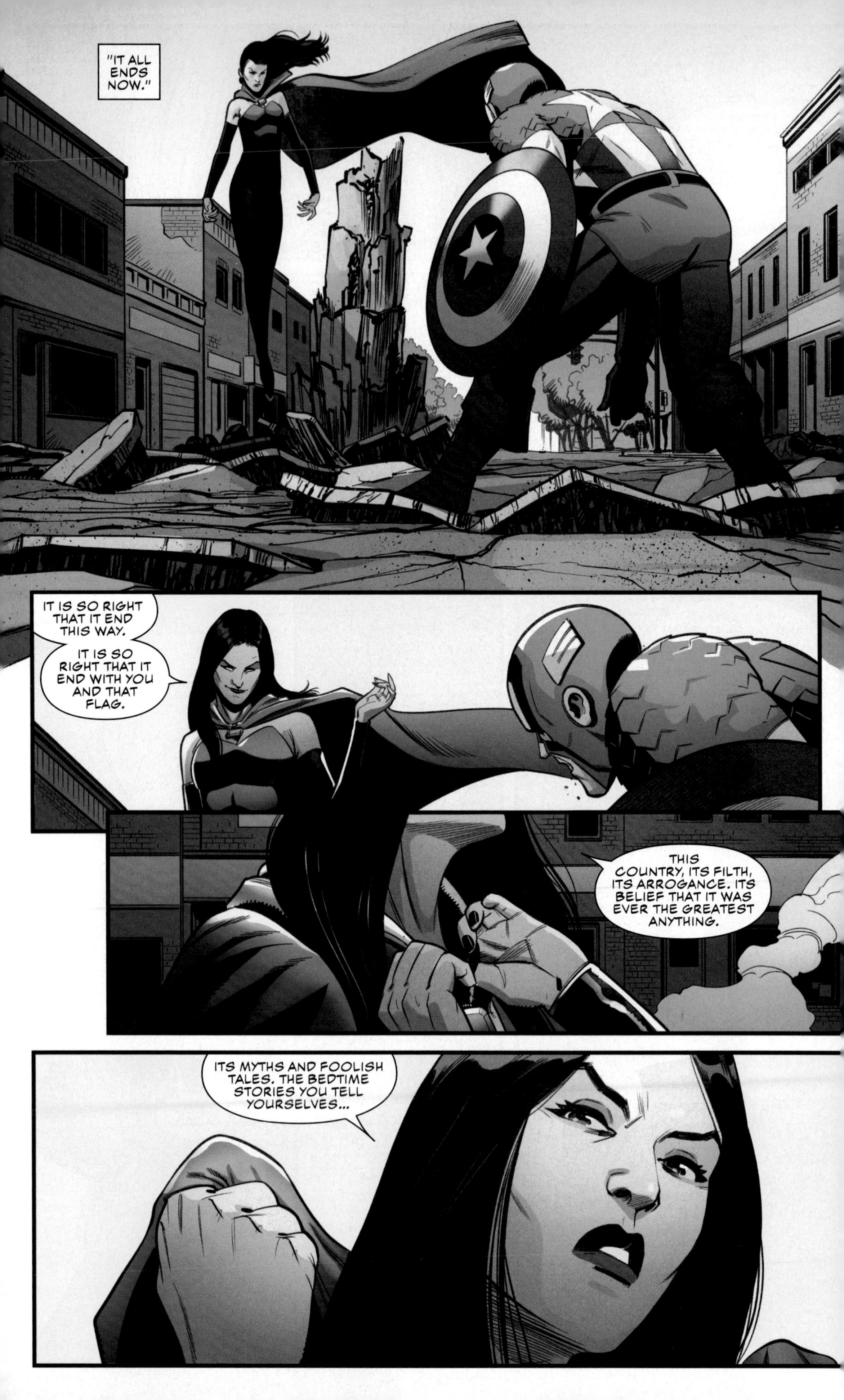
"IT ALL ENDS NOW."
IT IS SO RIGHT THAT IT END THIS WAY.
IT IS SO RIGHT THAT IT END WITH YOU AND THAT FLAG.
THIS COUNTRY, ITS FILTH, ITS ARROGANCE. ITS BELIEF THAT IT WAS EVER THE GREATEST ANYTHING.
ITS MYTHS AND FOOLISH TALES. THE BEDTIME STORIES YOU TELL YOURSELVES...

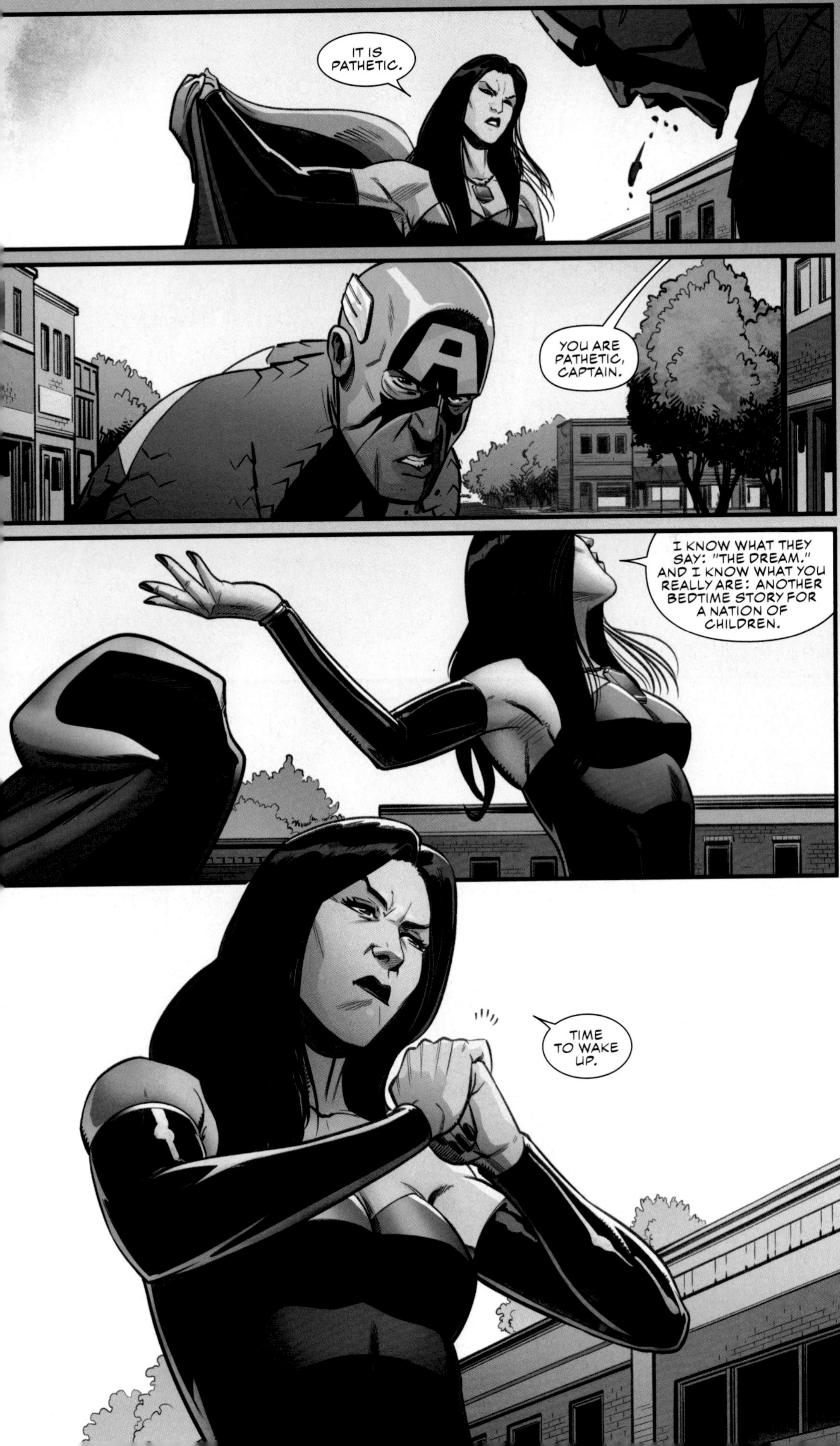

IT IS PATHETIC.
YOU ARE PATHETIC, CAPTAIN.
I KNOW WHAT THEY SAY: "THE DREAM." AND I KNOW WHAT YOU REALLY ARE: ANOTHER BEDTIME STORY FOR A NATION OF CHILDREN.
TIME TO WAKE UP.

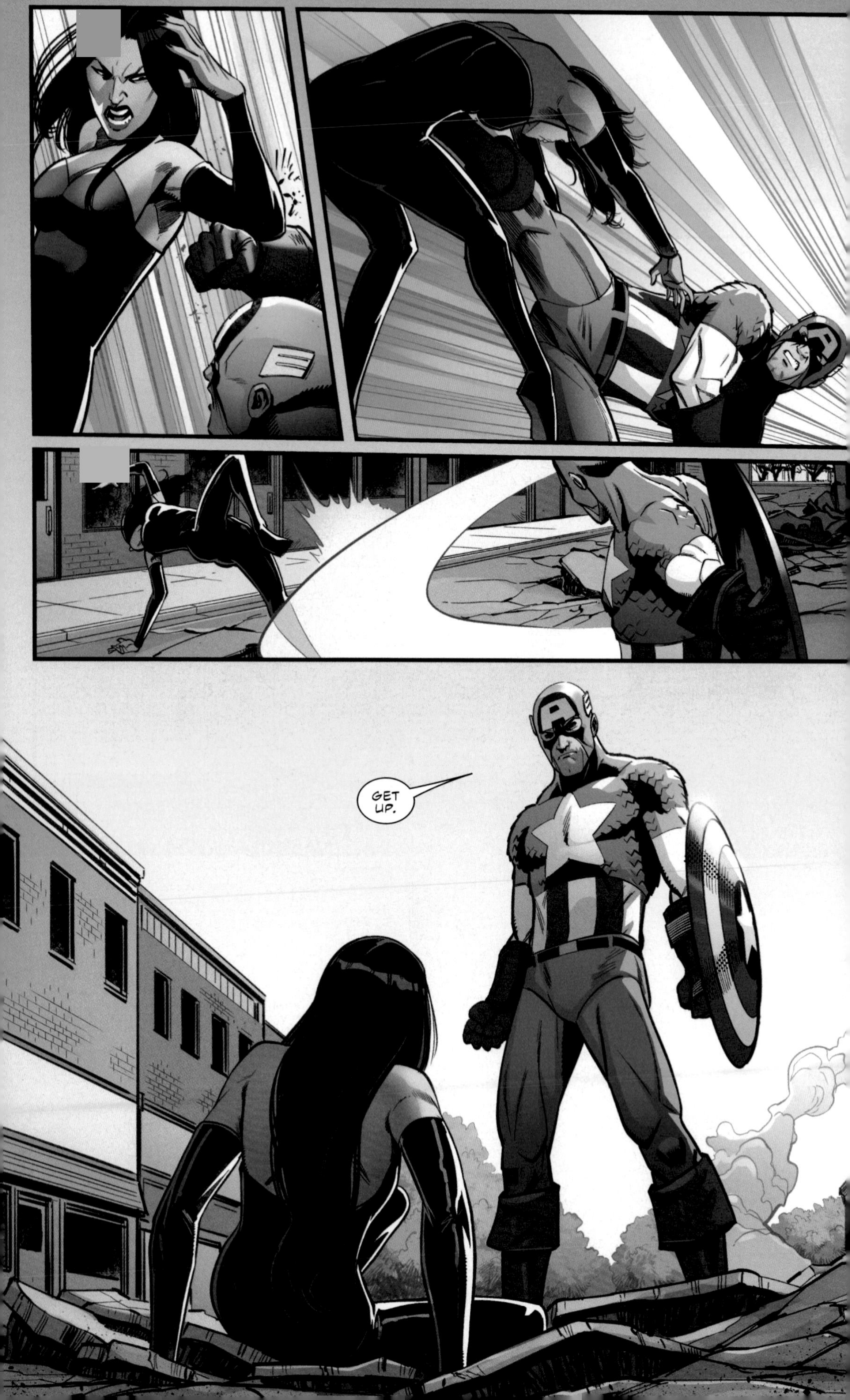
GET UP.

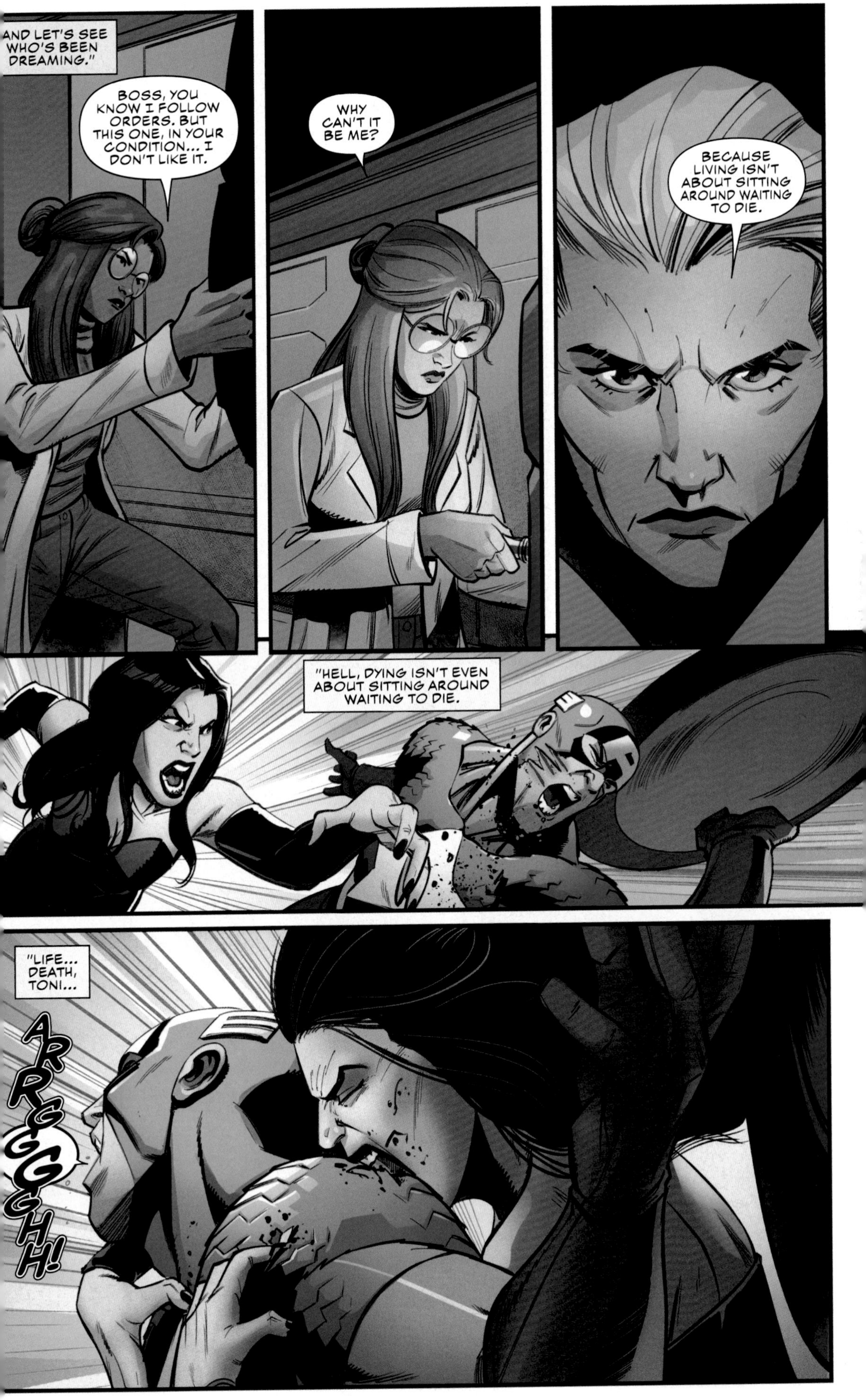

AND LET'S SEE WHO'S BEEN DREAMING."
BOSS, YOU KNOW I FOLLOW ORDERS. BUT THIS ONE, IN YOUR CONDITION... I DON'T LIKE IT.
WHY CAN'T IT BE ME?
BECAUSE LIVING ISN'T ABOUT SITTING AROUND WAITING TO DIE.
"HELL, DYING ISN'T EVEN ABOUT SITTING AROUND WAITING TO DIE.
"LIFE... DEATH, TONI...
ARRGGGHH!

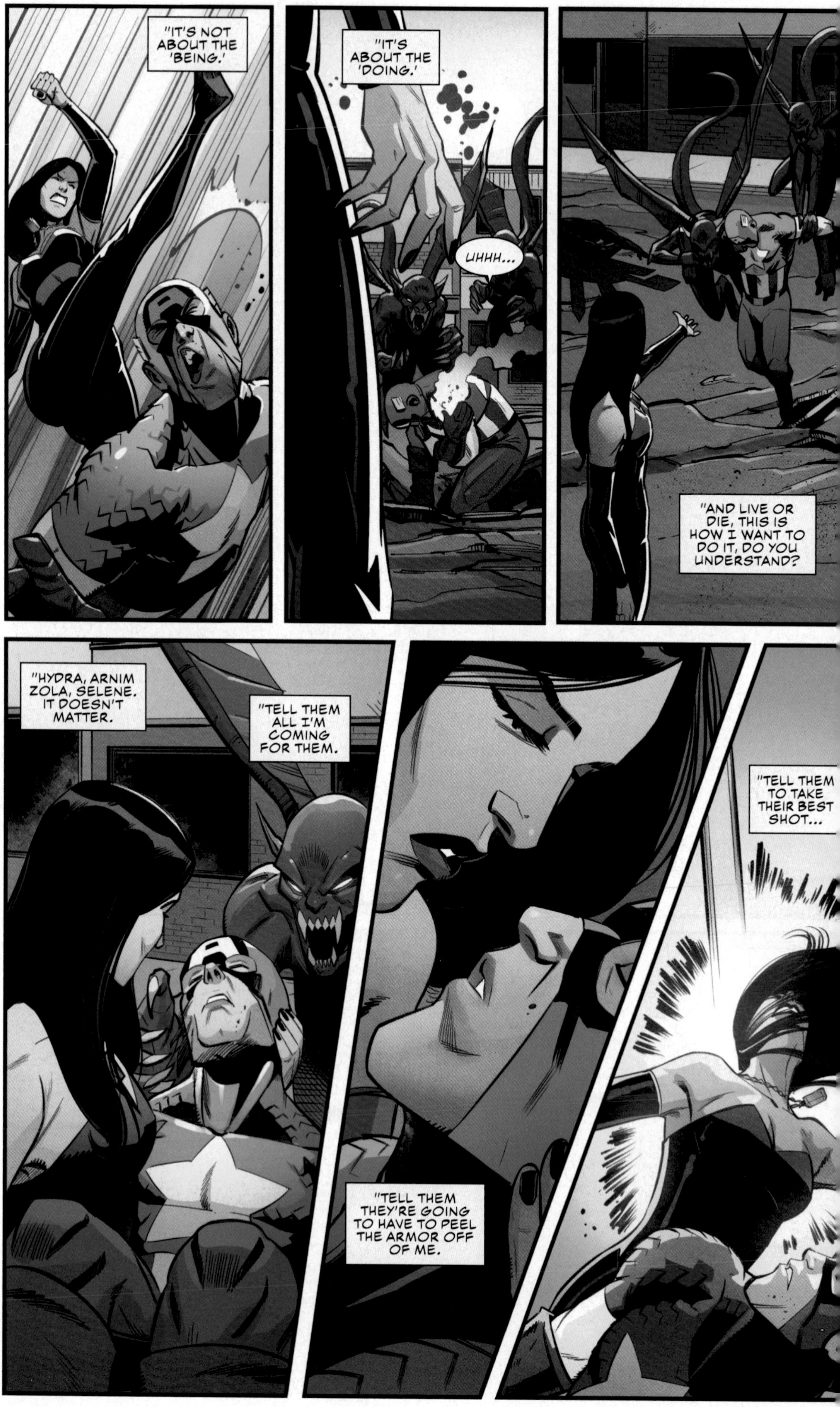
"IT'S NOT ABOUT THE 'BEING.'
"IT'S ABOUT THE 'DOING.'
UHHH...
"AND LIVE OR DIE, THIS IS HOW I WANT TO DO IT, DO YOU UNDERSTAND?
"HYDRA, ARNIM ZOLA, SELENE. IT DOESN'T MATTER.
"TELL THEM ALL I'M COMING FOR THEM.
"TELL THEM THEY'RE GOING TO HAVE TO PEEL THE ARMOR OFF OF ME.
"TELL THEM TO TAKE THEIR BEST SHOT...

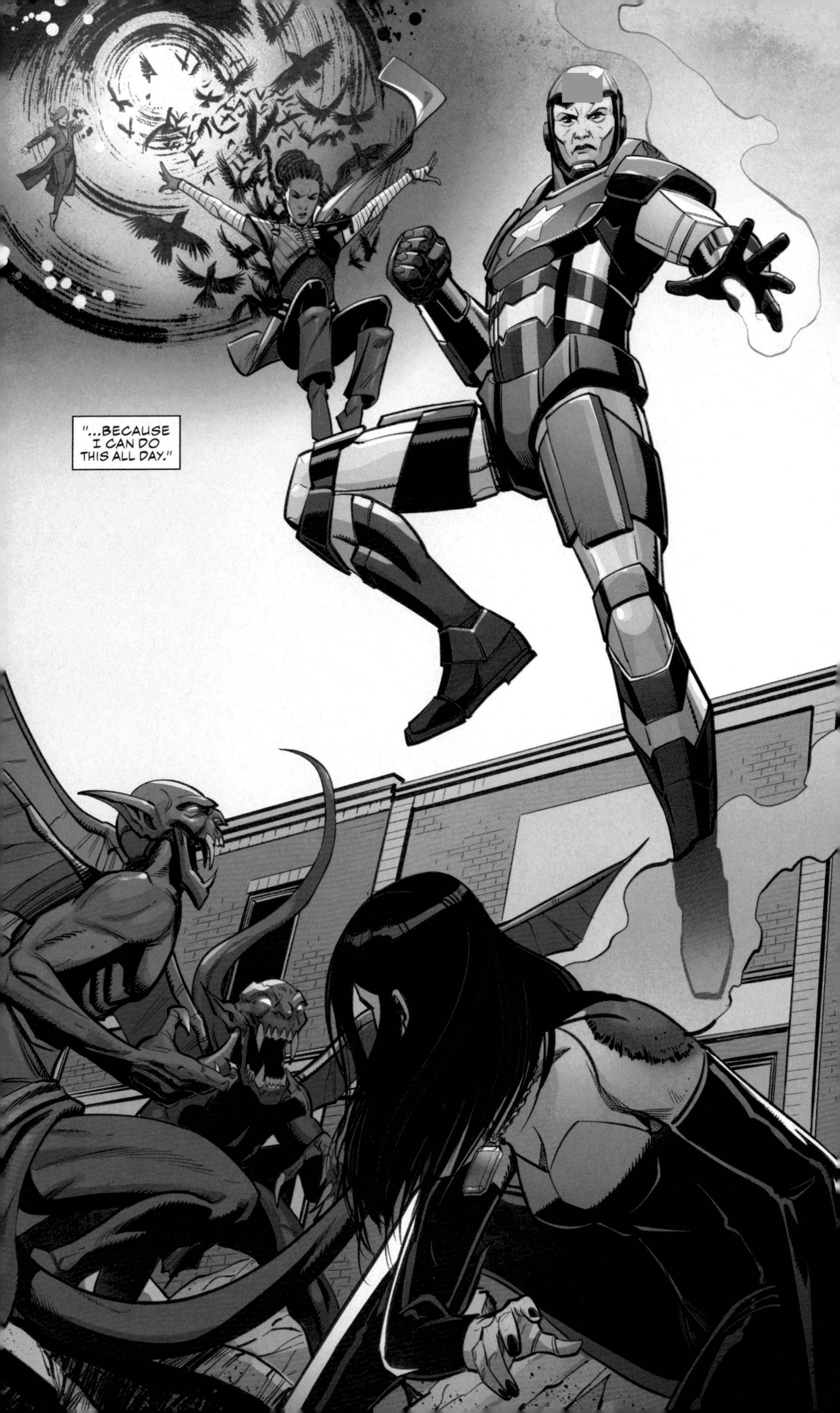
"...BECAUSE I CAN DO THIS ALL DAY."

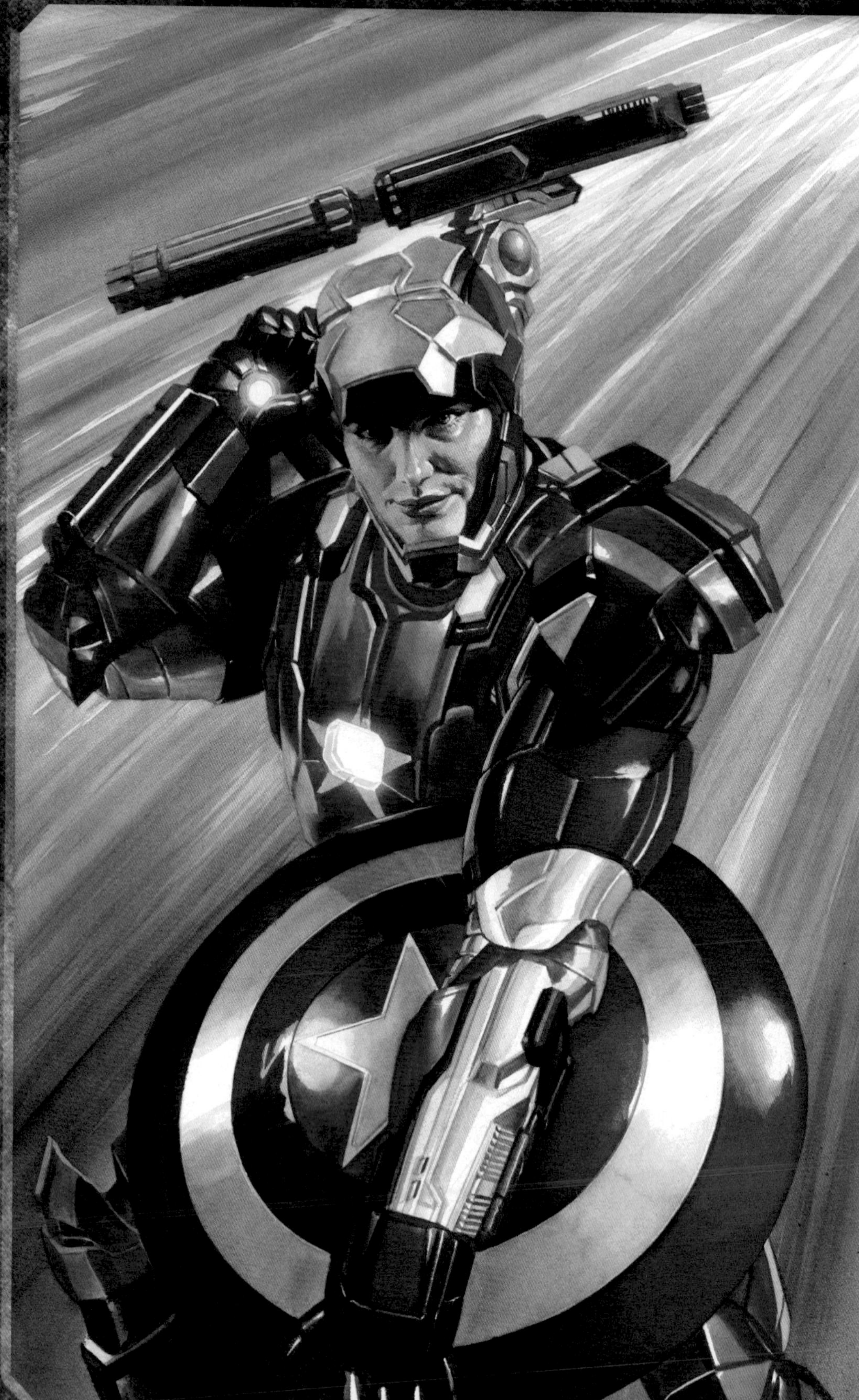

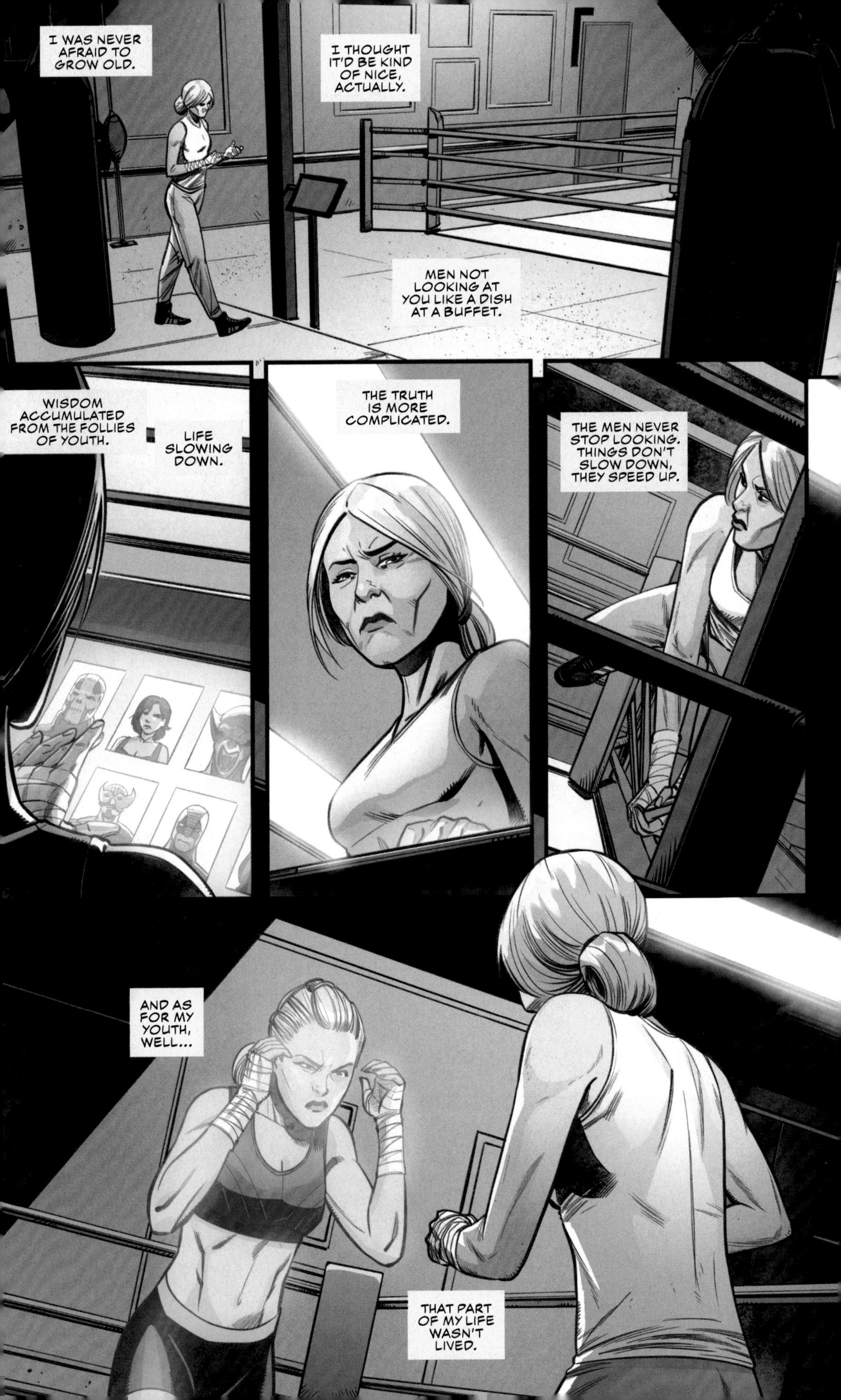
I WAS NEVER AFRAID TO GROW OLD.
I THOUGHT IT'D BE KIND OF NICE, ACTUALLY.
MEN NOT LOOKING AT YOU LIKE A DISH AT A BUFFET.
WISDOM ACCUMULATED FROM THE FOLLIES OF YOUTH.
LIFE SLOWING DOWN.
THE TRUTH IS MORE COMPLICATED.
THE MEN NEVER STOP LOOKING. THINGS DON'T SLOW DOWN, THEY SPEED UP.
AND AS FOR MY YOUTH, WELL...
THAT PART OF MY LIFE WASN'T LIVED.

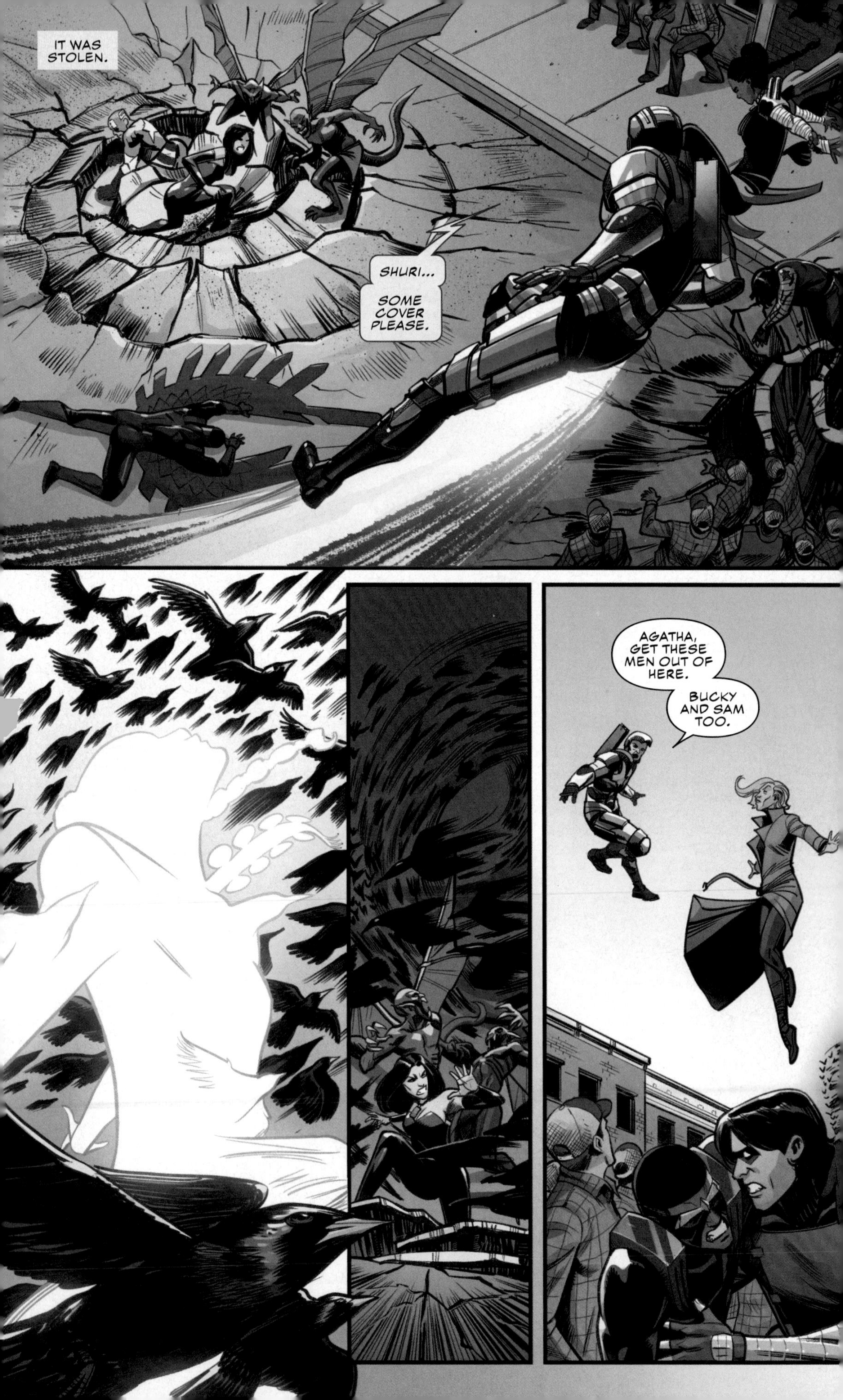
IT WAS STOLEN.
SHURI...
SOME COVER PLEASE.
AGATHA, GET THESE MEN OUT OF HERE.
BUCKY AND SAM TOO.

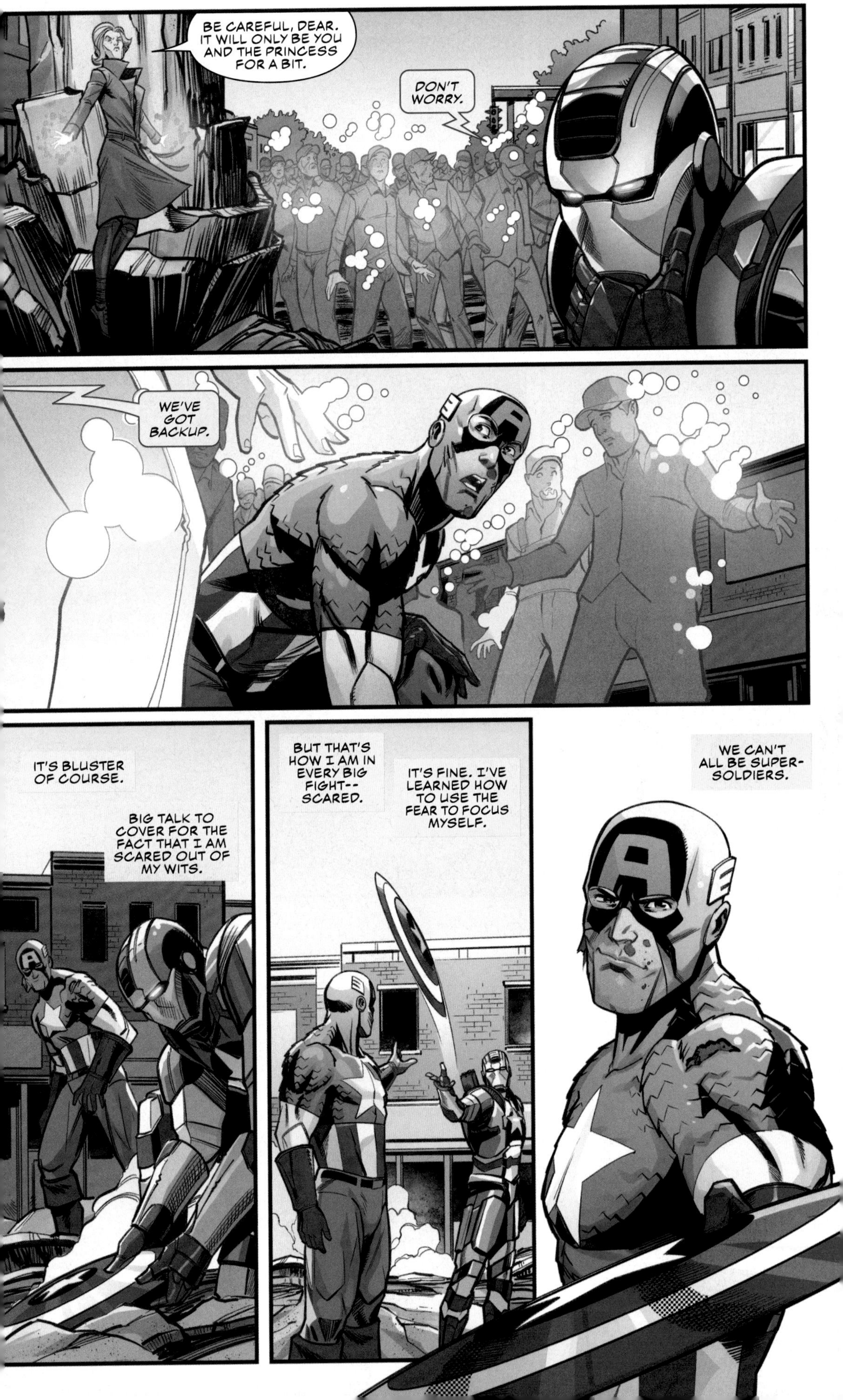
BE CAREFUL, DEAR. IT WILL ONLY BE YOU AND THE PRINCESS FOR A BIT.
DON'T WORRY.
WE'VE GOT BACKUP.
IT'S BLUSTER OF COURSE.
BIG TALK TO COVER FOR THE FACT THAT I AM SCARED OUT OF MY WITS.
BUT THAT'S HOW I AM IN EVERY BIG FIGHT-- SCARED.
IT'S FINE. I'VE LEARNED HOW TO USE THE FEAR TO FOCUS MYSELF.
WE CAN'T ALL BE SUPER-SOLDIERS.

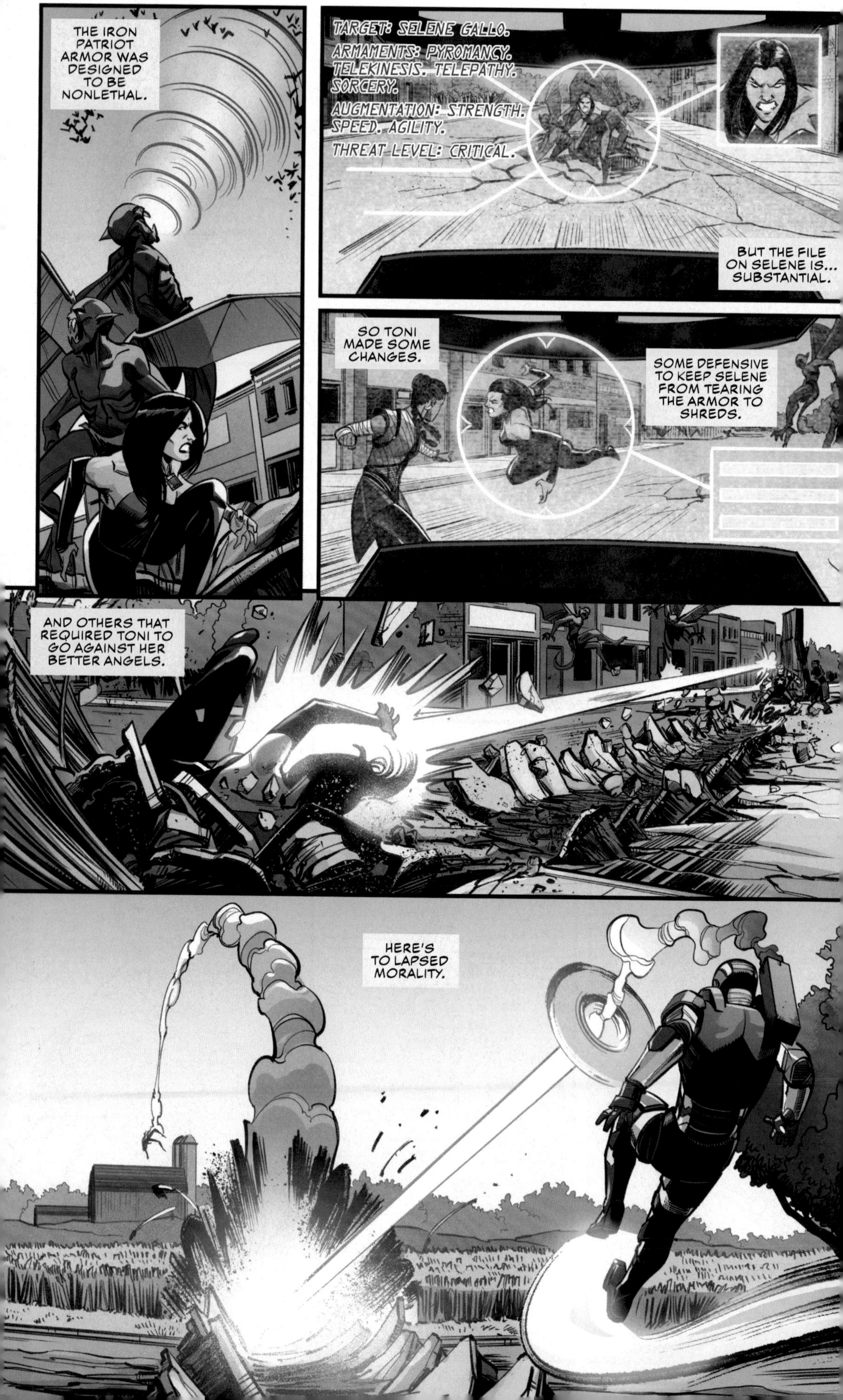

THE IRON PATRIOT ARMOR WAS DESIGNED TO BE NONLETHAL.
TARGET: SELENE GALLO.
ARMAMENTS: PYROMANCY. TELEKINESIS. TELEPATHY. SORCERY.
AUGMENTATION: STRENGTH. SPEED. AGILITY.
THREAT LEVEL: CRITICAL.
BUT THE FILE ON SELENE IS... SUBSTANTIAL.
SO TONI MADE SOME CHANGES.
SOME DEFENSIVE TO KEEP SELENE FROM TEARING THE ARMOR TO SHREDS.
AND OTHERS THAT REQUIRED TONI TO GO AGAINST HER BETTER ANGELS.
HERE'S TO LAPSED MORALITY.

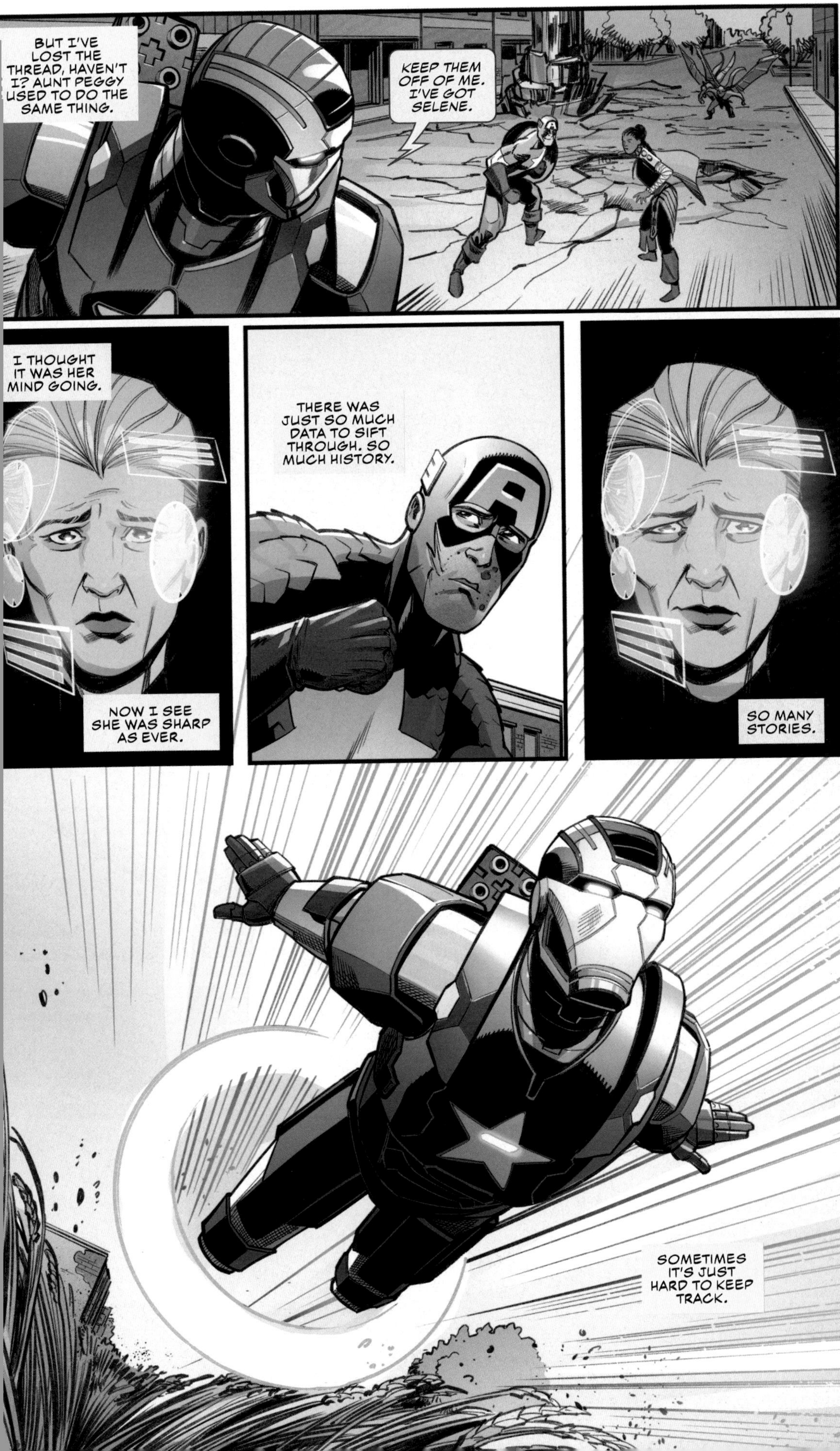
BUT I'VE LOST THE THREAD, HAVEN'T I? AUNT PEGGY USED TO DO THE SAME THING.
KEEP THEM OFF OF ME. I'VE GOT SELENE.
I THOUGHT IT WAS HER MIND GOING.
NOW I SEE SHE WAS SHARP AS EVER.
THERE WAS JUST SO MUCH DATA TO SIFT THROUGH. SO MUCH HISTORY.
SO MANY STORIES.
SOMETIMES IT'S JUST HARD TO KEEP TRACK.

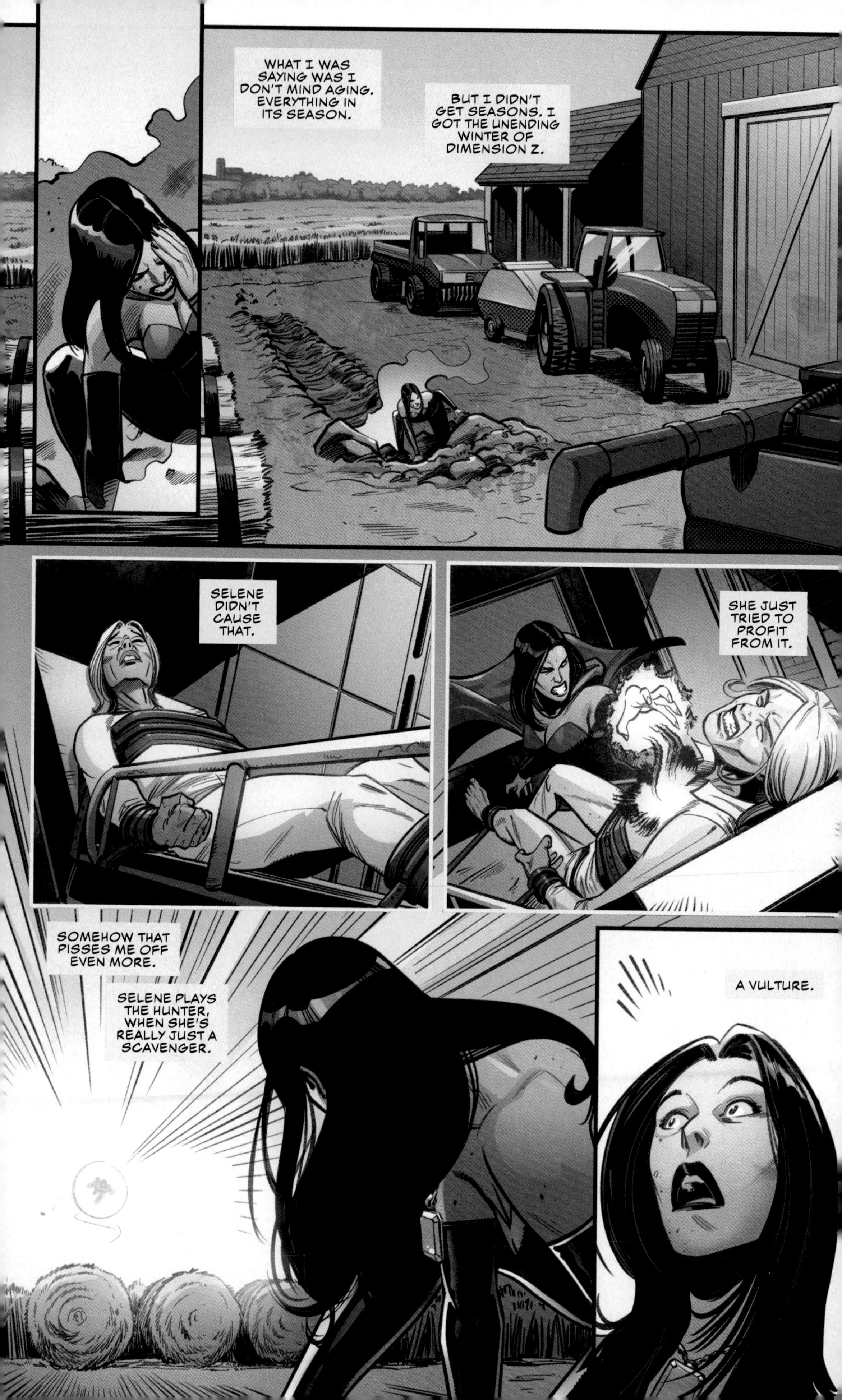
WHAT I WAS SAYING WAS I DON'T MIND AGING. EVERYTHING IN ITS SEASON.
BUT I DIDN'T GET SEASONS. I GOT THE UNENDING WINTER OF DIMENSION Z.
SELENE DIDN'T CAUSE THAT.
SHE JUST TRIED TO PROFIT FROM IT.
SOMEHOW THAT PISSES ME OFF EVEN MORE.
SELENE PLAYS THE HUNTER, WHEN SHE'S REALLY JUST A SCAVENGER.
A VULTURE.

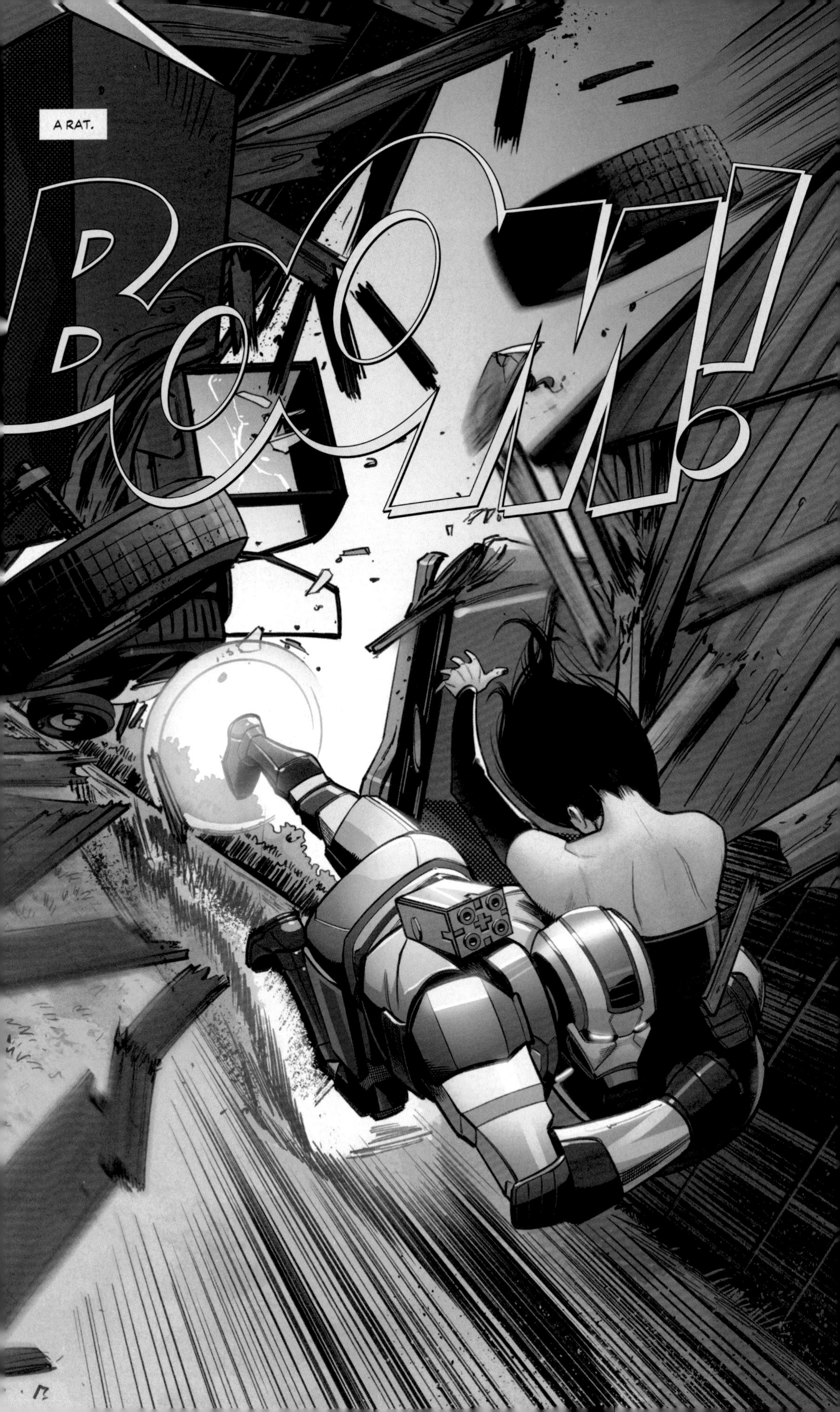
A RAT.
BOOM!

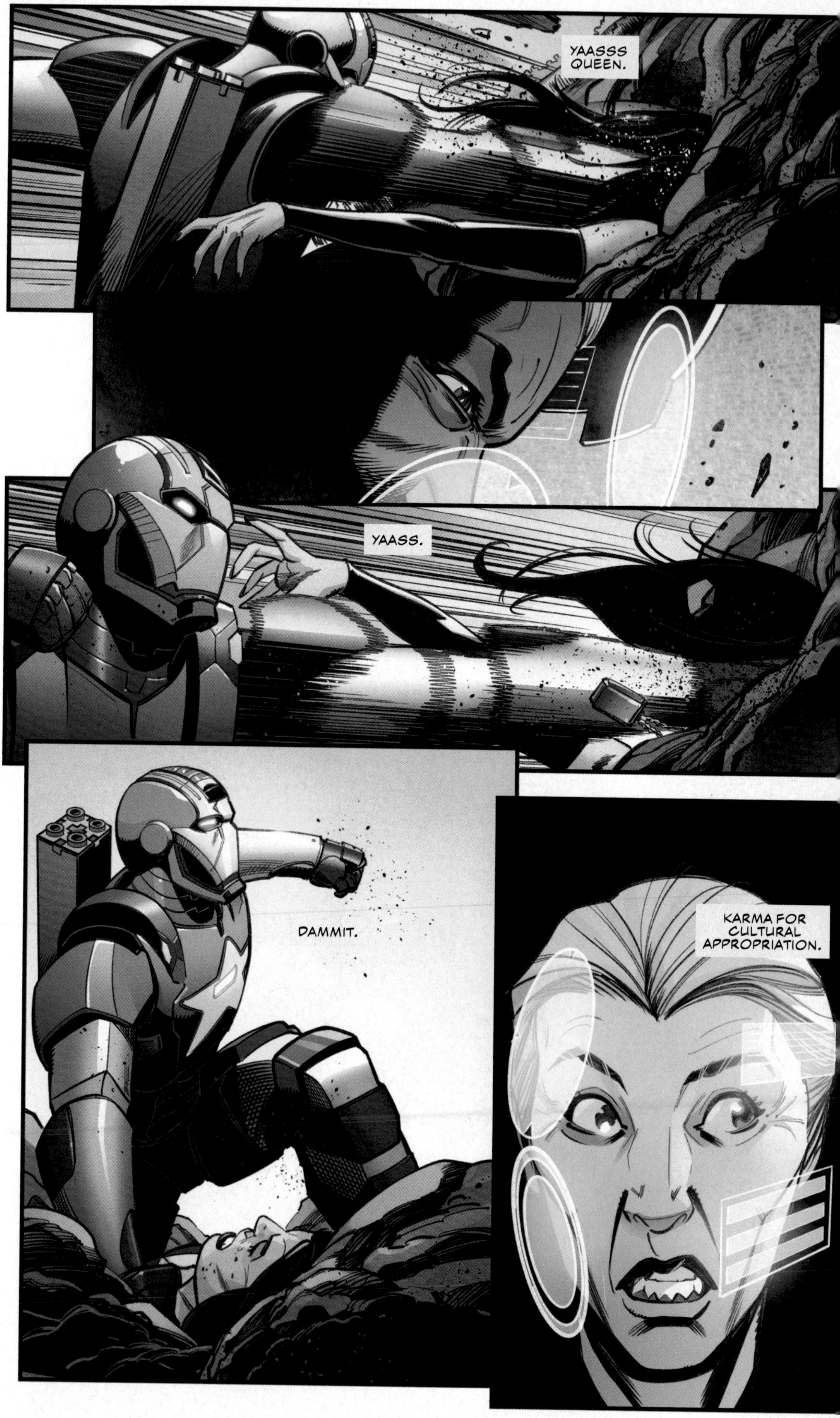
YAASSS QUEEN.
YAASS.
DAMMIT.
KARMA FOR CULTURAL APPROPRIATION.

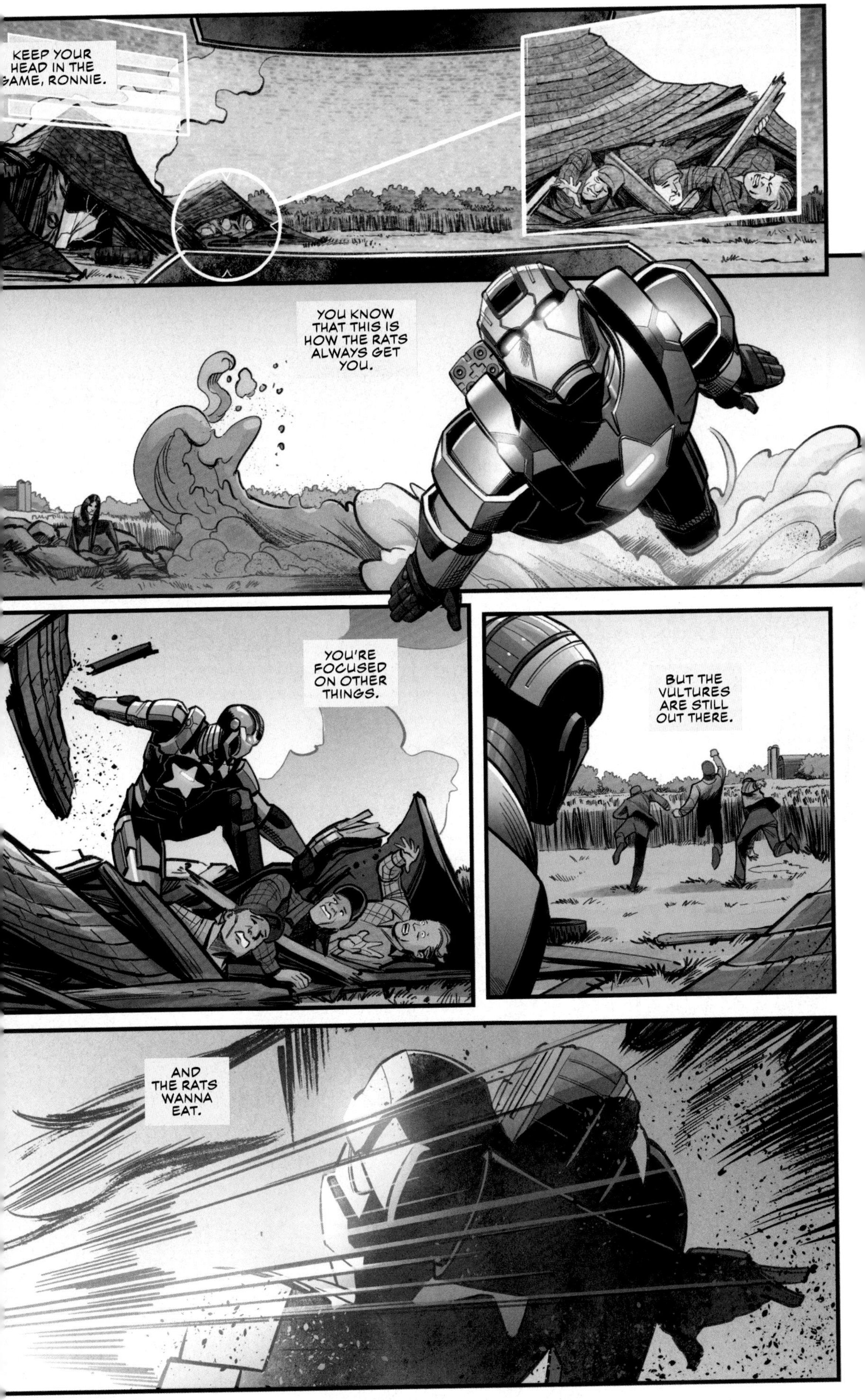
KEEP YOUR HEAD IN THE GAME, RONNIE.
YOU KNOW THAT THIS IS HOW THE RATS ALWAYS GET YOU.
YOU'RE FOCUSED ON OTHER THINGS.
BUT THE VULTURES ARE STILL OUT THERE.
AND THE RATS WANNA EAT.

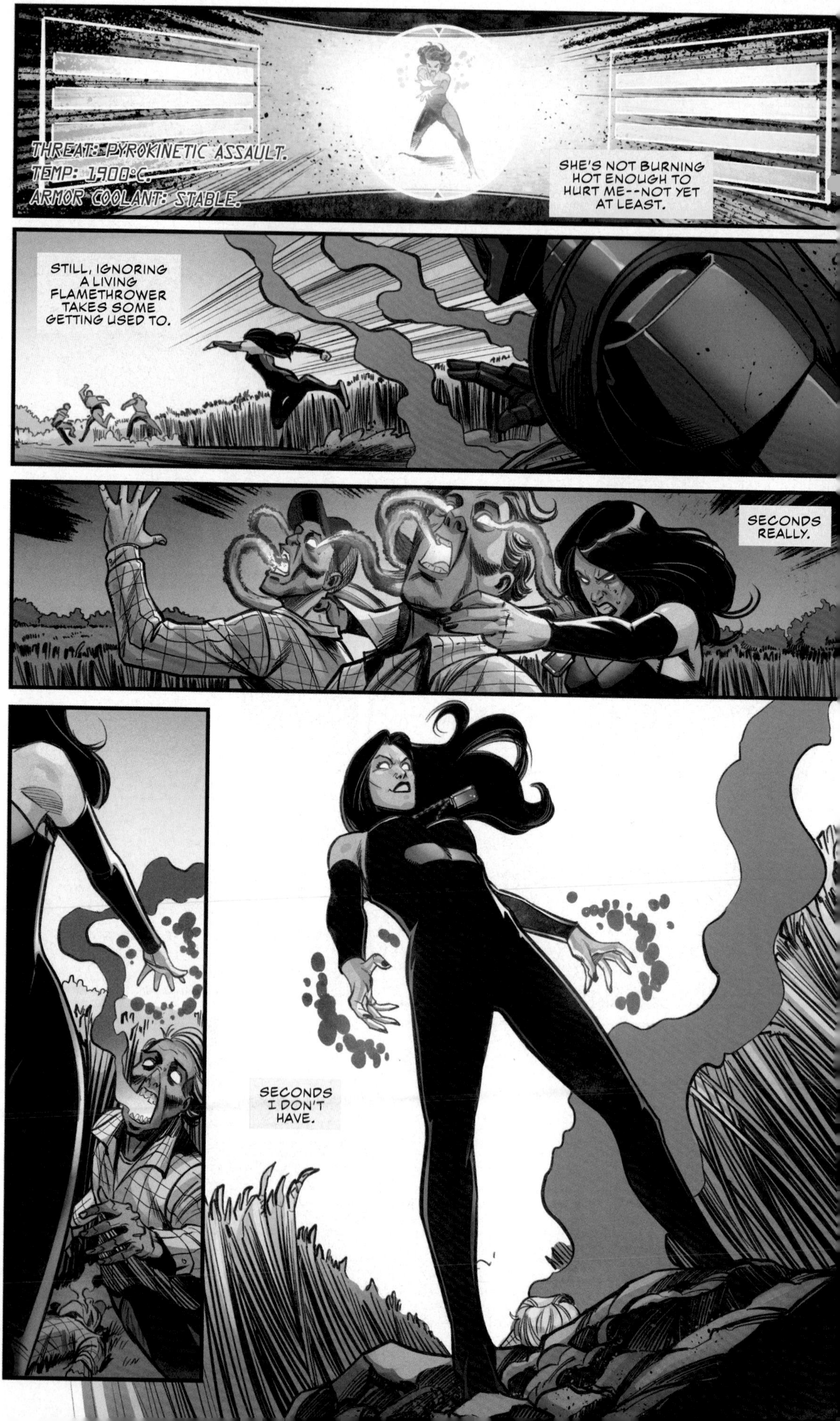
THREAT: PYROKINETIC ASSAULT.
TEMP: 1900°C.
ARMOR COOLANT: STABLE.
SHE'S NOT BURNING HOT ENOUGH TO HURT ME--NOT YET AT LEAST.
STILL, IGNORING A LIVING FLAMETHROWER TAKES SOME GETTING USED TO.
SECONDS REALLY.
SECONDS I DON'T HAVE.

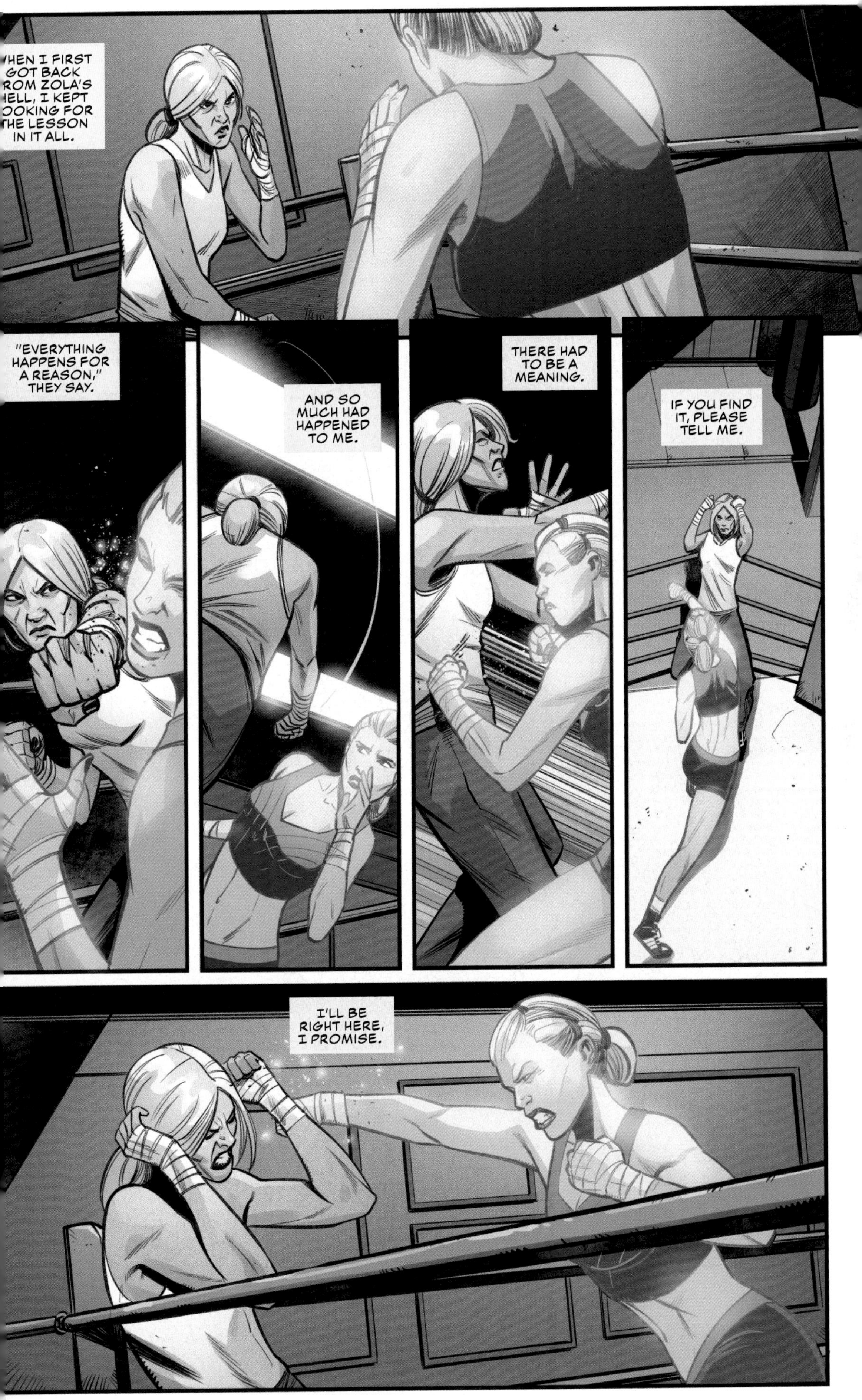
WHEN I FIRST GOT BACK FROM ZOLA'S HELL, I KEPT LOOKING FOR THE LESSON IN IT ALL.
"EVERYTHING HAPPENS FOR A REASON," THEY SAY.
AND SO MUCH HAD HAPPENED TO ME.
THERE HAD TO BE A MEANING.
IF YOU FIND IT, PLEASE TELL ME.
I'LL BE RIGHT HERE, I PROMISE.

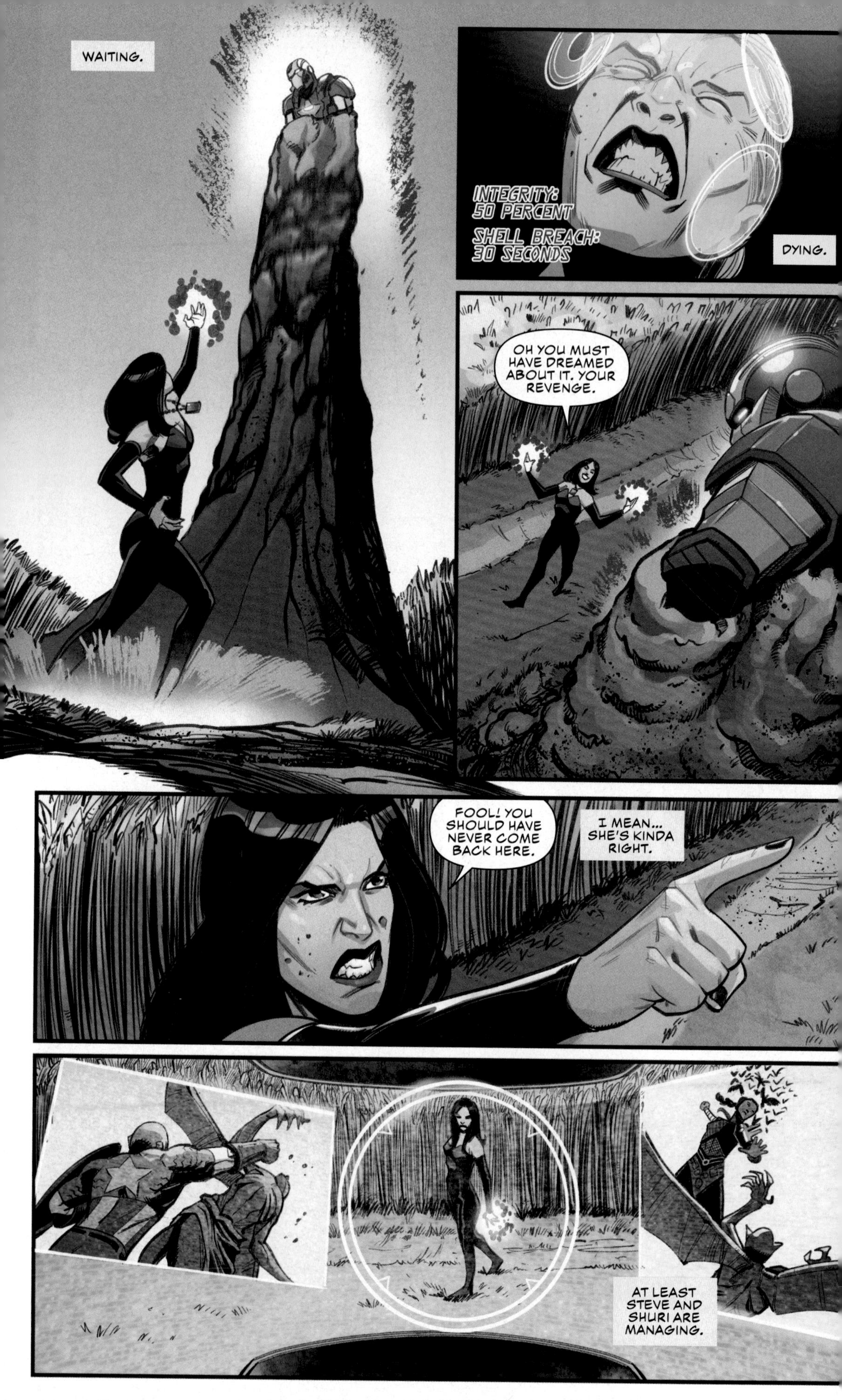
WAITING.
INTEGRITY:
50 PERCENT
SHELL BREACH:
30 SECONDS
DYING.
OH YOU MUST HAVE DREAMED ABOUT IT. YOUR REVENGE.
FOOL! YOU SHOULD HAVE NEVER COME BACK HERE.
I MEAN... SHE'S KINDA RIGHT.
AT LEAST STEVE AND SHURI ARE MANAGING.

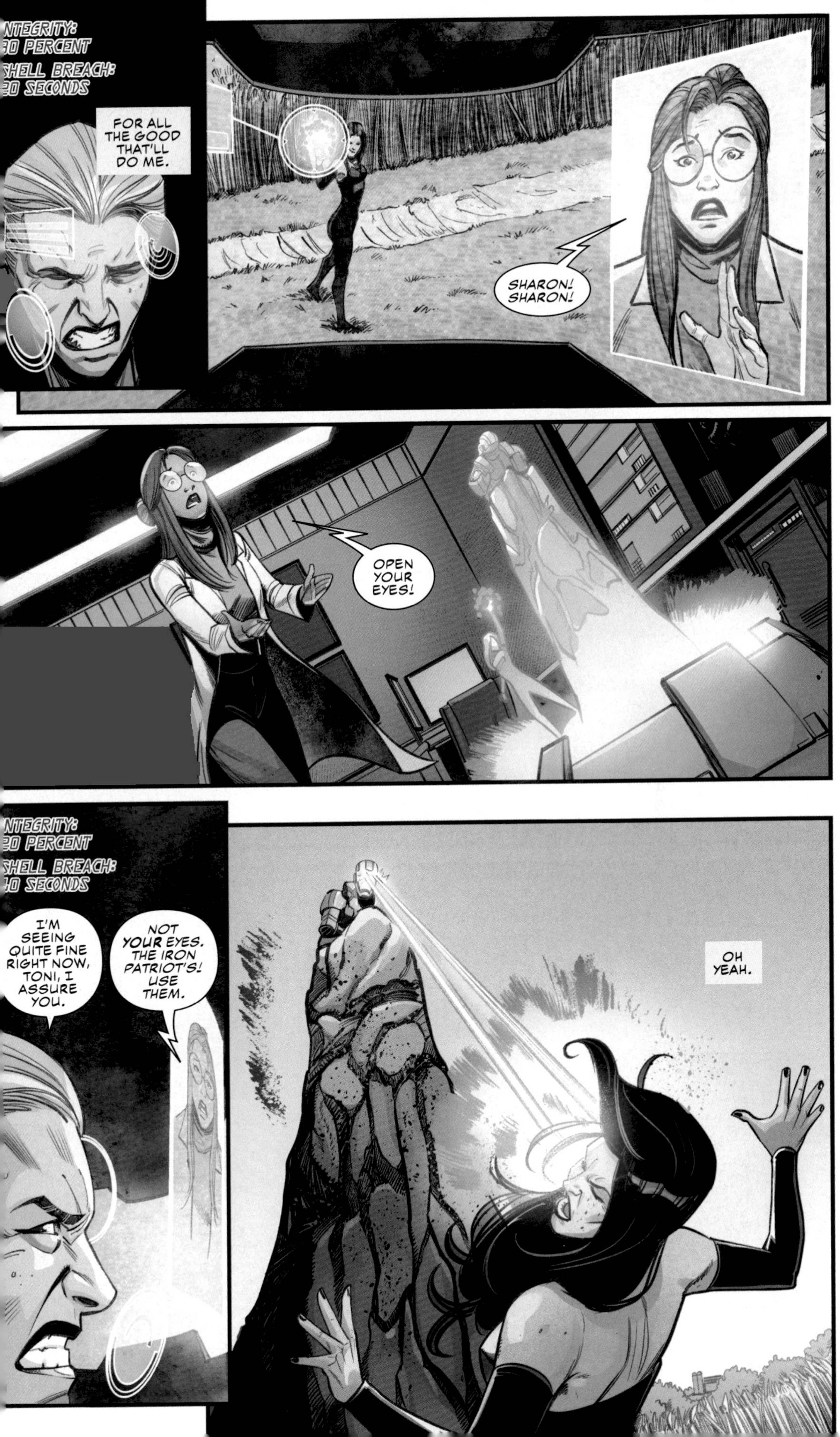
NTEGRITY:
0 PERCENT
SHELL BREACH:
0 SECONDS
FOR ALL THE GOOD THAT'LL DO ME.
SHARON! SHARON!
OPEN YOUR EYES!
NTEGRITY:
0 PERCENT
SHELL BREACH:
0 SECONDS
I'M SEEING QUITE FINE RIGHT NOW, TONI, I ASSURE YOU.
NOT YOUR EYES. THE IRON PATRIOT'S! USE THEM.
OH YEAH.

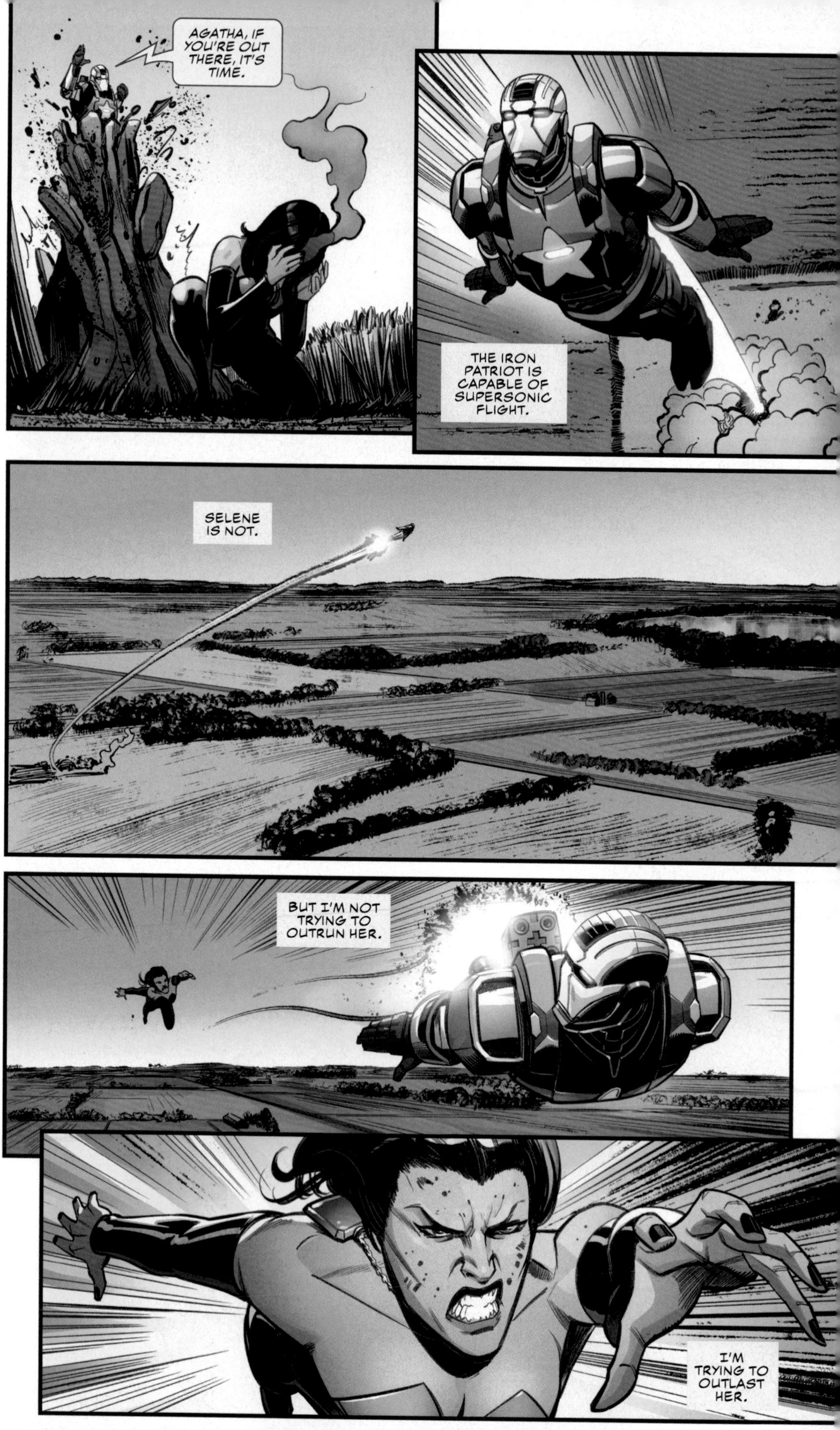
AGATHA, IF YOU'RE OUT THERE, IT'S TIME.
THE IRON PATRIOT IS CAPABLE OF SUPERSONIC FLIGHT.
SELENE IS NOT.
BUT I'M NOT TRYING TO OUTRUN HER.
I'M TRYING TO OUTLAST HER.

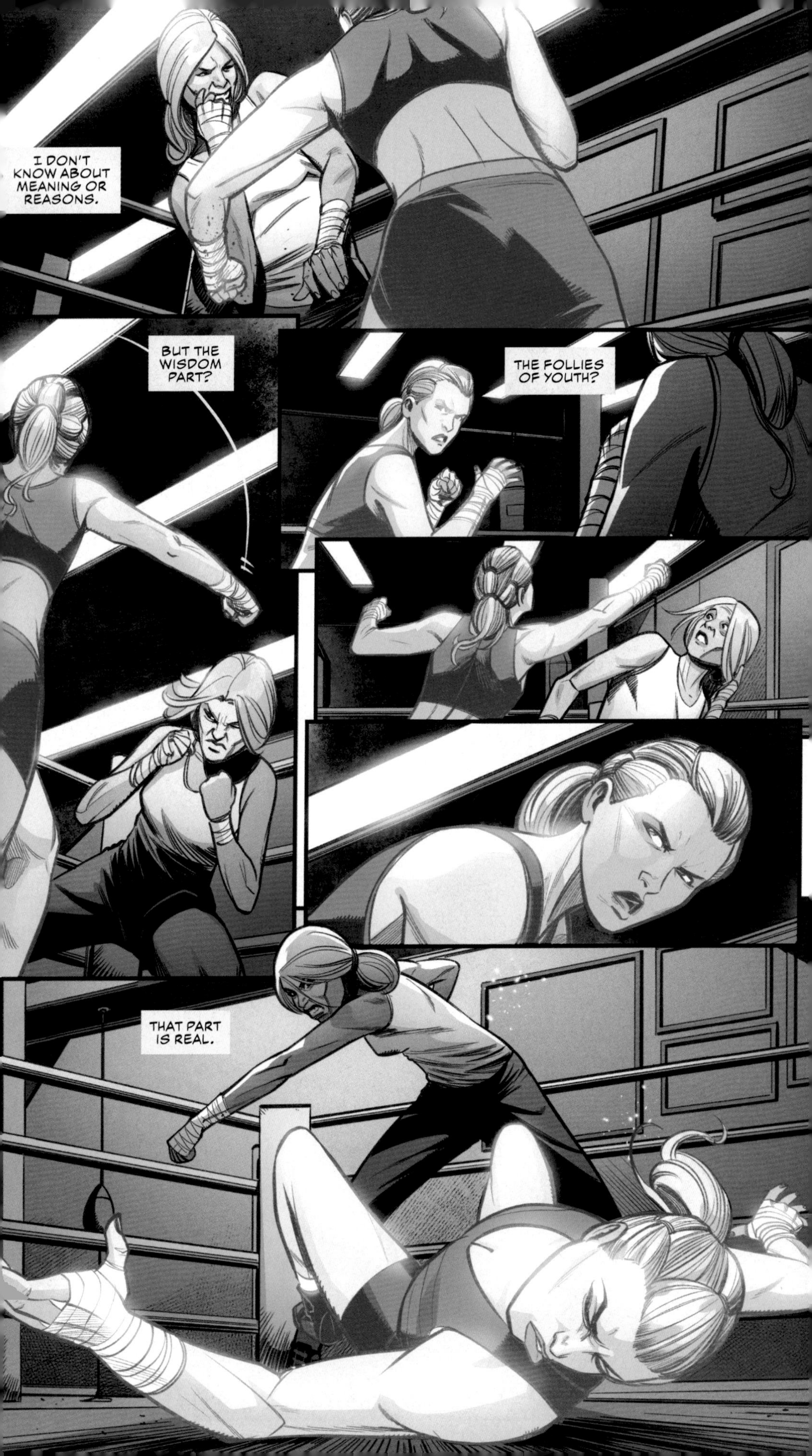
I DON'T KNOW ABOUT MEANING OR REASONS.
BUT THE WISDOM PART?
THE FOLLIES OF YOUTH?
THAT PART IS REAL.

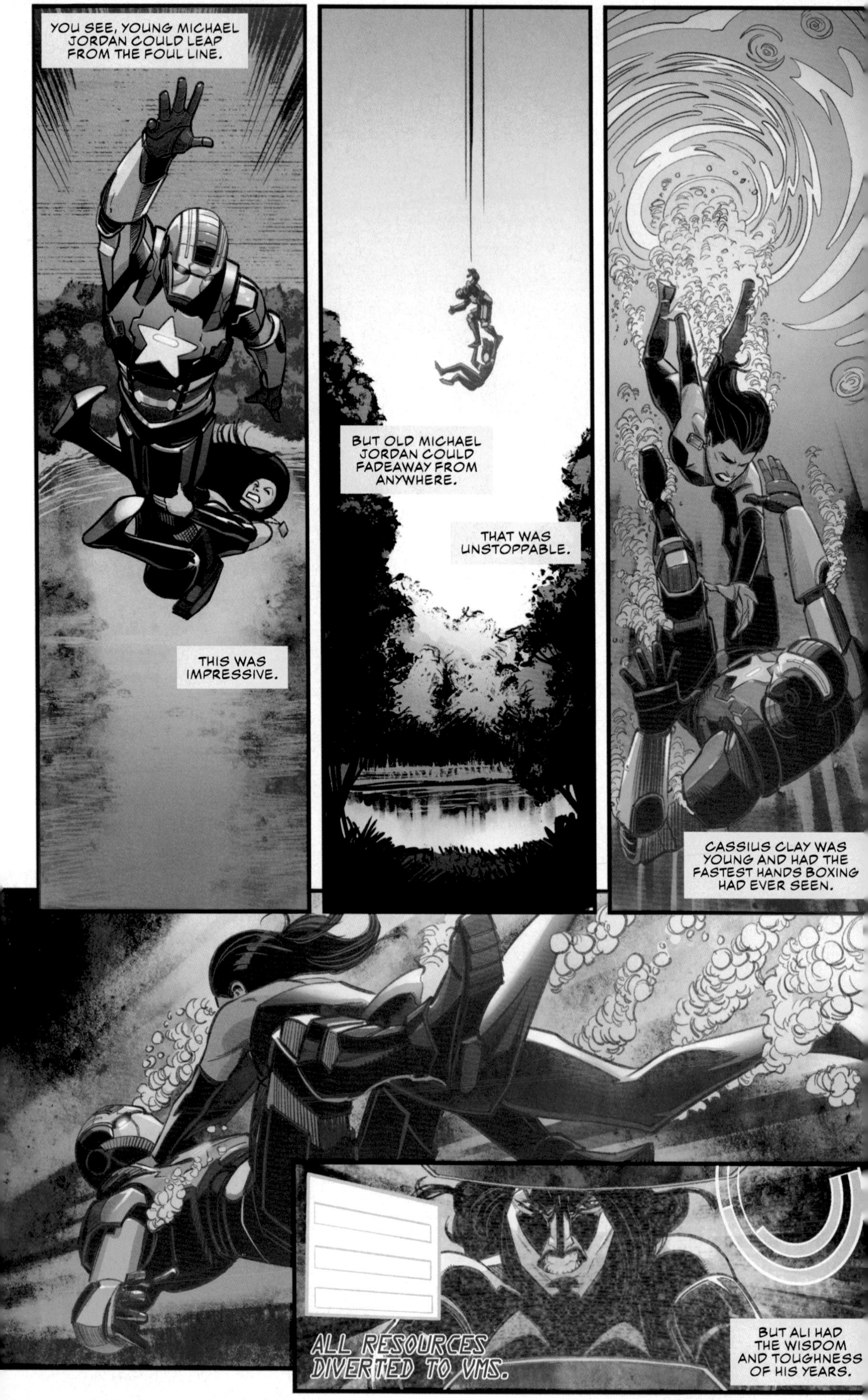
YOU SEE, YOUNG MICHAEL JORDAN COULD LEAP FROM THE FOUL LINE.
THIS WAS IMPRESSIVE.
BUT OLD MICHAEL JORDAN COULD FADEAWAY FROM ANYWHERE.
THAT WAS UNSTOPPABLE.
CASSIUS CLAY WAS YOUNG AND HAD THE FASTEST HANDS BOXING HAD EVER SEEN.
ALL RESOURCES DIVERTED TO VMS.
BUT ALI HAD THE WISDOM AND TOUGHNESS OF HIS YEARS.

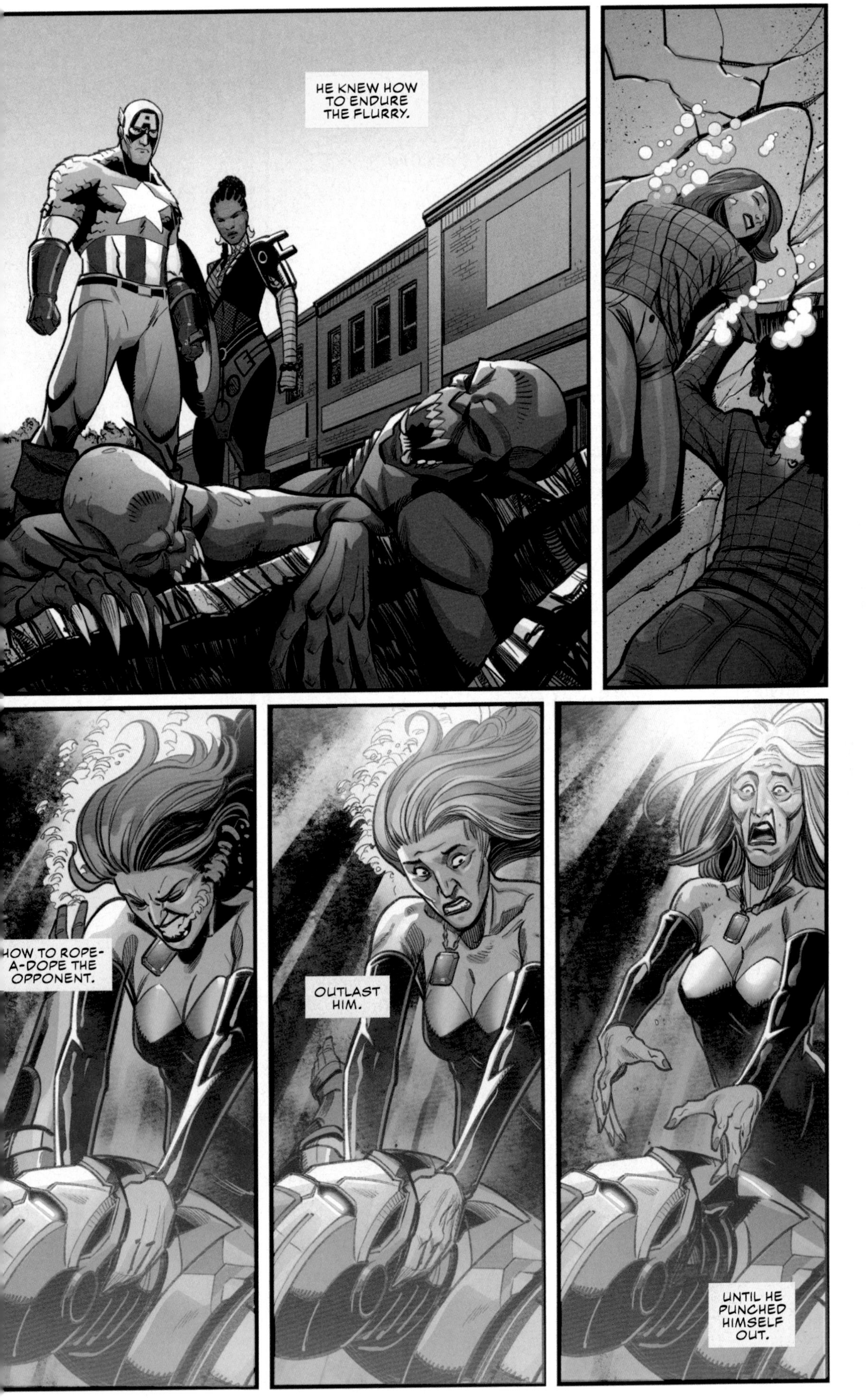
HE KNEW HOW TO ENDURE THE FLURRY.
HOW TO ROPE-A-DOPE THE OPPONENT.
OUTLAST HIM.
UNTIL HE PUNCHED HIMSELF OUT.

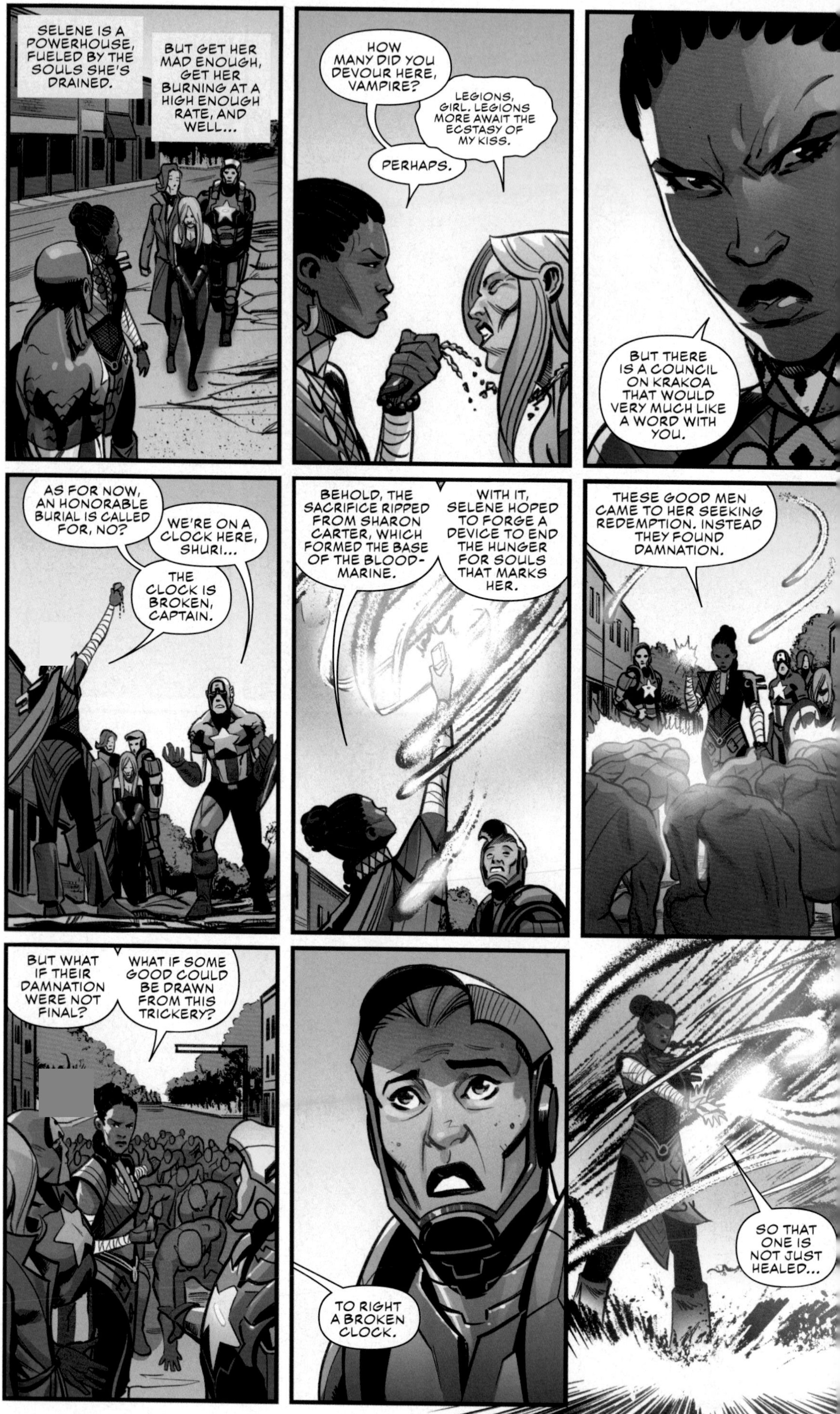
SELENE IS A POWERHOUSE, FUELED BY THE SOULS SHE'S DRAINED.
BUT GET HER MAD ENOUGH, GET HER BURNING AT A HIGH ENOUGH RATE, AND WELL...
HOW MANY DID YOU DEVOUR HERE, VAMPIRE?
PERHAPS.
LEGIONS, GIRL. LEGIONS MORE AWAIT THE ECSTASY OF MY KISS.
BUT THERE IS A COUNCIL ON KRAKOA THAT WOULD VERY MUCH LIKE A WORD WITH YOU.
AS FOR NOW, AN HONORABLE BURIAL IS CALLED FOR, NO?
WE'RE ON A CLOCK HERE, SHURI...
THE CLOCK IS BROKEN, CAPTAIN.
BEHOLD, THE SACRIFICE RIPPED FROM SHARON CARTER, WHICH FORMED THE BASE OF THE BLOOD-MARINE.
WITH IT, SELENE HOPED TO FORGE A DEVICE TO END THE HUNGER FOR SOULS THAT MARKS HER.
THESE GOOD MEN CAME TO HER SEEKING REDEMPTION. INSTEAD THEY FOUND DAMNATION.
BUT WHAT IF THEIR DAMNATION WERE NOT FINAL?
WHAT IF SOME GOOD COULD BE DRAWN FROM THIS TRICKERY?
TO RIGHT A BROKEN CLOCK.
SO THAT ONE IS NOT JUST HEALED...

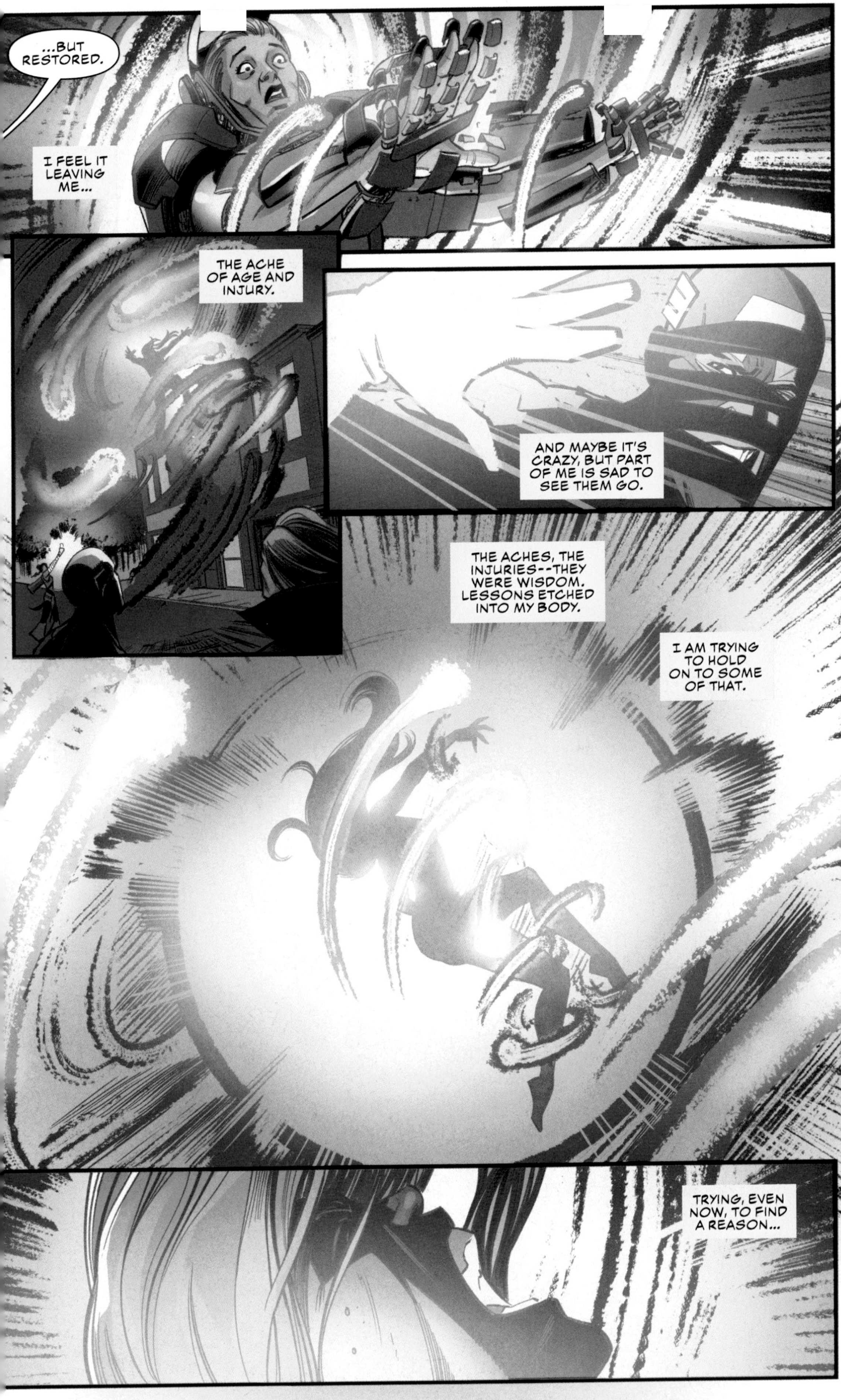
...BUT RESTORED.
I FEEL IT LEAVING ME...
THE ACHE OF AGE AND INJURY.
AND MAYBE IT'S CRAZY, BUT PART OF ME IS SAD TO SEE THEM GO.
THE ACHES, THE INJURIES--THEY WERE WISDOM. LESSONS ETCHED INTO MY BODY.
I AM TRYING TO HOLD ON TO SOME OF THAT.
TRYING, EVEN NOW, TO FIND A REASON...

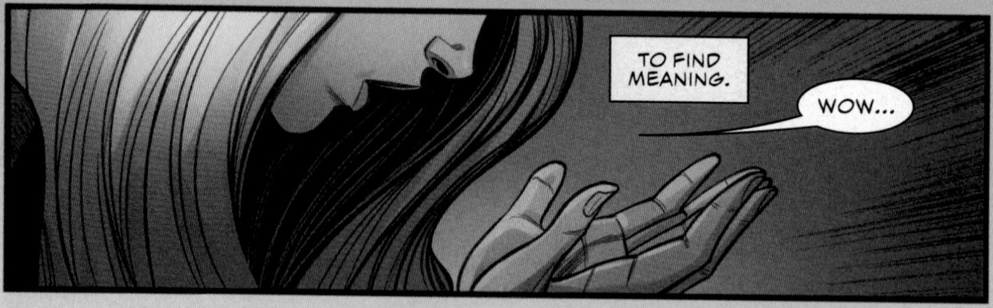
TO FIND MEANING.
WOW...
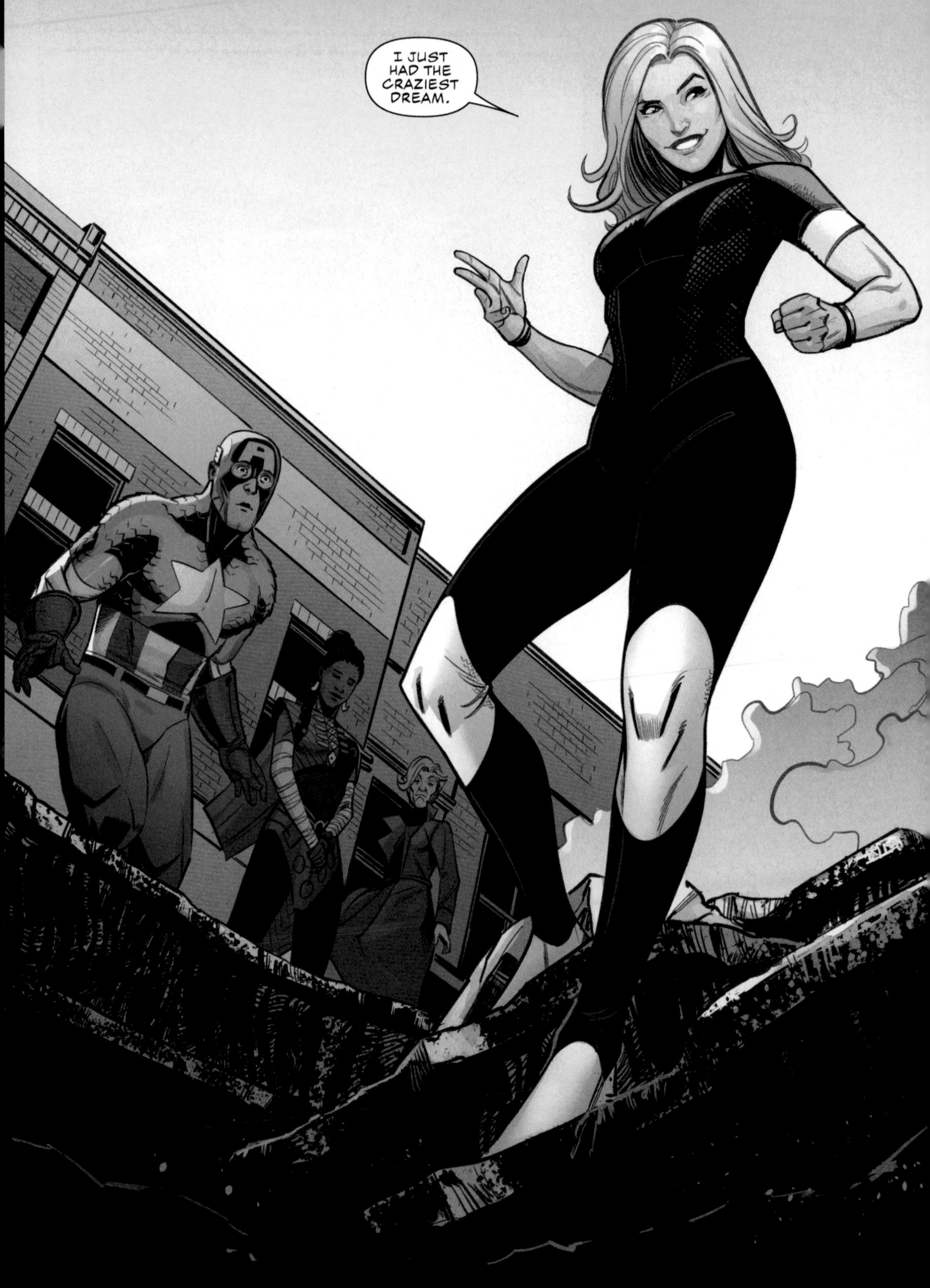
I JUST HAD THE CRAZIEST DREAM.

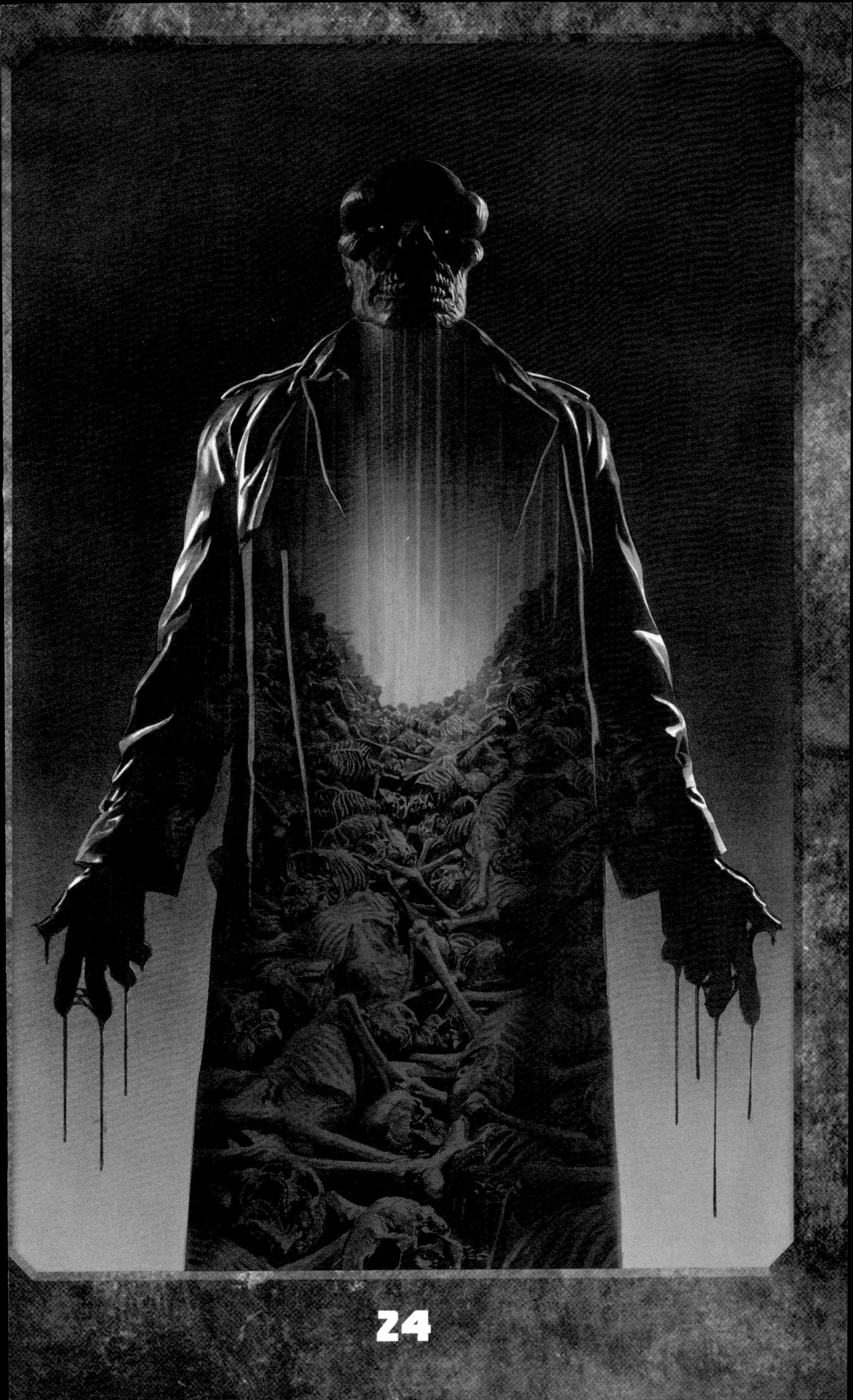

24

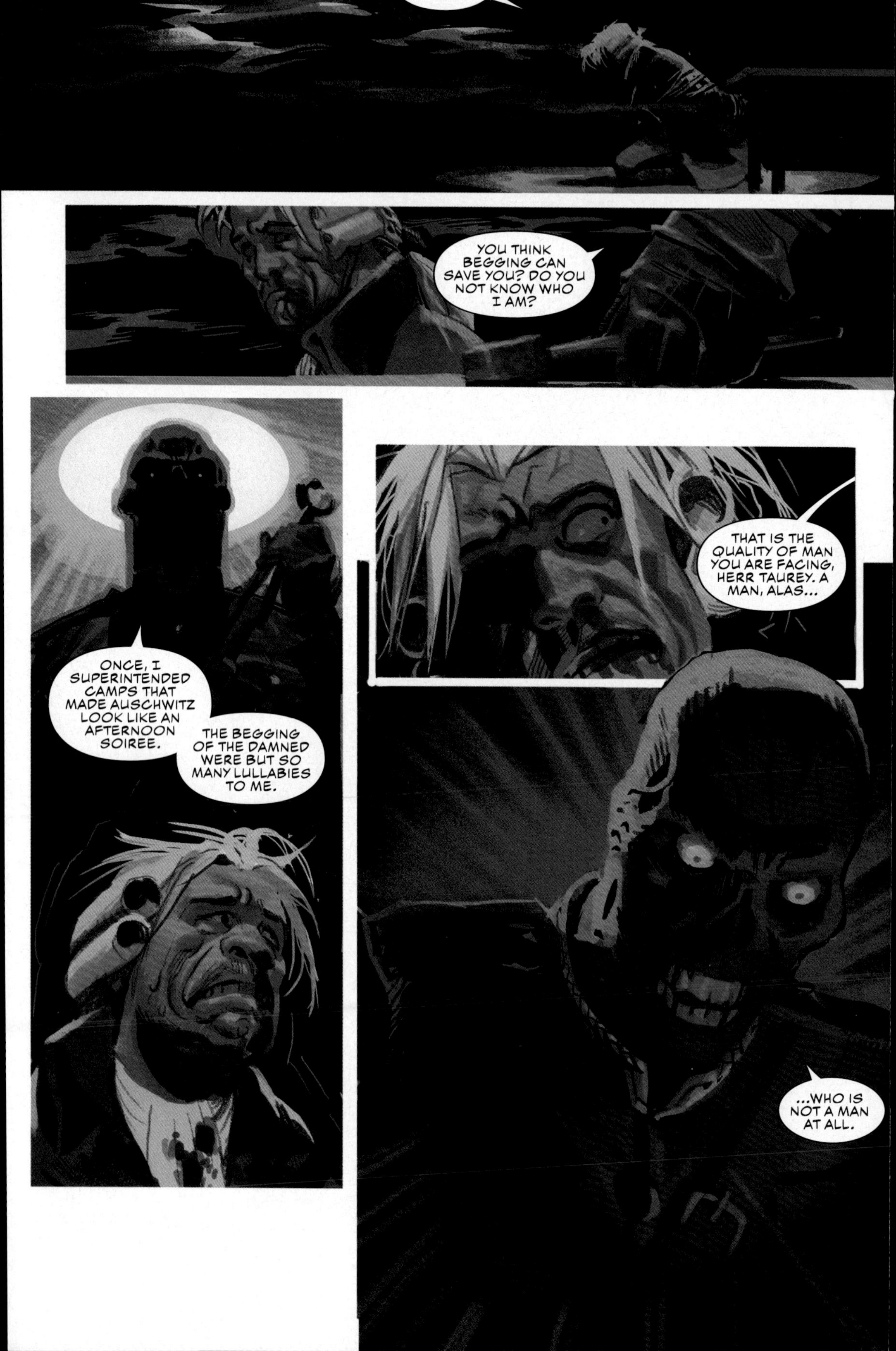
YOU THINK BEGGING CAN SAVE YOU? DO YOU NOT KNOW WHO I AM?
ONCE, I SUPERINTENDED CAMPS THAT MADE AUSCHWITZ LOOK LIKE AN AFTERNOON SOIREE.
THE BEGGING OF THE DAMNED WERE BUT SO MANY LULLABIES TO ME.
THAT IS THE QUALITY OF MAN YOU ARE FACING, HERR TAUREY. A MAN, ALAS...
...WHO IS NOT A MAN AT ALL.

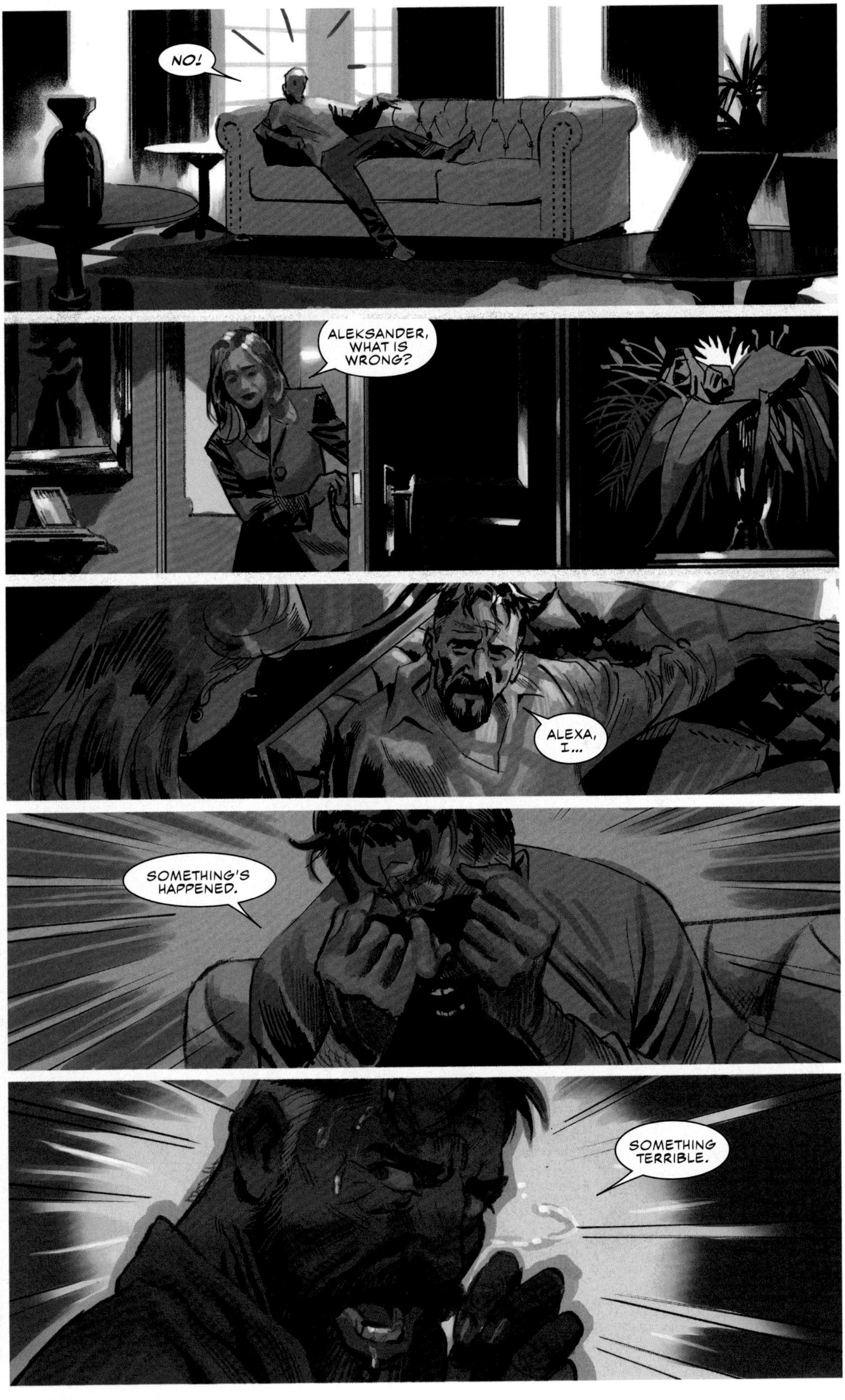
NO!
ALEKSANDER, WHAT IS WRONG?
ALEXA, I...
SOMETHING'S HAPPENED.
SOMETHING TERRIBLE.

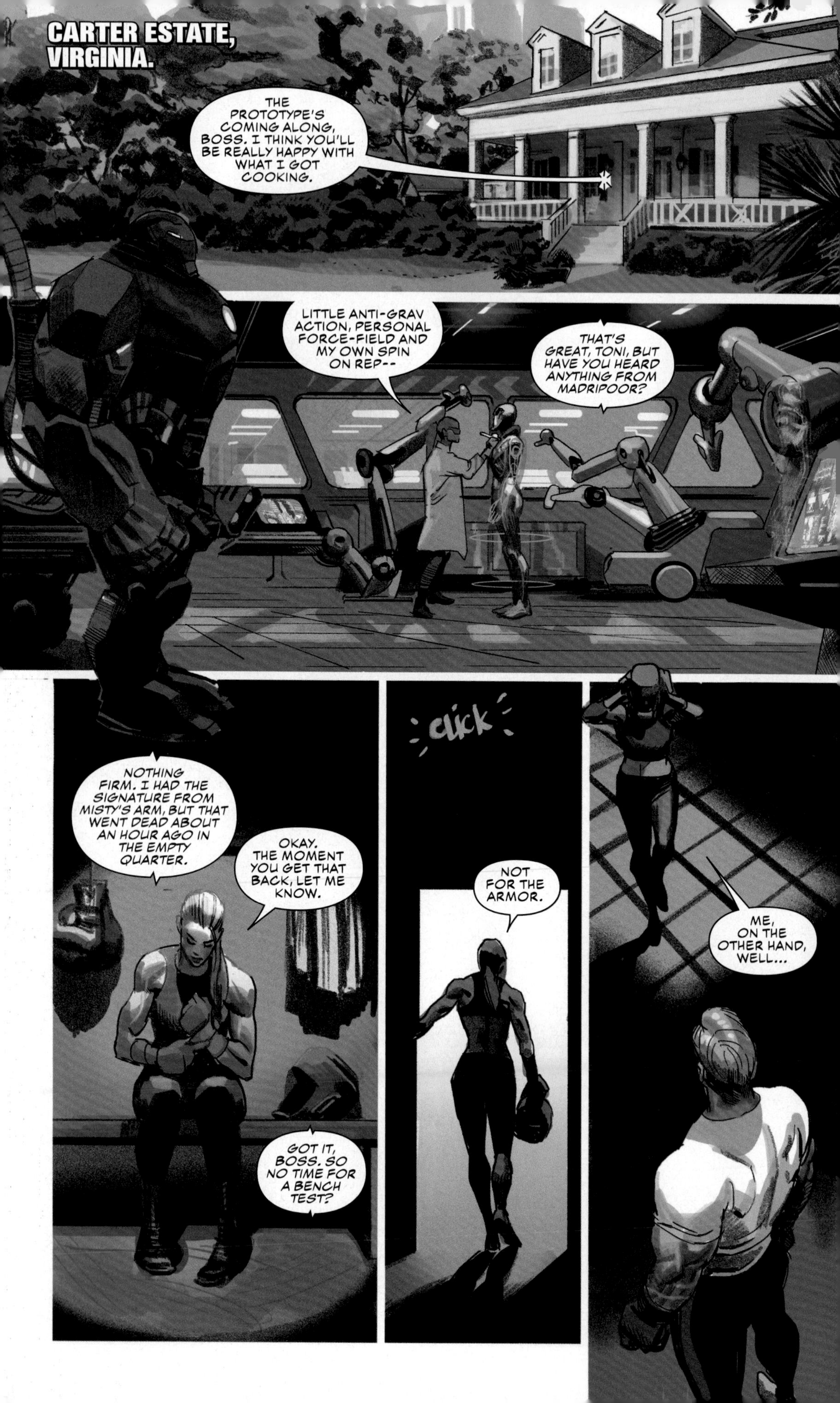
CARTER ESTATE, VIRGINIA.
THE PROTOTYPE'S COMING ALONG, BOSS. I THINK YOU'LL BE REALLY HAPPY WITH WHAT I GOT COOKING.
LITTLE ANTI-GRAV ACTION, PERSONAL FORCE-FIELD AND MY OWN SPIN ON REP--
THAT'S GREAT, TONI, BUT HAVE YOU HEARD ANYTHING FROM MADRIPOOR?
NOTHING FIRM. I HAD THE SIGNATURE FROM MISTY'S ARM, BUT THAT WENT DEAD ABOUT AN HOUR AGO IN THE EMPTY QUARTER.
OKAY. THE MOMENT YOU GET THAT BACK, LET ME KNOW.
GOT IT, BOSS. SO NO TIME FOR A BENCH TEST?
click
NOT FOR THE ARMOR.
ME, ON THE OTHER HAND, WELL...

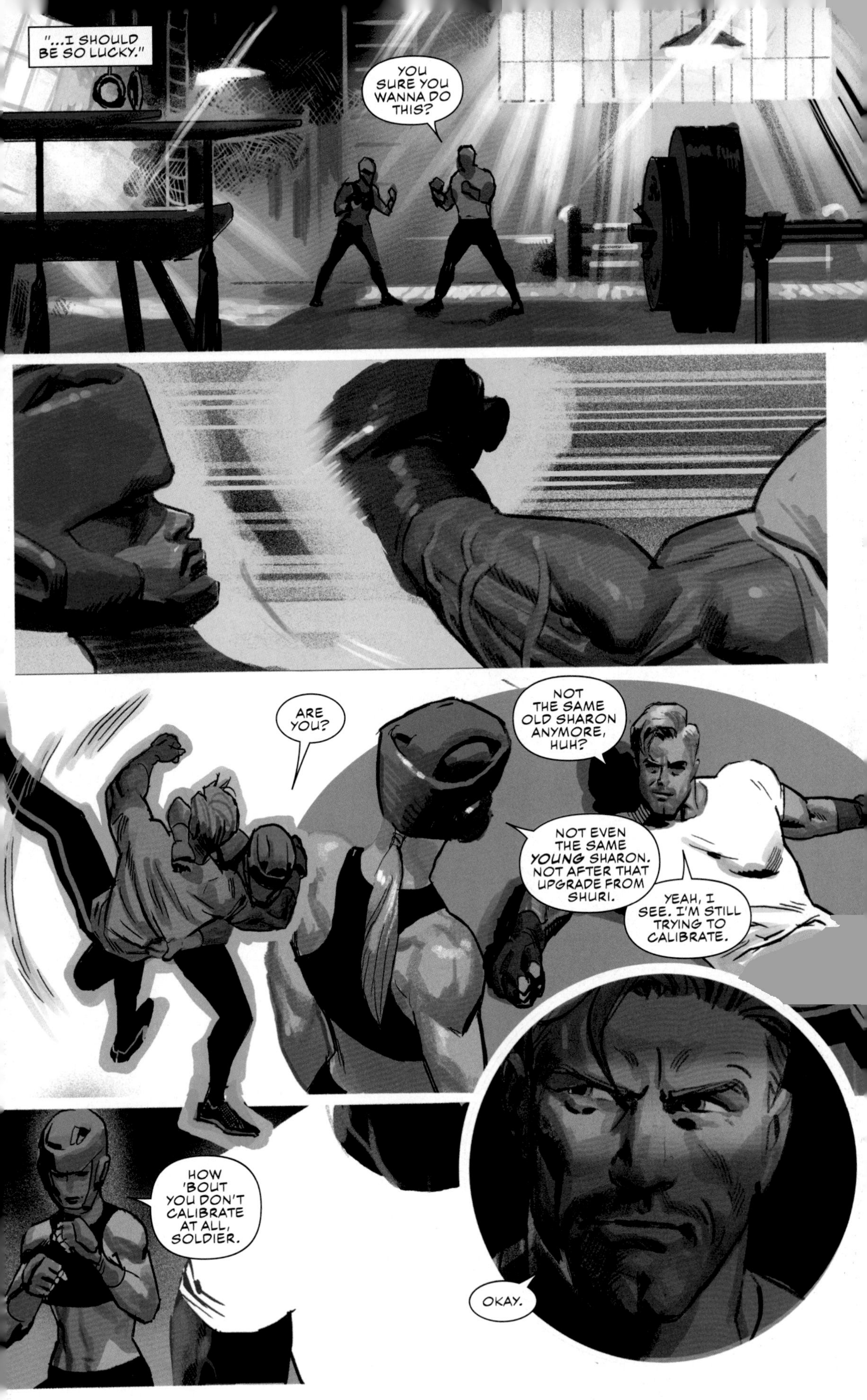
"...I SHOULD BE SO LUCKY."
YOU SURE YOU WANNA DO THIS?
ARE YOU?
NOT THE SAME OLD SHARON ANYMORE, HUH?
NOT EVEN THE SAME *YOUNG* SHARON. NOT AFTER THAT UPGRADE FROM SHURI.
YEAH, I SEE. I'M STILL TRYING TO CALIBRATE.
HOW 'BOUT YOU DON'T CALIBRATE AT ALL, SOLDIER.
OKAY.

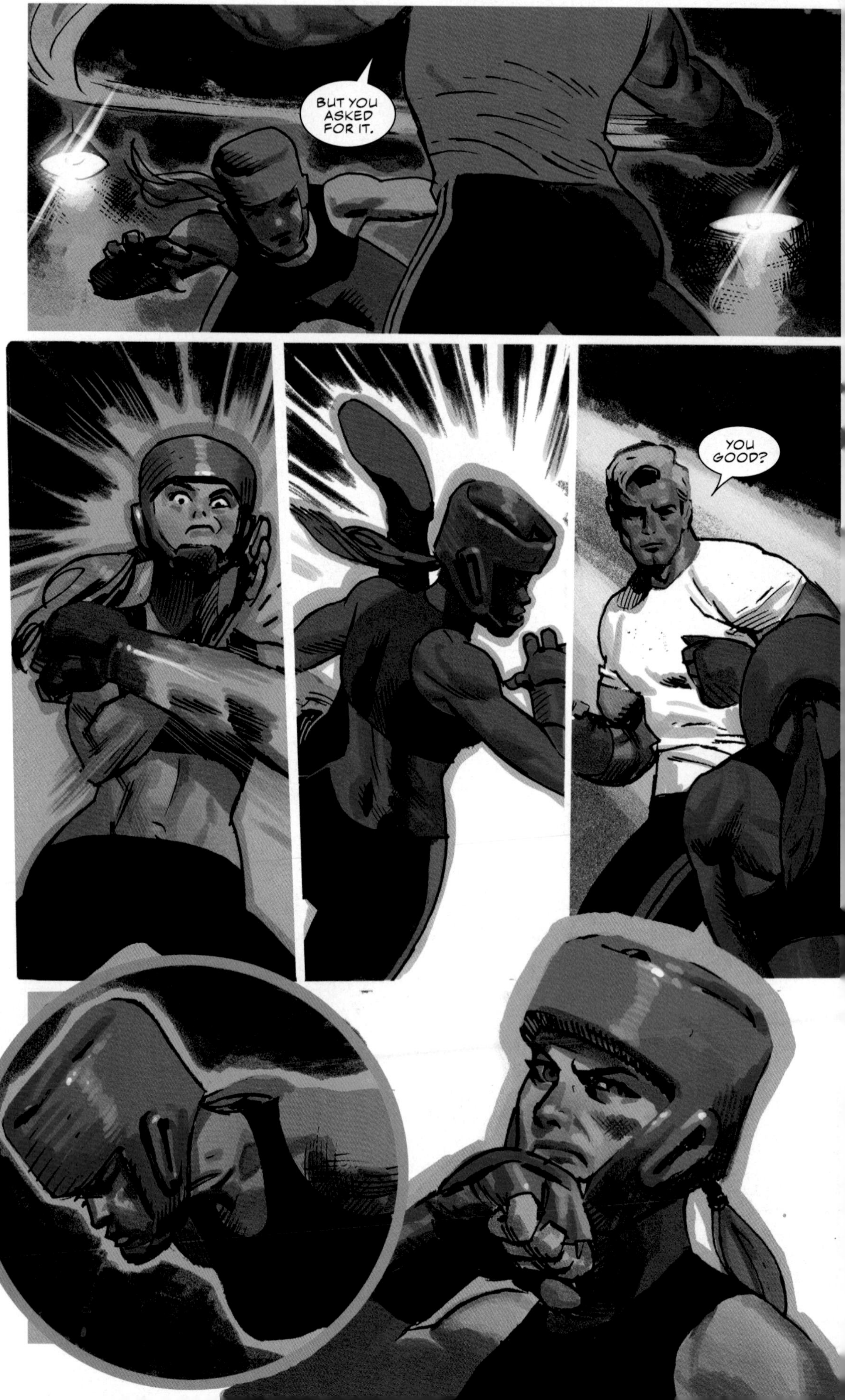
BUT YOU ASKED FOR IT.
YOU GOOD?

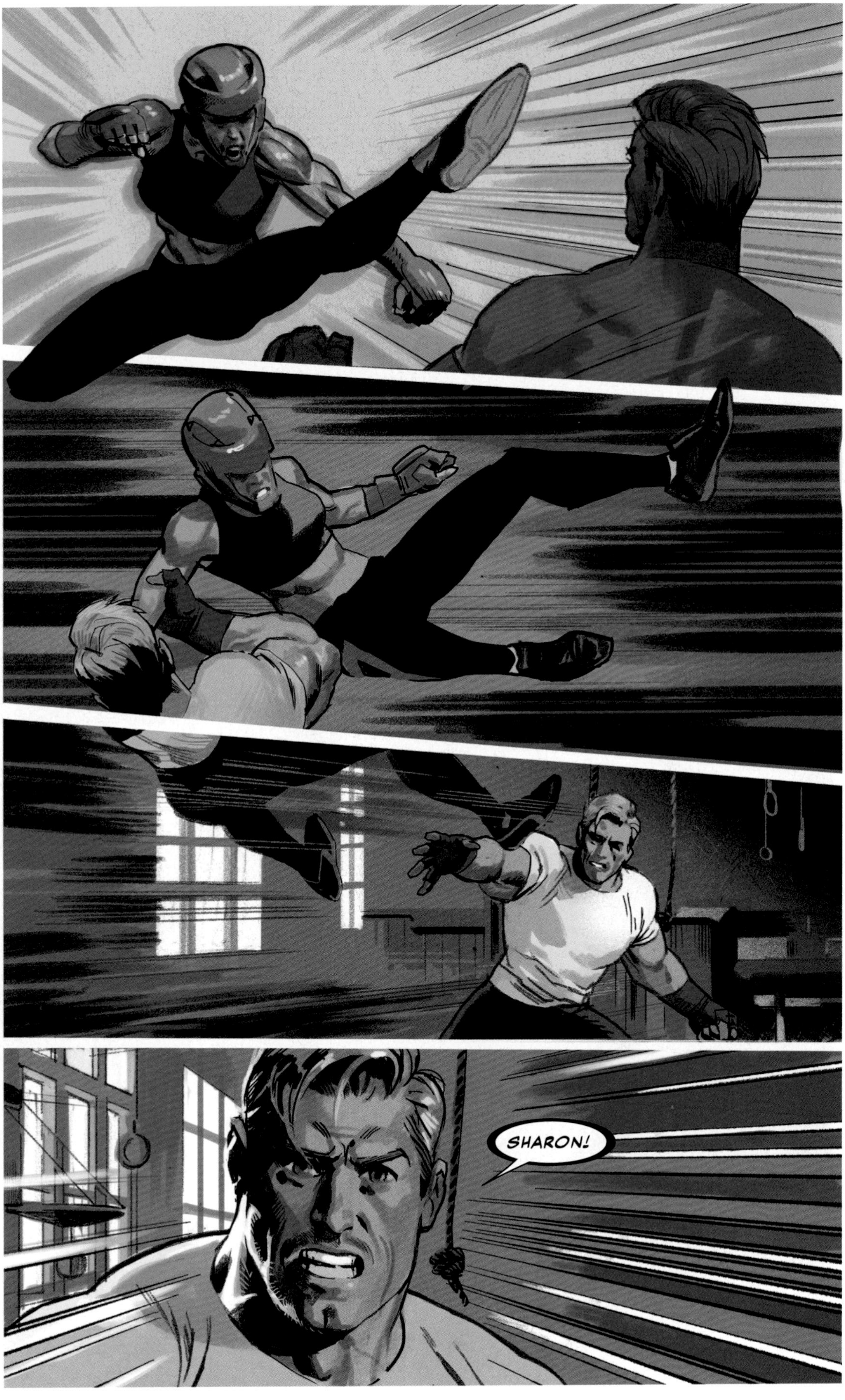

SHARON!

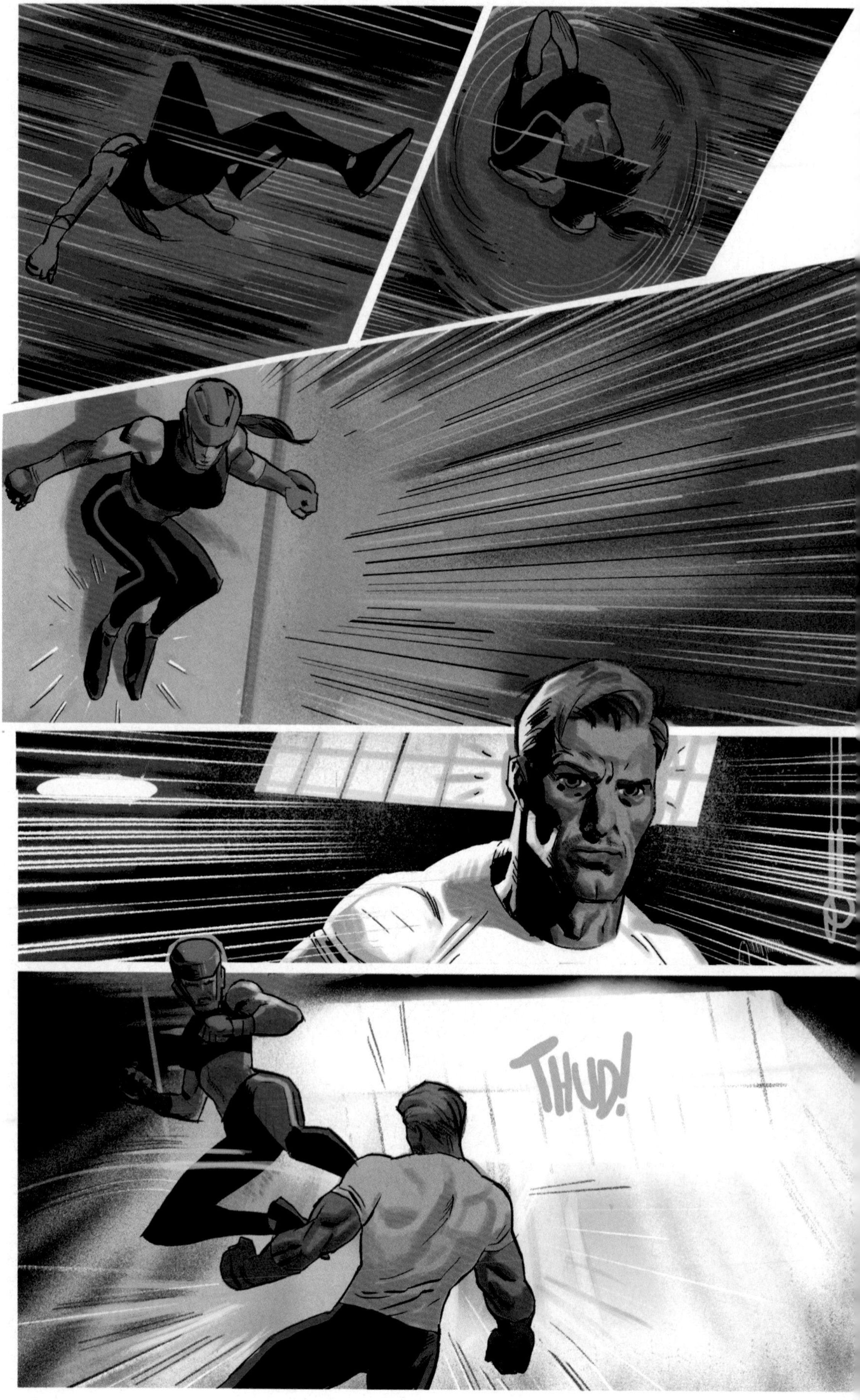
THUD!

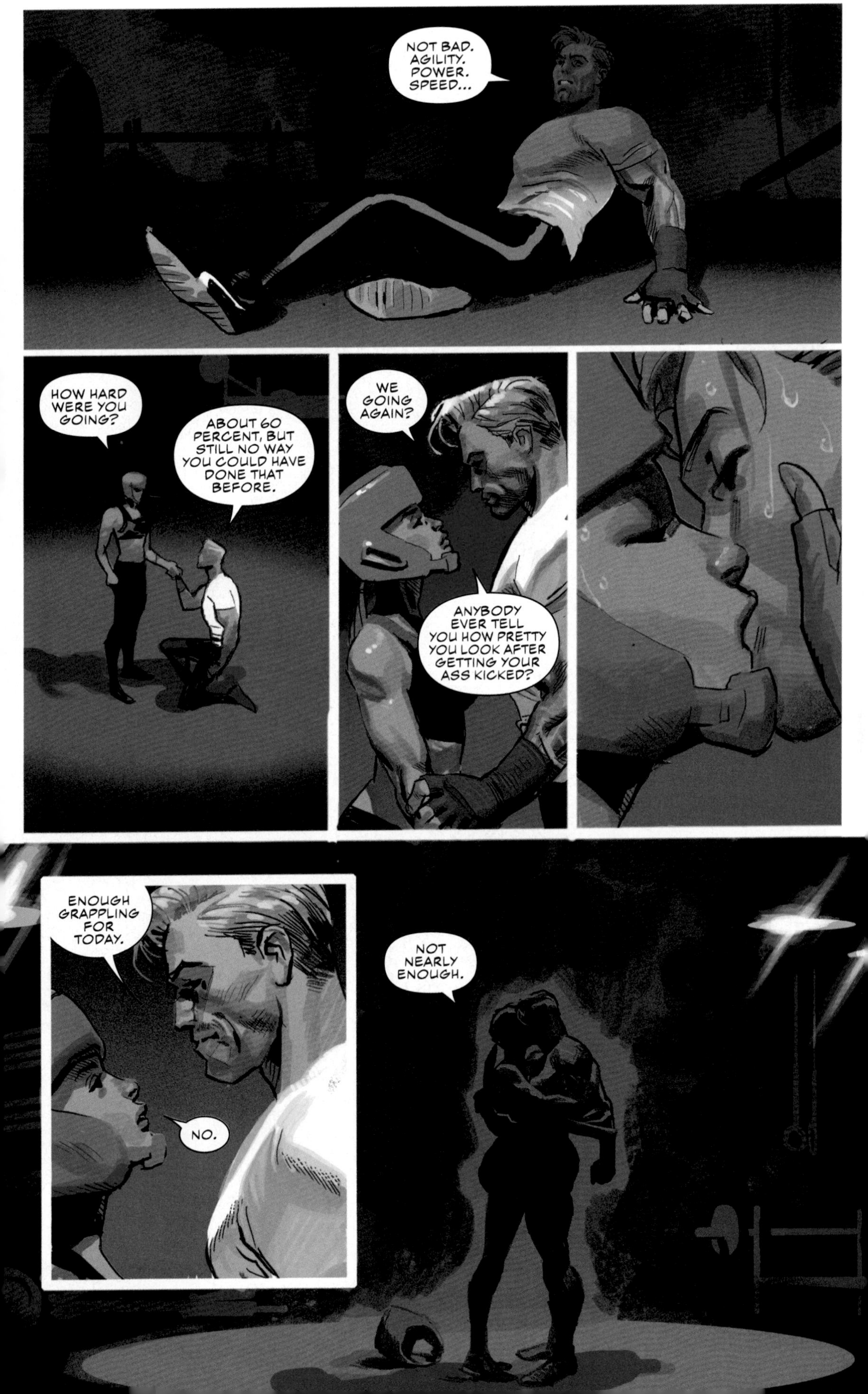
NOT BAD. AGILITY. POWER. SPEED...
HOW HARD WERE YOU GOING?
ABOUT 60 PERCENT, BUT STILL NO WAY YOU COULD HAVE DONE THAT BEFORE.
WE GOING AGAIN?
ANYBODY EVER TELL YOU HOW PRETTY YOU LOOK AFTER GETTING YOUR ASS KICKED?
ENOUGH GRAPPLING FOR TODAY.
NO.
NOT NEARLY ENOUGH.

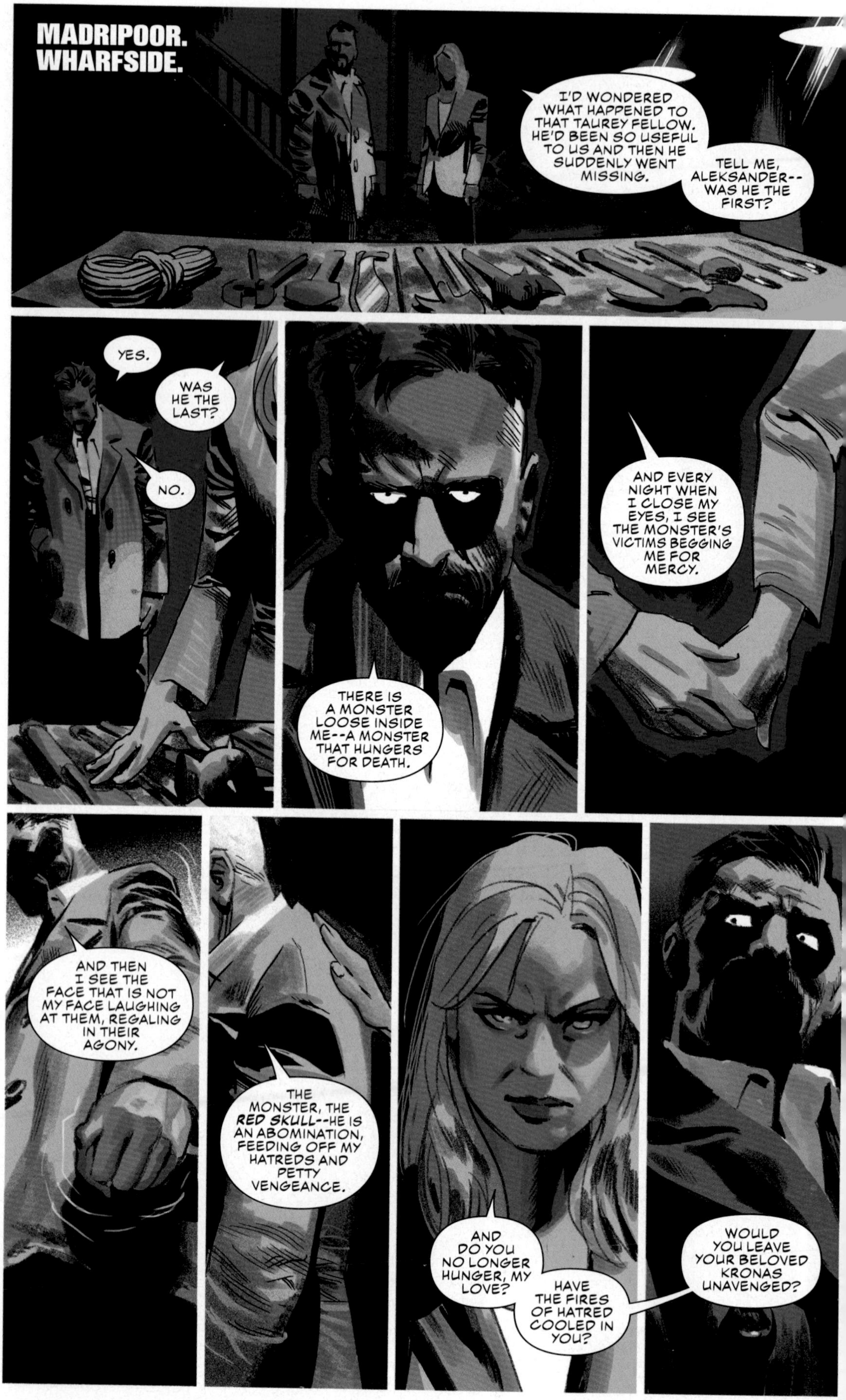
MADRIPOOR. WHARFSIDE.
I'D WONDERED WHAT HAPPENED TO THAT TAUREY FELLOW. HE'D BEEN SO USEFUL TO US AND THEN HE SUDDENLY WENT MISSING.
TELL ME, ALEKSANDER--WAS HE THE FIRST?
YES.
WAS HE THE LAST?
NO.
THERE IS A MONSTER LOOSE INSIDE ME--A MONSTER THAT HUNGERS FOR DEATH.
AND EVERY NIGHT WHEN I CLOSE MY EYES, I SEE THE MONSTER'S VICTIMS BEGGING ME FOR MERCY.
AND THEN I SEE THE FACE THAT IS NOT MY FACE LAUGHING AT THEM, REGALING IN THEIR AGONY.
THE MONSTER, THE RED SKULL--HE IS AN ABOMINATION, FEEDING OFF MY HATREDS AND PETTY VENGEANCE.
AND DO YOU NO LONGER HUNGER, MY LOVE?
HAVE THE FIRES OF HATRED COOLED IN YOU?
WOULD YOU LEAVE YOUR BELOVED KRONAS UNAVENGED?

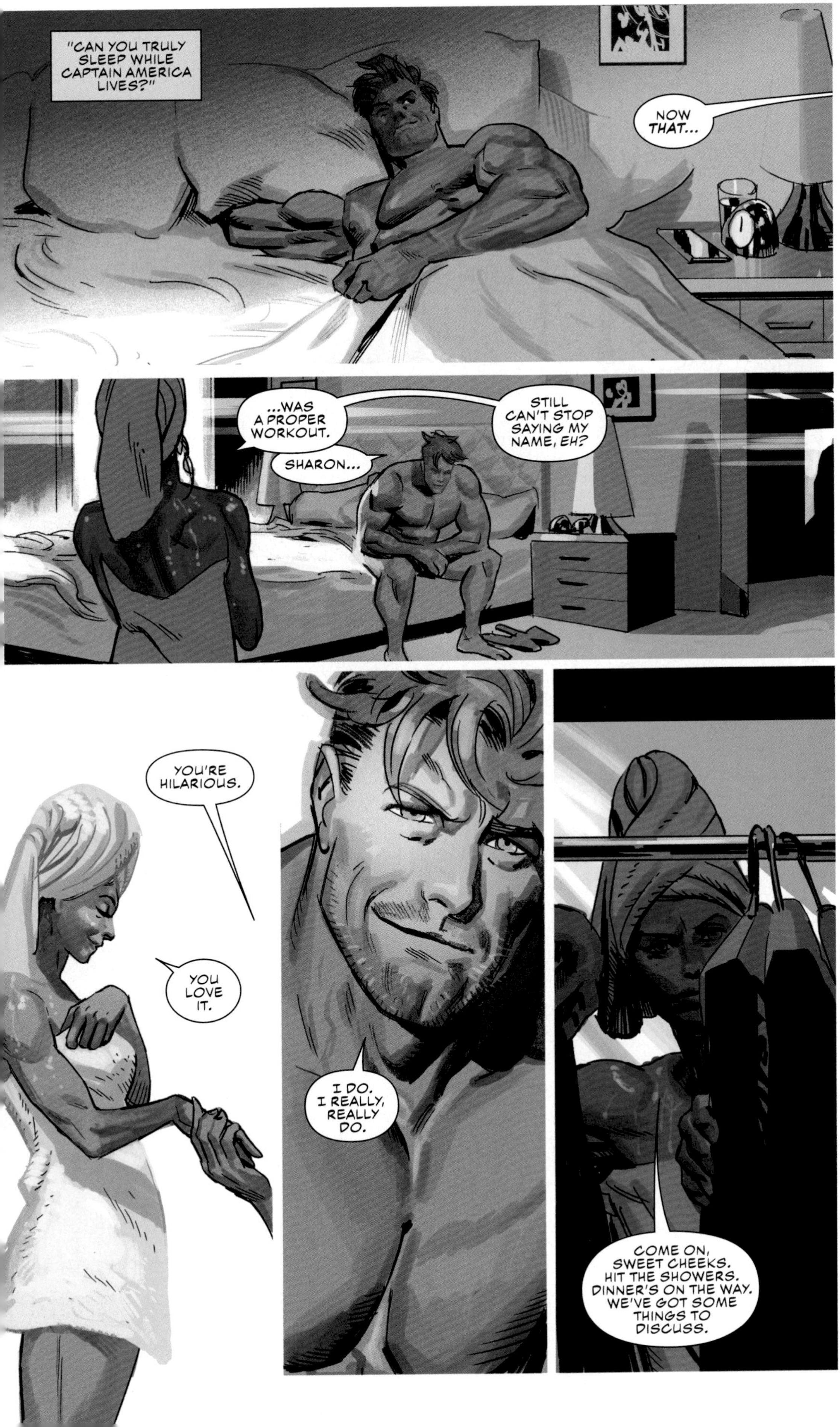
"CAN YOU TRULY SLEEP WHILE CAPTAIN AMERICA LIVES?"
NOW THAT...
...WAS A PROPER WORKOUT.
SHARON...
STILL CAN'T STOP SAYING MY NAME, EH?
YOU'RE HILARIOUS.
YOU LOVE IT.
I DO. I REALLY, REALLY DO.
COME ON, SWEET CHEEKS. HIT THE SHOWERS. DINNER'S ON THE WAY. WE'VE GOT SOME THINGS TO DISCUSS.

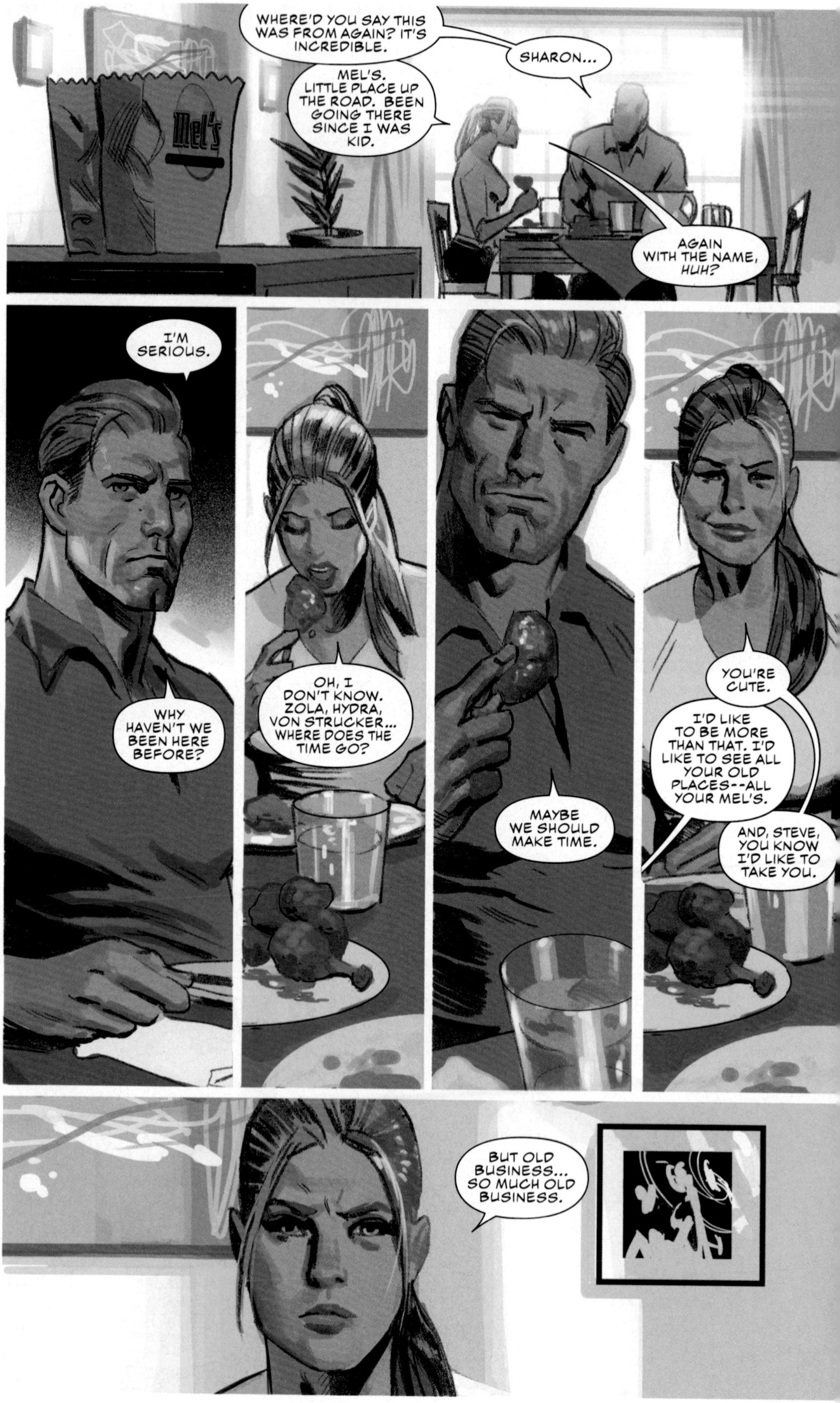
WHERE'D YOU SAY THIS WAS FROM AGAIN? IT'S INCREDIBLE.
SHARON...
MEL'S. LITTLE PLACE UP THE ROAD. BEEN GOING THERE SINCE I WAS KID.
Mel's
AGAIN WITH THE NAME, HUH?
I'M SERIOUS.
WHY HAVEN'T WE BEEN HERE BEFORE?
OH, I DON'T KNOW. ZOLA, HYDRA, VON STRUCKER... WHERE DOES THE TIME GO?
MAYBE WE SHOULD MAKE TIME.
YOU'RE CUTE.
I'D LIKE TO BE MORE THAN THAT. I'D LIKE TO SEE ALL YOUR OLD PLACES--ALL YOUR MEL'S.
AND, STEVE, YOU KNOW I'D LIKE TO TAKE YOU.
BUT OLD BUSINESS... SO MUCH OLD BUSINESS.

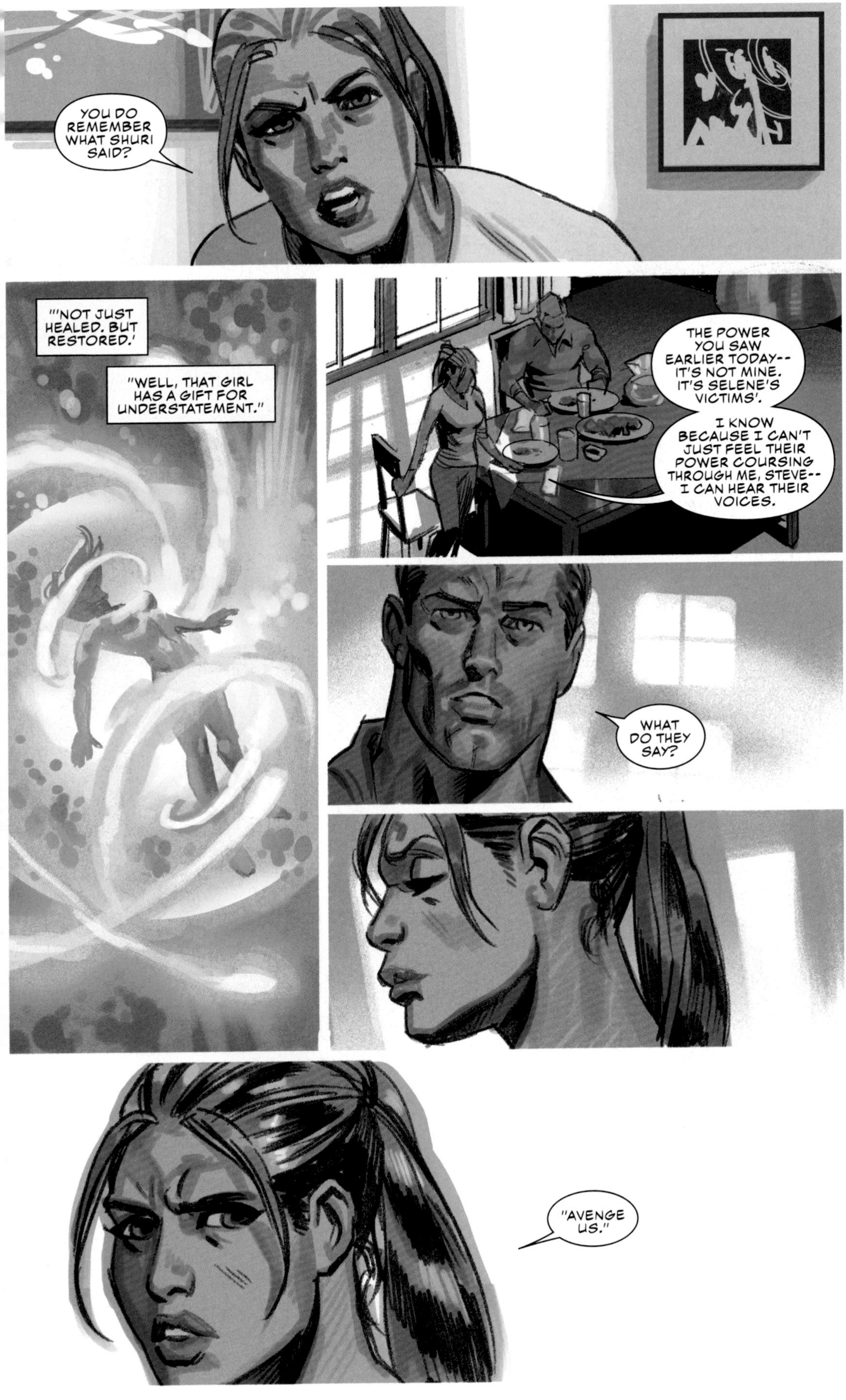
YOU DO REMEMBER WHAT SHURI SAID?
"'NOT JUST HEALED. BUT RESTORED.'
"WELL, THAT GIRL HAS A GIFT FOR UNDERSTATEMENT."
THE POWER YOU SAW EARLIER TODAY-- IT'S NOT MINE. IT'S SELENE'S VICTIMS'.
I KNOW BECAUSE I CAN'T JUST FEEL THEIR POWER COURSING THROUGH ME, STEVE-- I CAN HEAR THEIR VOICES.
WHAT DO THEY SAY?
"AVENGE US."

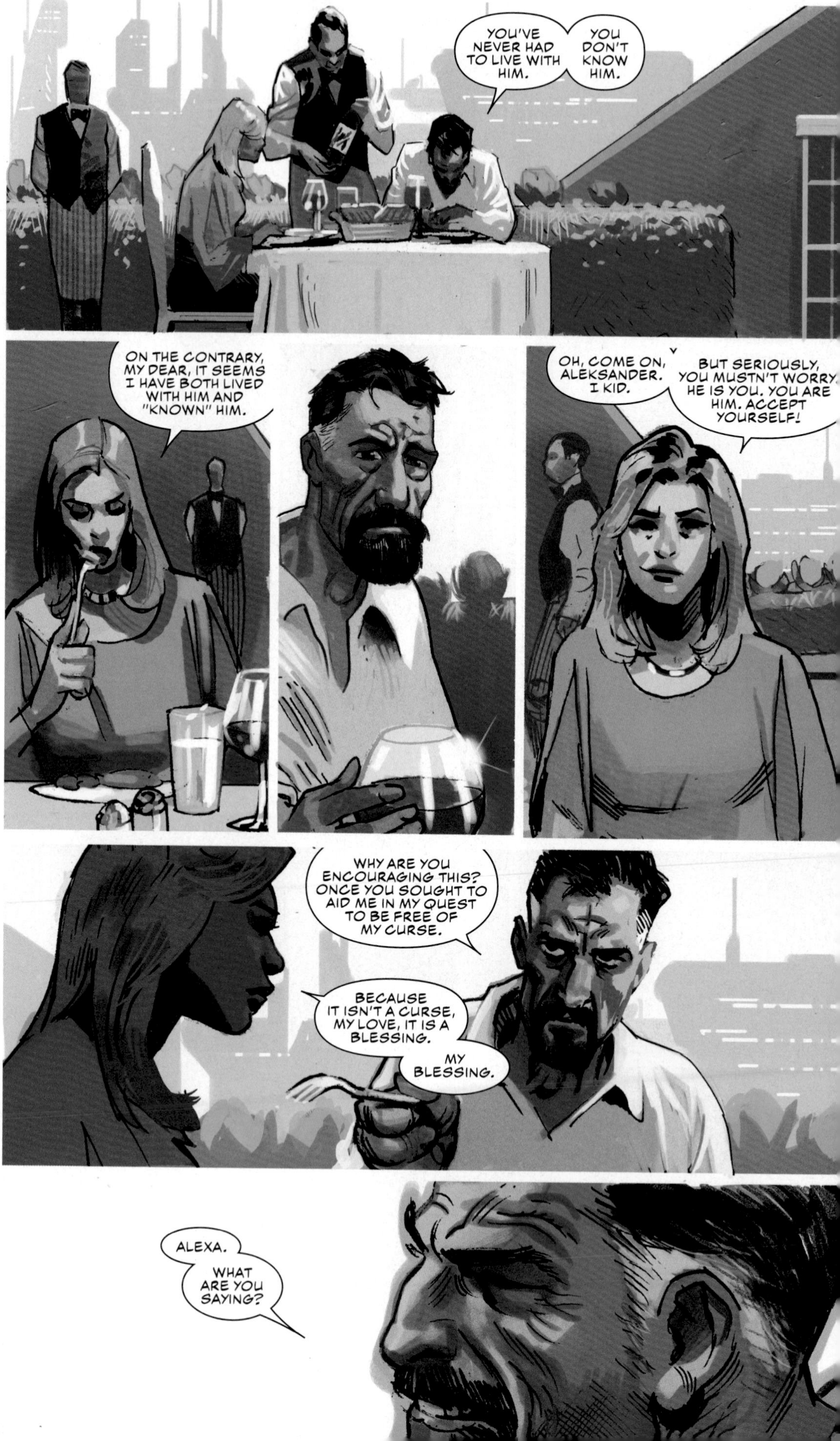

YOU'VE NEVER HAD TO LIVE WITH HIM.
YOU DON'T KNOW HIM.
ON THE CONTRARY, MY DEAR, IT SEEMS I HAVE BOTH LIVED WITH HIM AND "KNOWN" HIM.
OH, COME ON, ALEKSANDER. I KID.
BUT SERIOUSLY, YOU MUSTN'T WORRY. HE IS YOU. YOU ARE HIM. ACCEPT YOURSELF!
WHY ARE YOU ENCOURAGING THIS? ONCE YOU SOUGHT TO AID ME IN MY QUEST TO BE FREE OF MY CURSE.
BECAUSE IT ISN'T A CURSE, MY LOVE, IT IS A BLESSING.
MY BLESSING.
ALEXA.
WHAT ARE YOU SAYING?

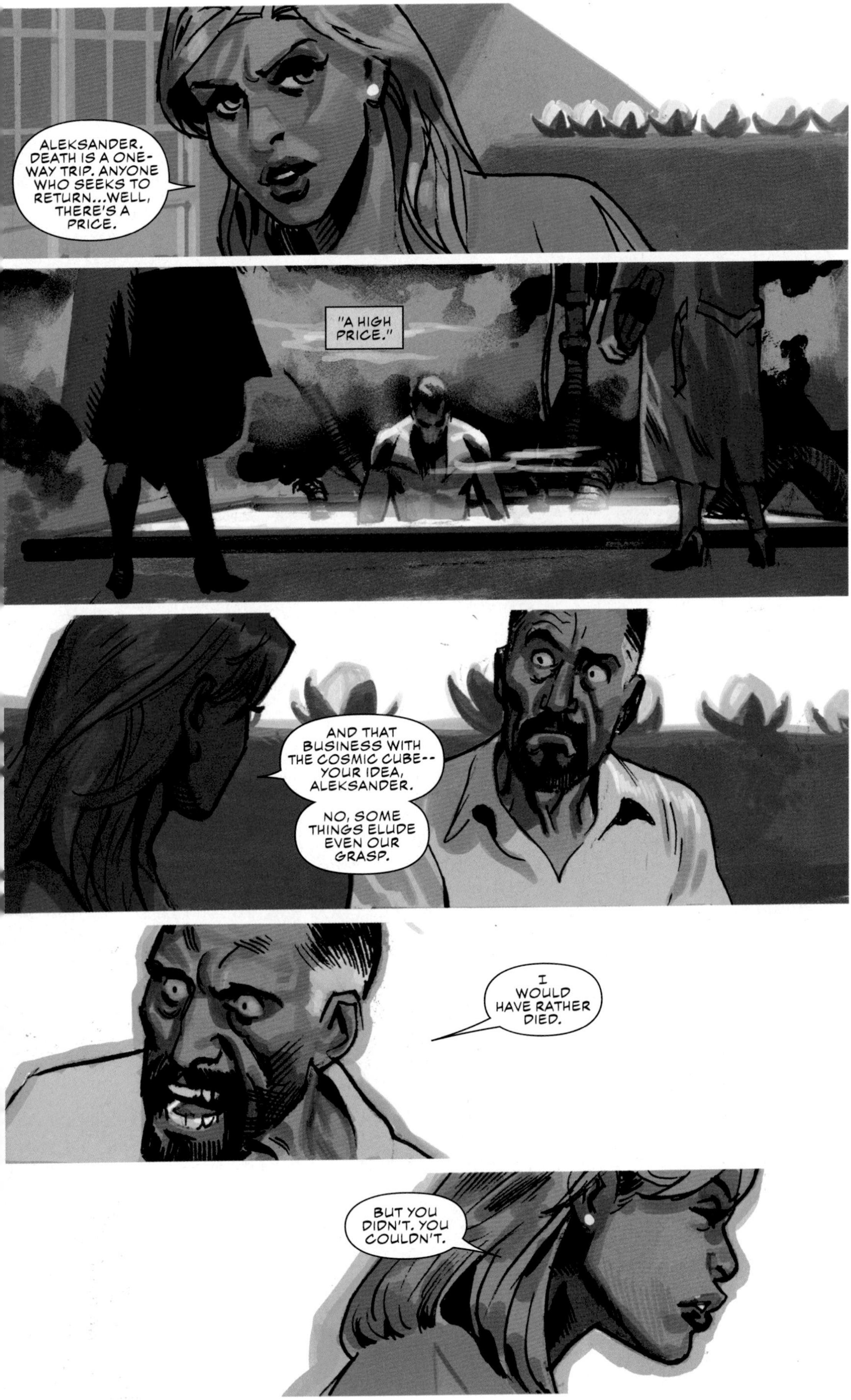
ALEKSANDER. DEATH IS A ONE-WAY TRIP. ANYONE WHO SEEKS TO RETURN...WELL, THERE'S A PRICE.
"A HIGH PRICE."
AND THAT BUSINESS WITH THE COSMIC CUBE--YOUR IDEA, ALEKSANDER.
NO, SOME THINGS ELUDE EVEN OUR GRASP.
I WOULD HAVE RATHER DIED.
BUT YOU DIDN'T. YOU COULDN'T.

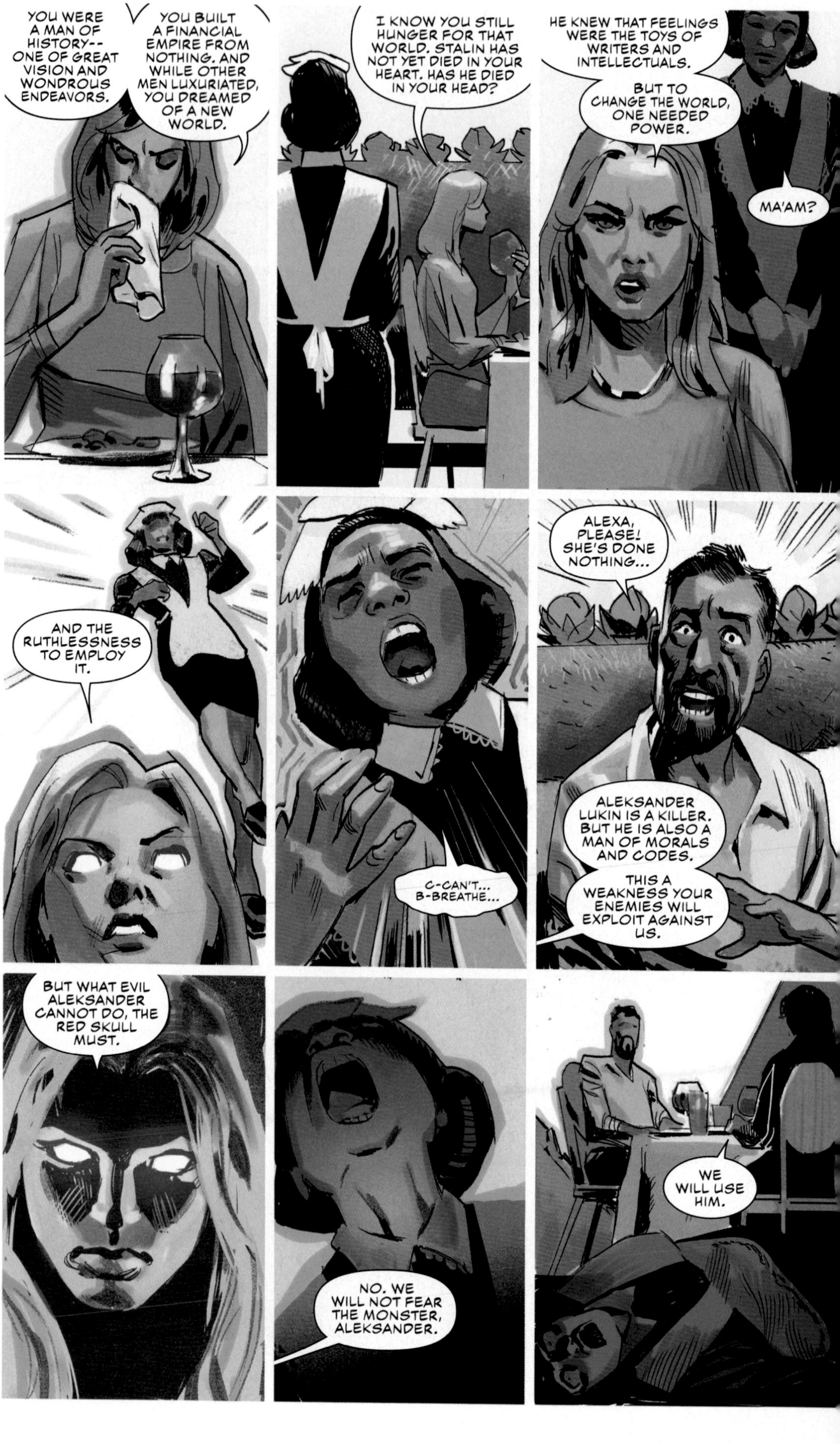
YOU WERE A MAN OF HISTORY-- ONE OF GREAT VISION AND WONDROUS ENDEAVORS.
YOU BUILT A FINANCIAL EMPIRE FROM NOTHING. AND WHILE OTHER MEN LUXURIATED, YOU DREAMED OF A NEW WORLD.
I KNOW YOU STILL HUNGER FOR THAT WORLD. STALIN HAS NOT YET DIED IN YOUR HEART. HAS HE DIED IN YOUR HEAD?
HE KNEW THAT FEELINGS WERE THE TOYS OF WRITERS AND INTELLECTUALS.
BUT TO CHANGE THE WORLD, ONE NEEDED POWER.
MA'AM?
AND THE RUTHLESSNESS TO EMPLOY IT.
C-CAN'T... B-BREATHE...
ALEXA, PLEASE! SHE'S DONE NOTHING...
ALEKSANDER LUKIN IS A KILLER. BUT HE IS ALSO A MAN OF MORALS AND CODES.
THIS A WEAKNESS YOUR ENEMIES WILL EXPLOIT AGAINST US.
BUT WHAT EVIL ALEKSANDER CANNOT DO, THE RED SKULL MUST.
NO. WE WILL NOT FEAR THE MONSTER, ALEKSANDER.
WE WILL USE HIM.

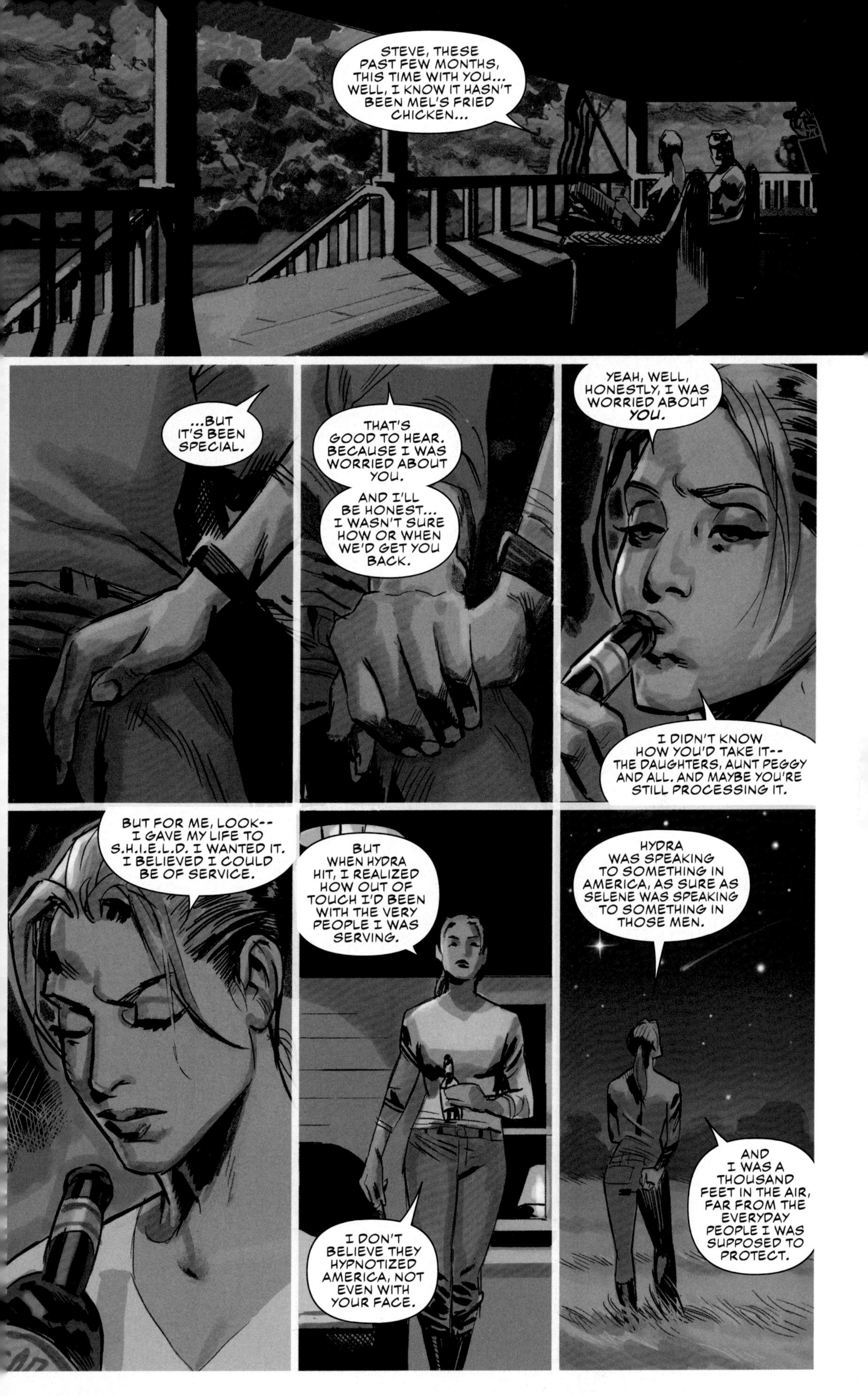
STEVE, THESE PAST FEW MONTHS, THIS TIME WITH YOU... WELL, I KNOW IT HASN'T BEEN MEL'S FRIED CHICKEN...
...BUT IT'S BEEN SPECIAL.
THAT'S GOOD TO HEAR. BECAUSE I WAS WORRIED ABOUT YOU.
AND I'LL BE HONEST... I WASN'T SURE HOW OR WHEN WE'D GET YOU BACK.
YEAH, WELL, HONESTLY, I WAS WORRIED ABOUT YOU.
I DIDN'T KNOW HOW YOU'D TAKE IT-- THE DAUGHTERS, AUNT PEGGY AND ALL. AND MAYBE YOU'RE STILL PROCESSING IT.
BUT FOR ME, LOOK-- I GAVE MY LIFE TO S.H.I.E.L.D. I WANTED IT. I BELIEVED I COULD BE OF SERVICE.
BUT WHEN HYDRA HIT, I REALIZED HOW OUT OF TOUCH I'D BEEN WITH THE VERY PEOPLE I WAS SERVING.
I DON'T BELIEVE THEY HYPNOTIZED AMERICA, NOT EVEN WITH YOUR FACE.
HYDRA WAS SPEAKING TO SOMETHING IN AMERICA, AS SURE AS SELENE WAS SPEAKING TO SOMETHING IN THOSE MEN.
AND I WAS A THOUSAND FEET IN THE AIR, FAR FROM THE EVERYDAY PEOPLE I WAS SUPPOSED TO PROTECT.

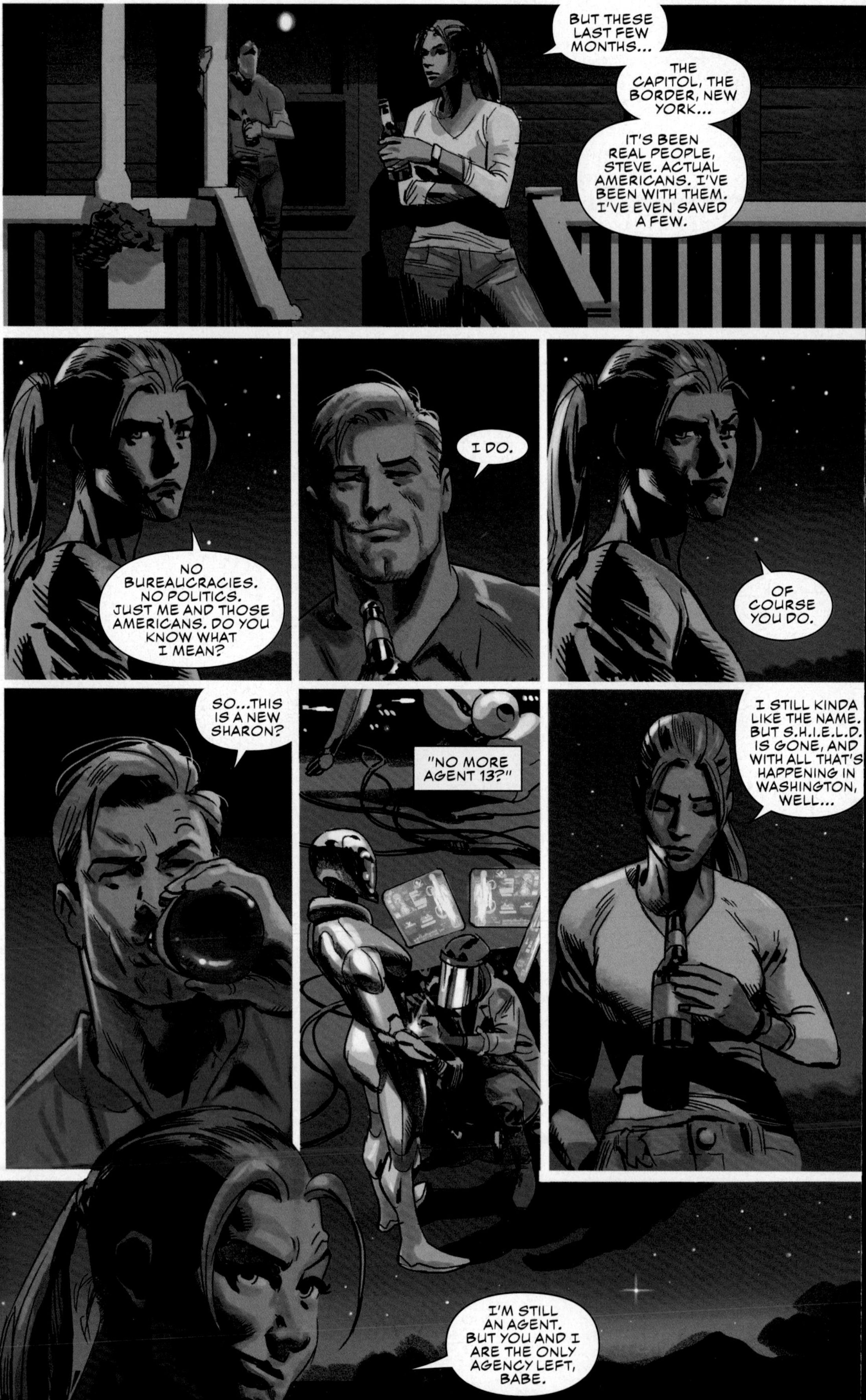
BUT THESE LAST FEW MONTHS...
THE CAPITOL, THE BORDER, NEW YORK...
IT'S BEEN REAL PEOPLE, STEVE. ACTUAL AMERICANS. I'VE BEEN WITH THEM. I'VE EVEN SAVED A FEW.
NO BUREAUCRACIES. NO POLITICS. JUST ME AND THOSE AMERICANS. DO YOU KNOW WHAT I MEAN?
I DO.
OF COURSE YOU DO.
SO...THIS IS A NEW SHARON?
"NO MORE AGENT 13?"
I STILL KINDA LIKE THE NAME. BUT S.H.I.E.L.D. IS GONE, AND WITH ALL THAT'S HAPPENING IN WASHINGTON, WELL...
I'M STILL AN AGENT. BUT YOU AND I ARE THE ONLY AGENCY LEFT, BABE.

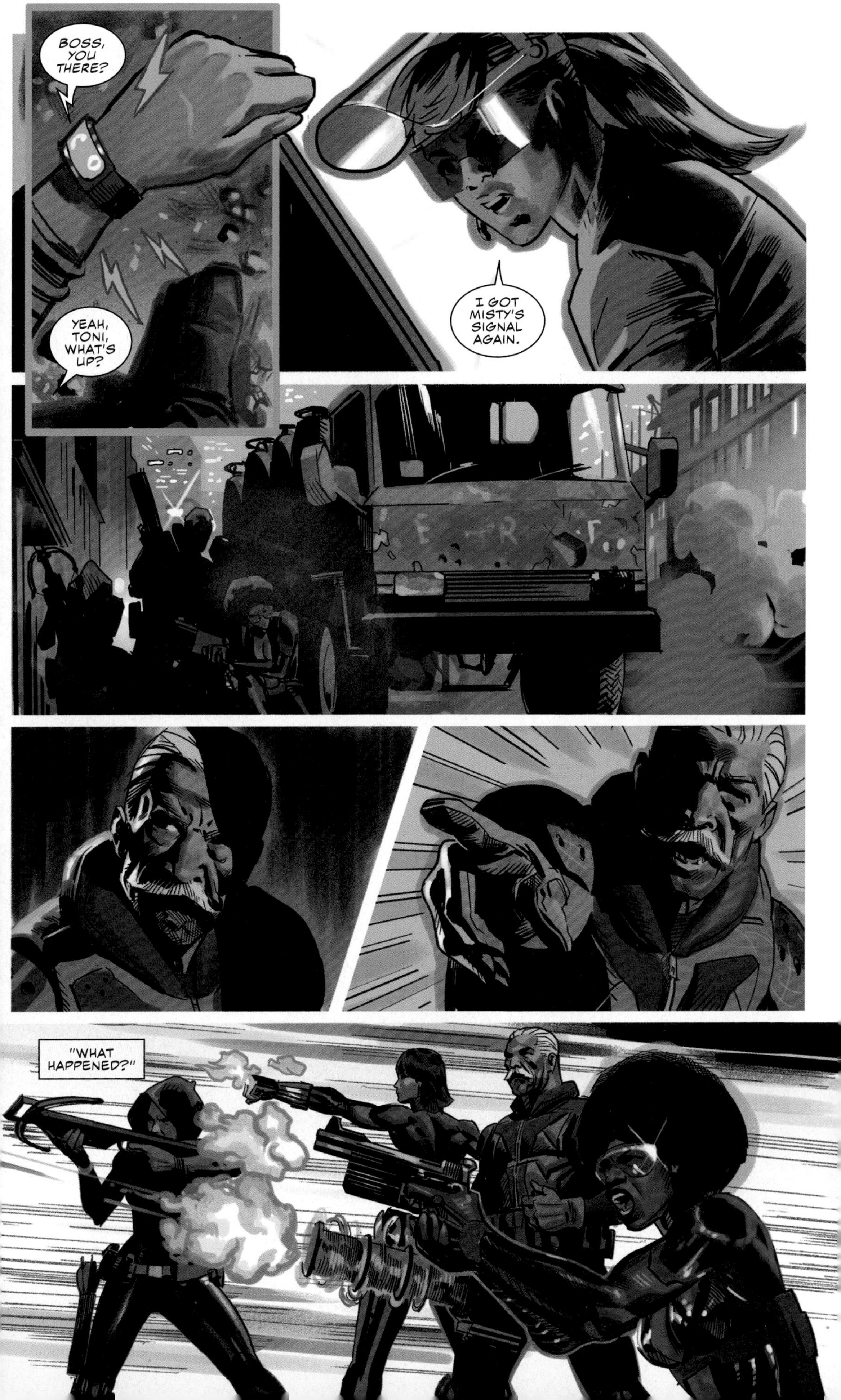
BOSS, YOU THERE?
YEAH, TONI, WHAT'S UP?
I GOT MISTY'S SIGNAL AGAIN.
"WHAT HAPPENED?"

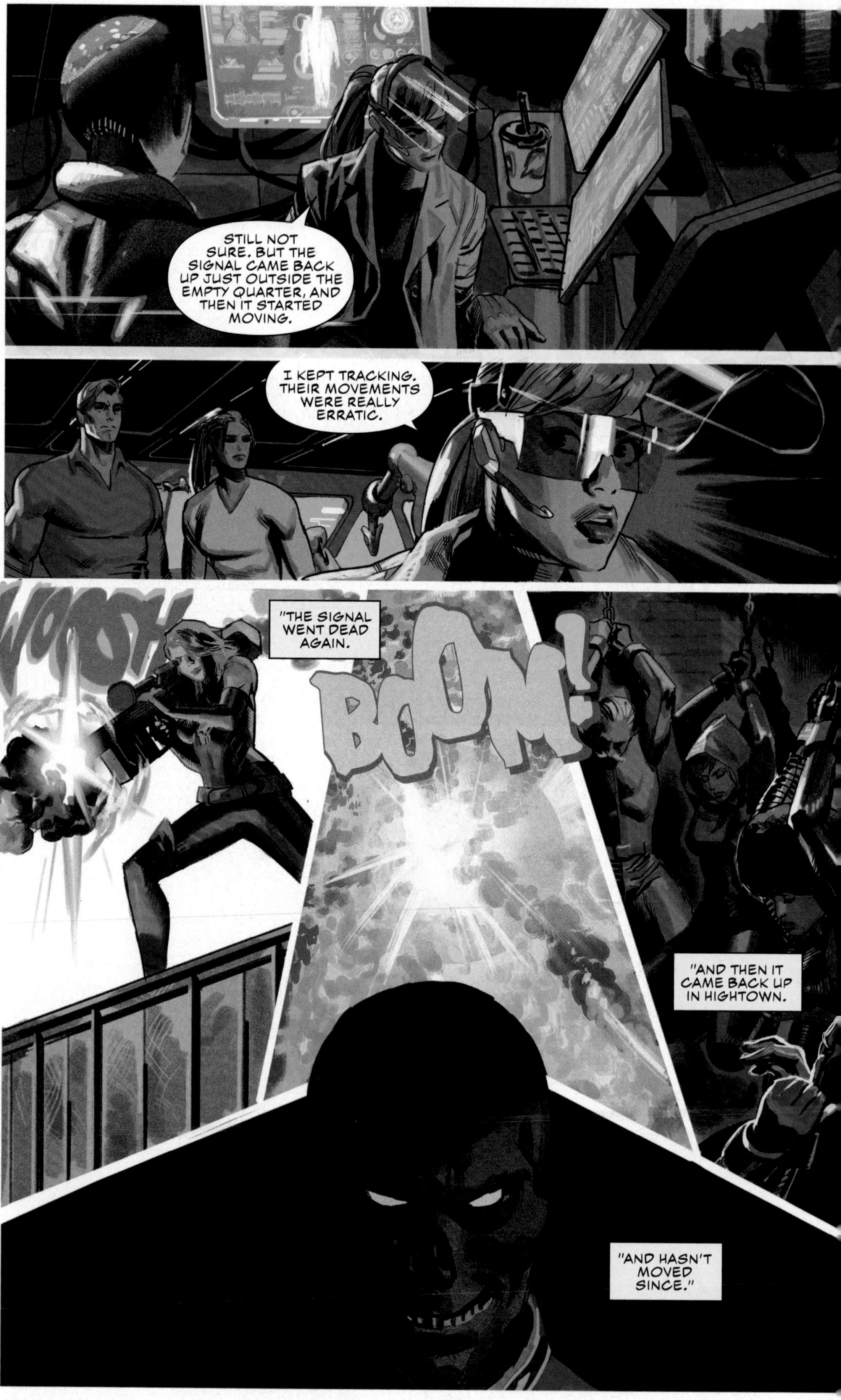
STILL NOT SURE. BUT THE SIGNAL CAME BACK UP JUST OUTSIDE THE EMPTY QUARTER, AND THEN IT STARTED MOVING.
I KEPT TRACKING. THEIR MOVEMENTS WERE REALLY ERRATIC.
FWOOOSH!
"THE SIGNAL WENT DEAD AGAIN.
BOOM!
"AND THEN IT CAME BACK UP IN HIGHTOWN.
"AND HASN'T MOVED SINCE."

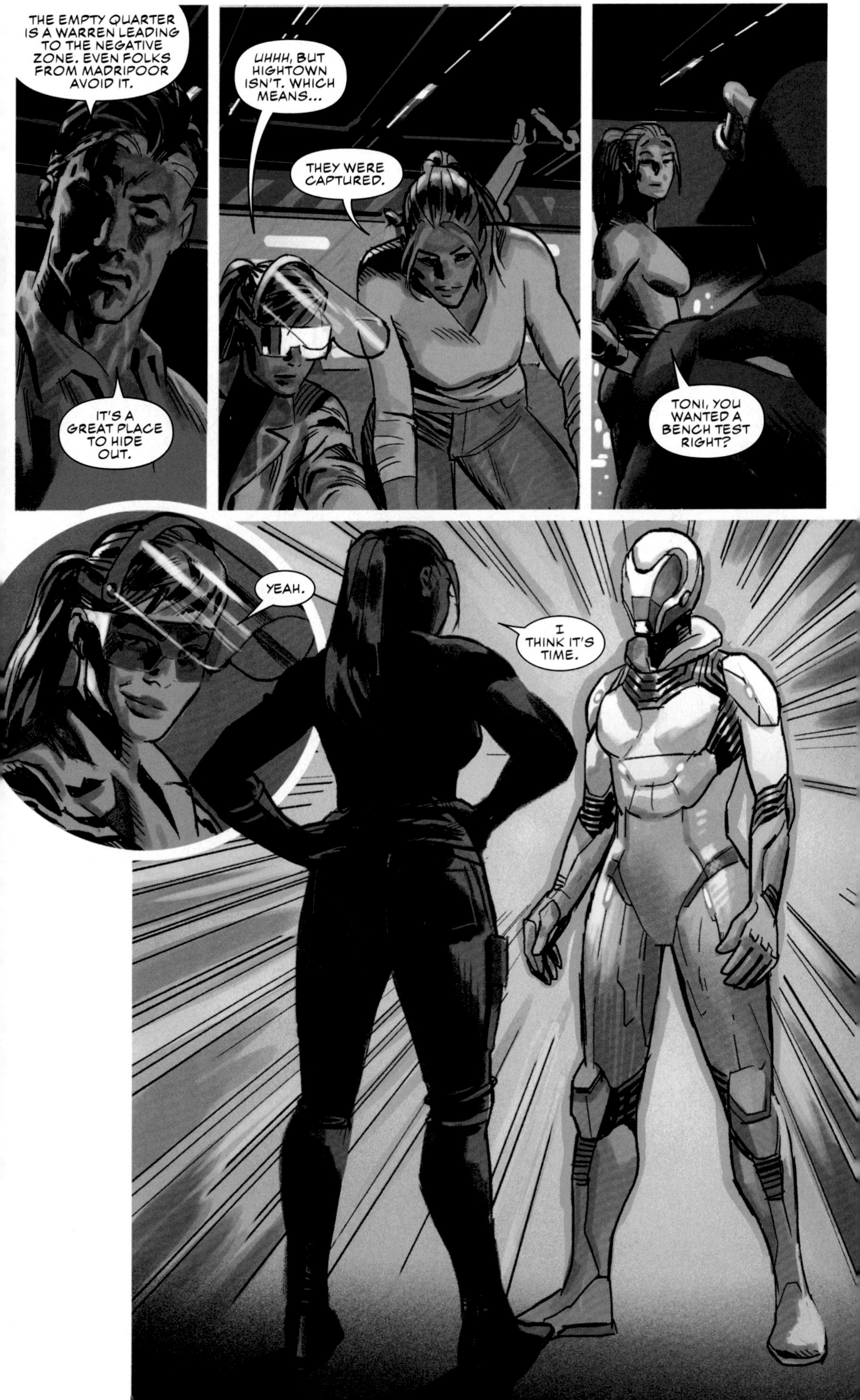
THE EMPTY QUARTER IS A WARREN LEADING TO THE NEGATIVE ZONE. EVEN FOLKS FROM MADRIPOOR AVOID IT.
IT'S A GREAT PLACE TO HIDE OUT.
UHHH, BUT HIGHTOWN ISN'T. WHICH MEANS...
THEY WERE CAPTURED.
TONI, YOU WANTED A BENCH TEST RIGHT?
YEAH.
I THINK IT'S TIME.

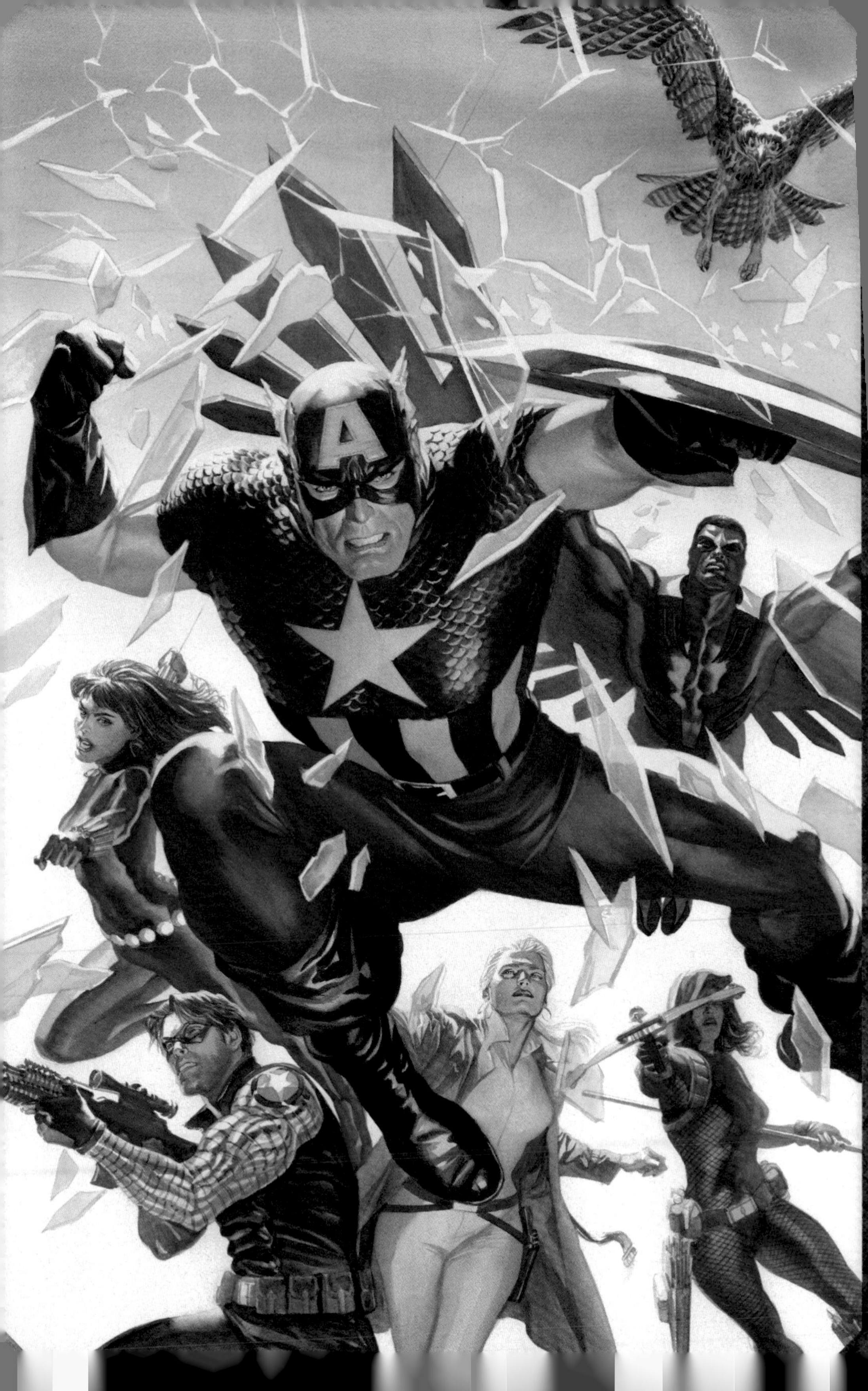

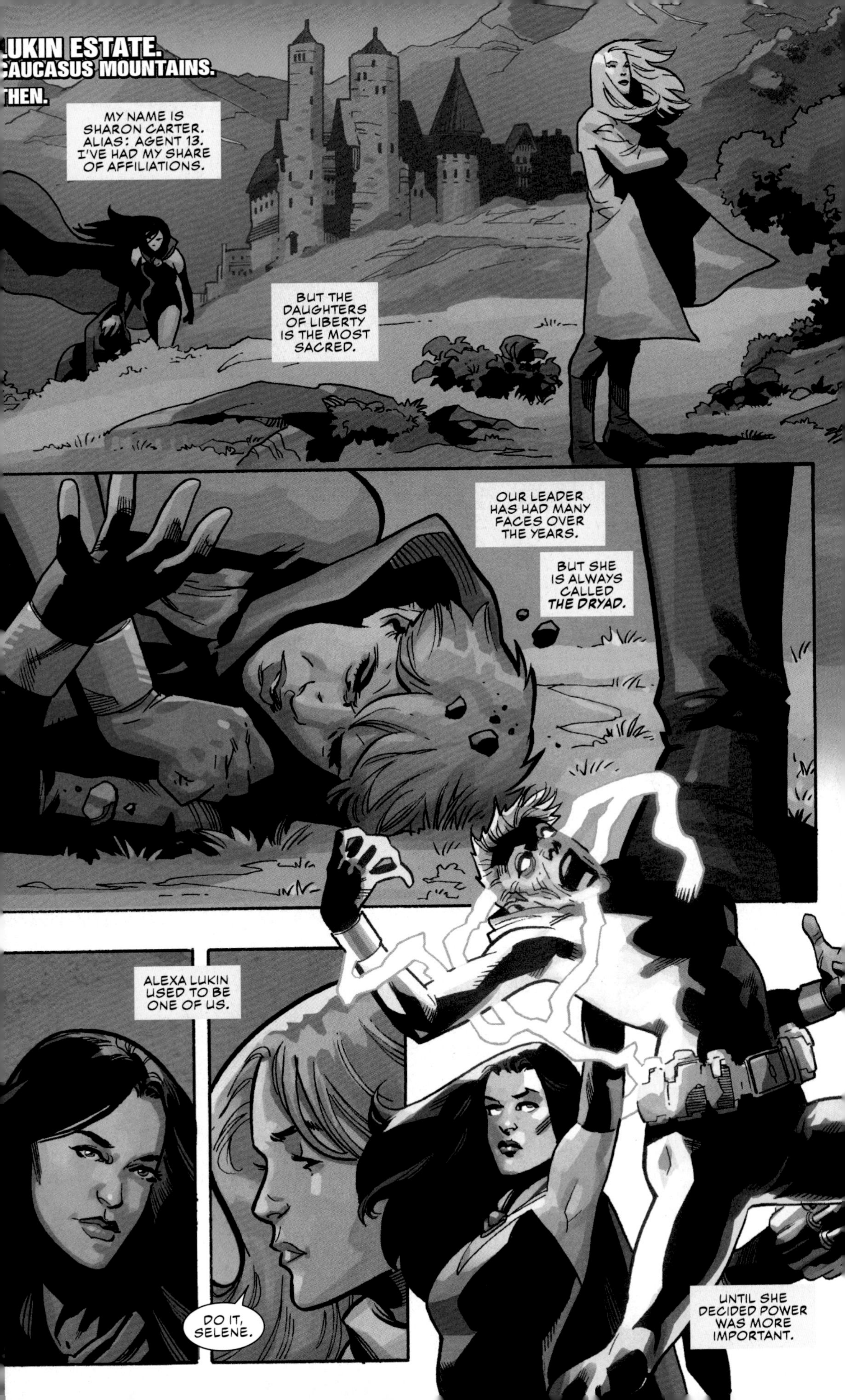
LUKIN ESTATE.
CAUCASUS MOUNTAINS.
THEN.
MY NAME IS SHARON CARTER. ALIAS: AGENT 13. I'VE HAD MY SHARE OF AFFILIATIONS.
BUT THE DAUGHTERS OF LIBERTY IS THE MOST SACRED.
OUR LEADER HAS HAD MANY FACES OVER THE YEARS.
BUT SHE IS ALWAYS CALLED THE DRYAD.
ALEXA LUKIN USED TO BE ONE OF US.
DO IT, SELENE.
UNTIL SHE DECIDED POWER WAS MORE IMPORTANT.

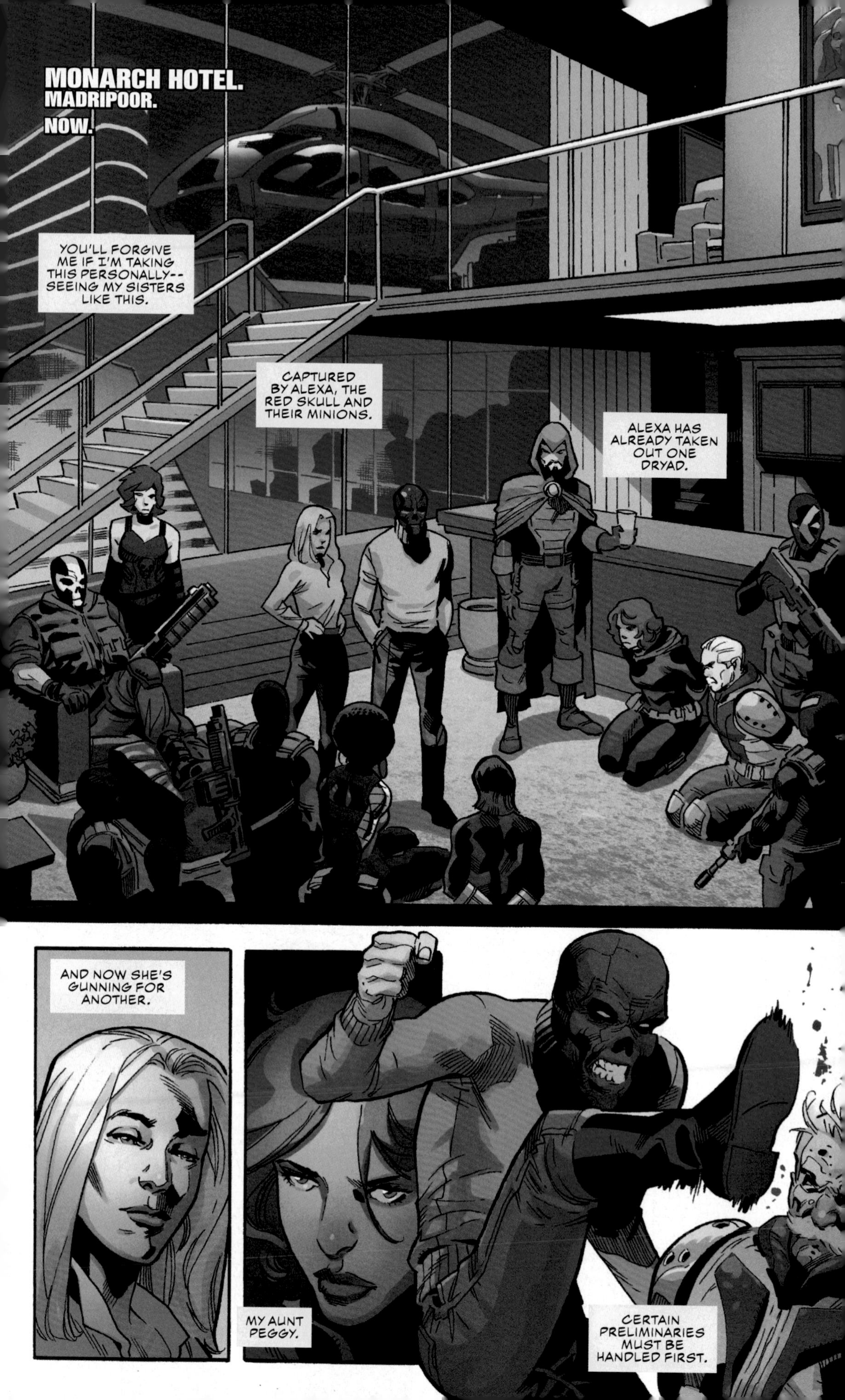
MONARCH HOTEL.
MADRIPOOR.
NOW.
YOU'LL FORGIVE ME IF I'M TAKING THIS PERSONALLY-- SEEING MY SISTERS LIKE THIS.
CAPTURED BY ALEXA, THE RED SKULL AND THEIR MINIONS.
ALEXA HAS ALREADY TAKEN OUT ONE DRYAD.
AND NOW SHE'S GUNNING FOR ANOTHER.
MY AUNT PEGGY.
CERTAIN PRELIMINARIES MUST BE HANDLED FIRST.

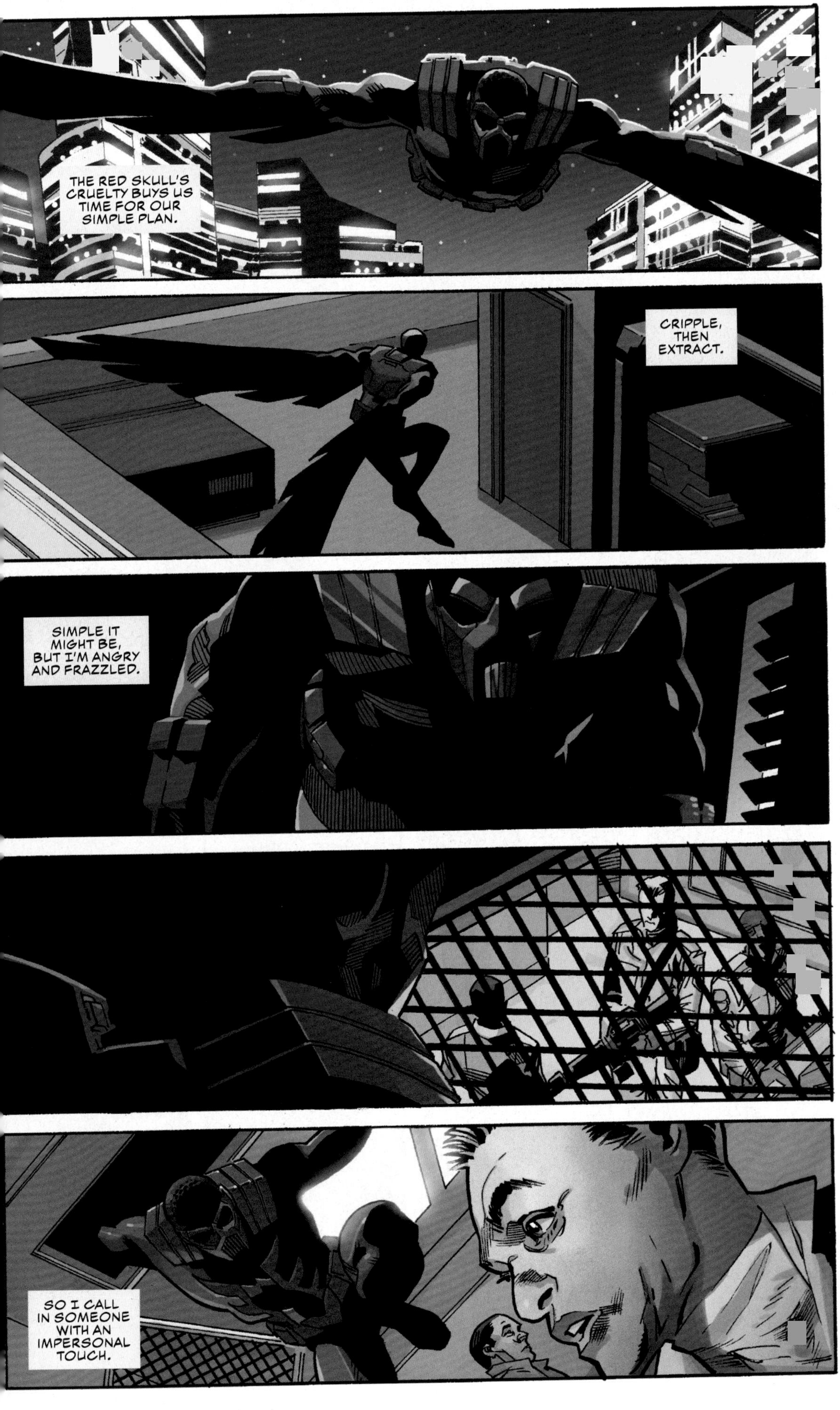
THE RED SKULL'S CRUELTY BUYS US TIME FOR OUR SIMPLE PLAN.
CRIPPLE, THEN EXTRACT.
SIMPLE IT MIGHT BE, BUT I'M ANGRY AND FRAZZLED.
SO I CALL IN SOMEONE WITH AN IMPERSONAL TOUCH.

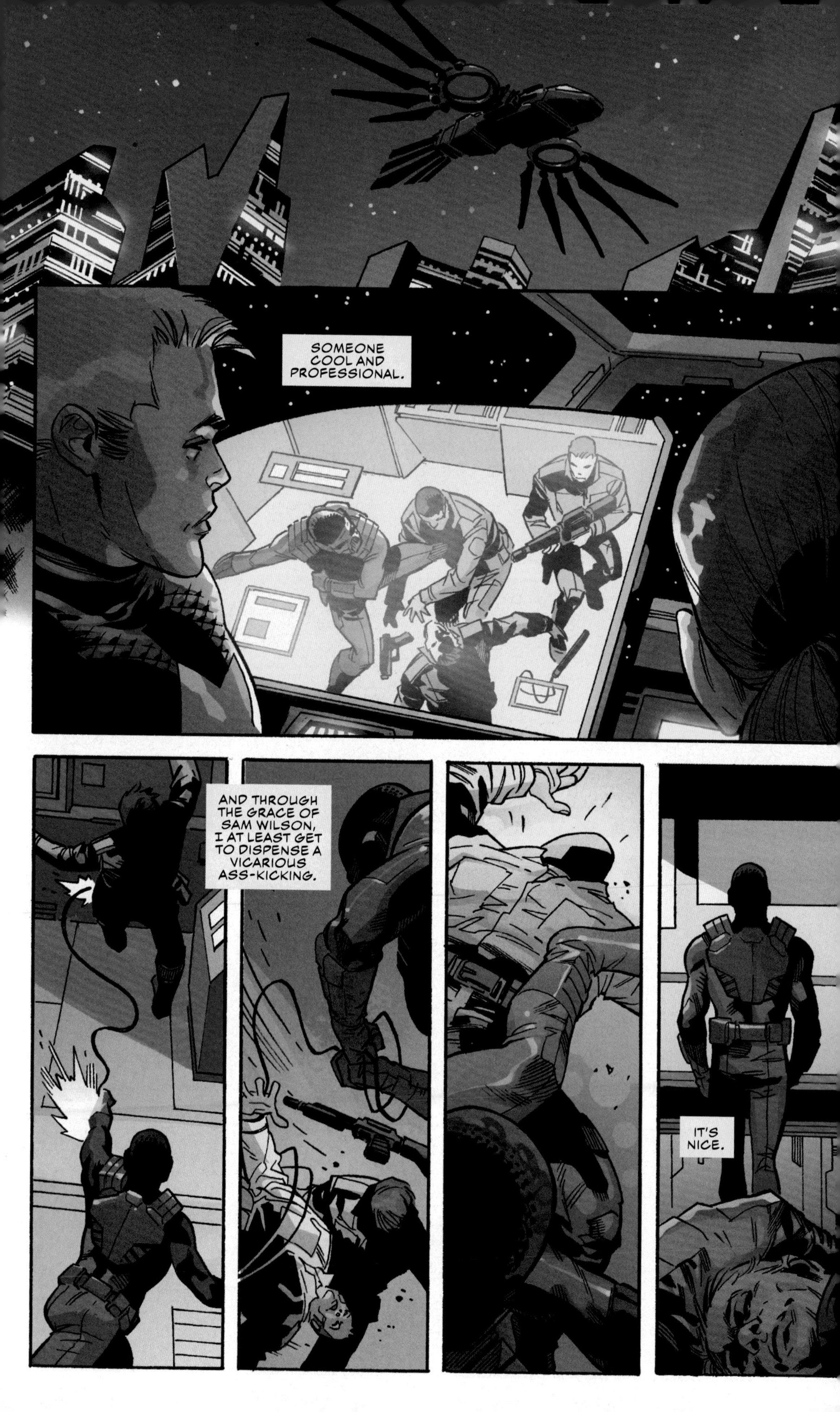
SOMEONE COOL AND PROFESSIONAL.
AND THROUGH THE GRACE OF SAM WILSON, I AT LEAST GET TO DISPENSE A VICARIOUS ASS-KICKING.
IT'S NICE.

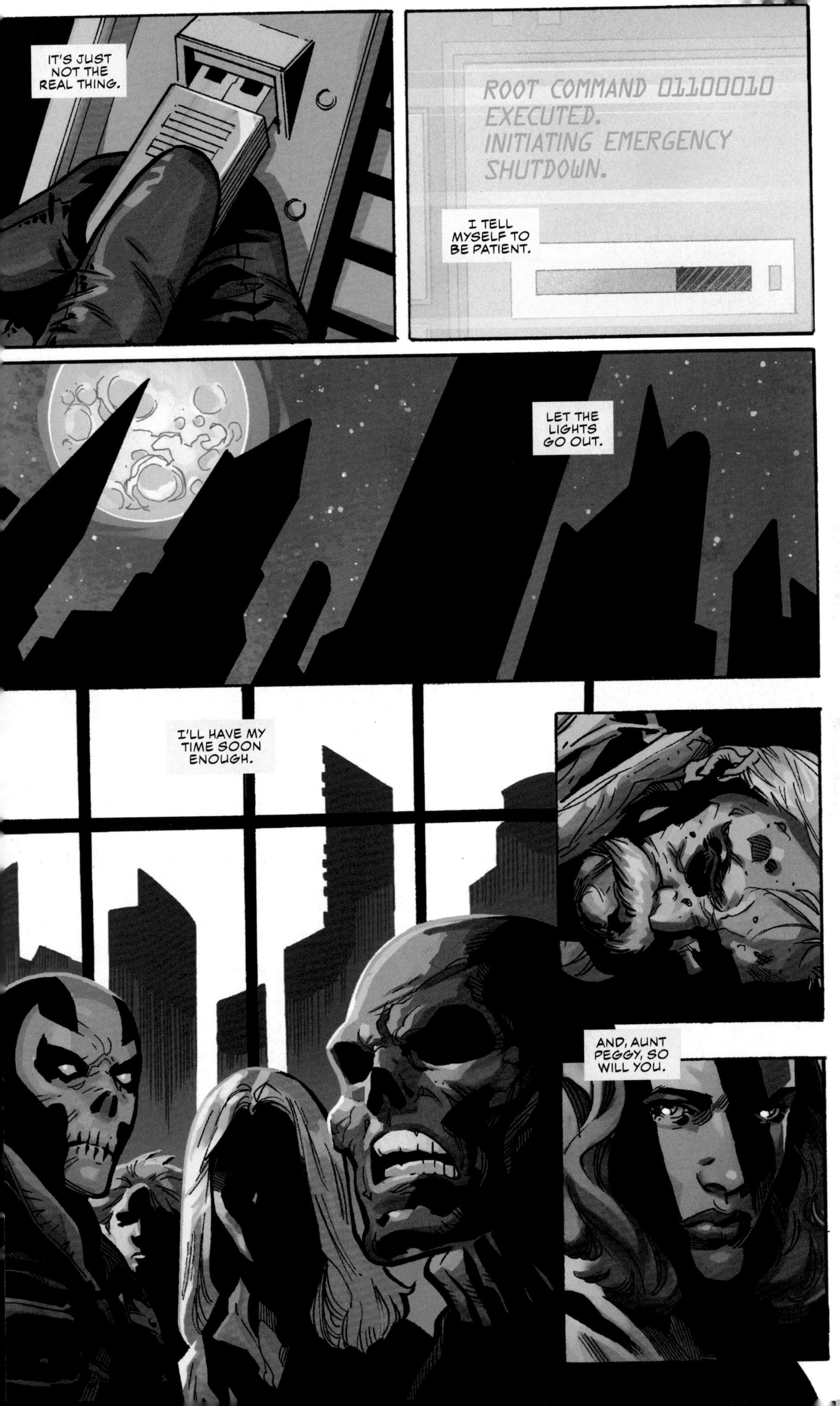

IT'S JUST NOT THE REAL THING.
ROOT COMMAND 01100010 EXECUTED.
INITIATING EMERGENCY SHUTDOWN.
I TELL MYSELF TO BE PATIENT.
LET THE LIGHTS GO OUT.
I'LL HAVE MY TIME SOON ENOUGH.
AND, AUNT PEGGY, SO WILL YOU.

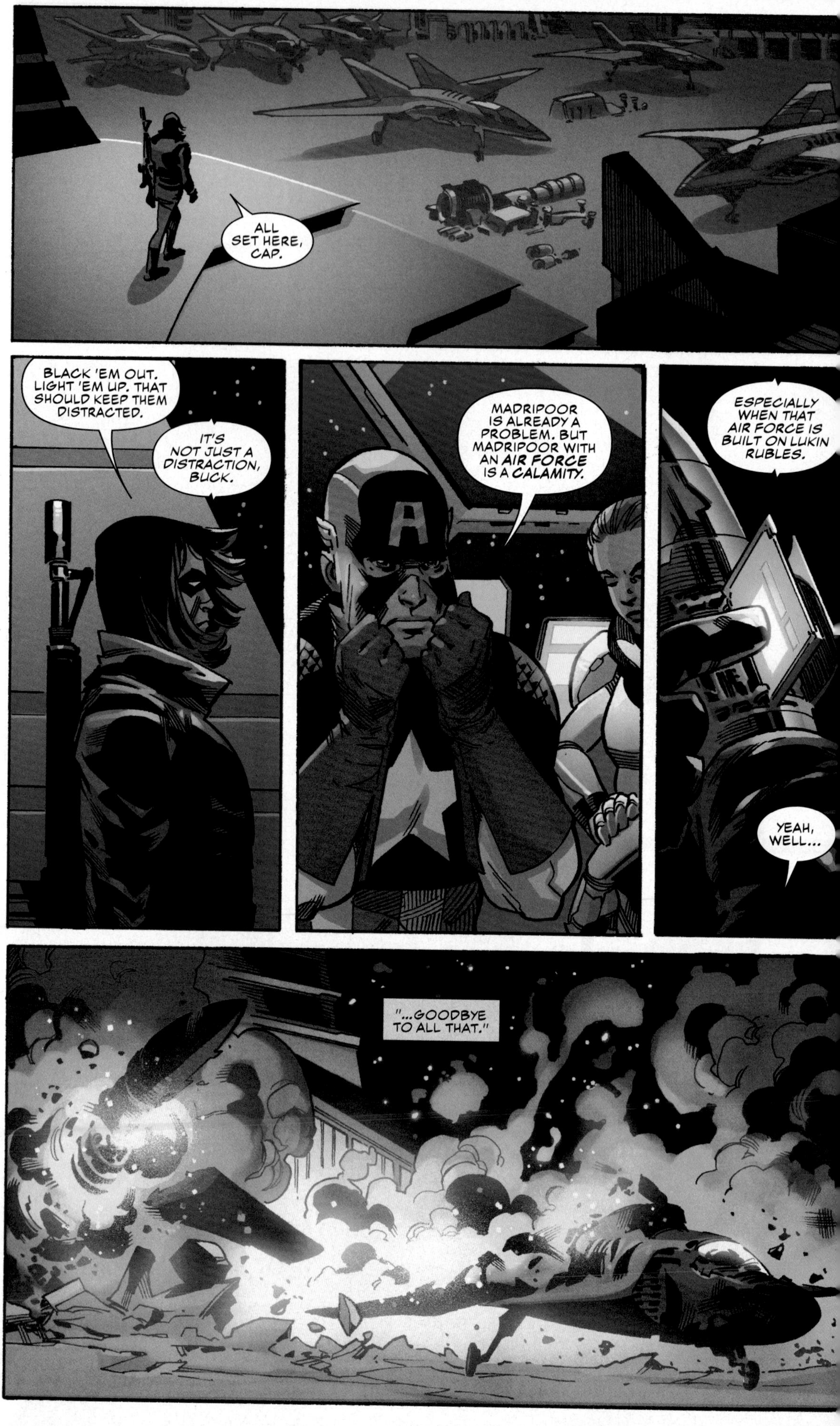
ALL SET HERE, CAP.
BLACK 'EM OUT. LIGHT 'EM UP. THAT SHOULD KEEP THEM DISTRACTED.
IT'S NOT JUST A DISTRACTION, BUCK.
MADRIPOOR IS ALREADY A PROBLEM. BUT MADRIPOOR WITH AN AIR FORCE IS A CALAMITY.
ESPECIALLY WHEN THAT AIR FORCE IS BUILT ON LUKIN RUBLES.
YEAH, WELL...
"...GOODBYE TO ALL THAT."

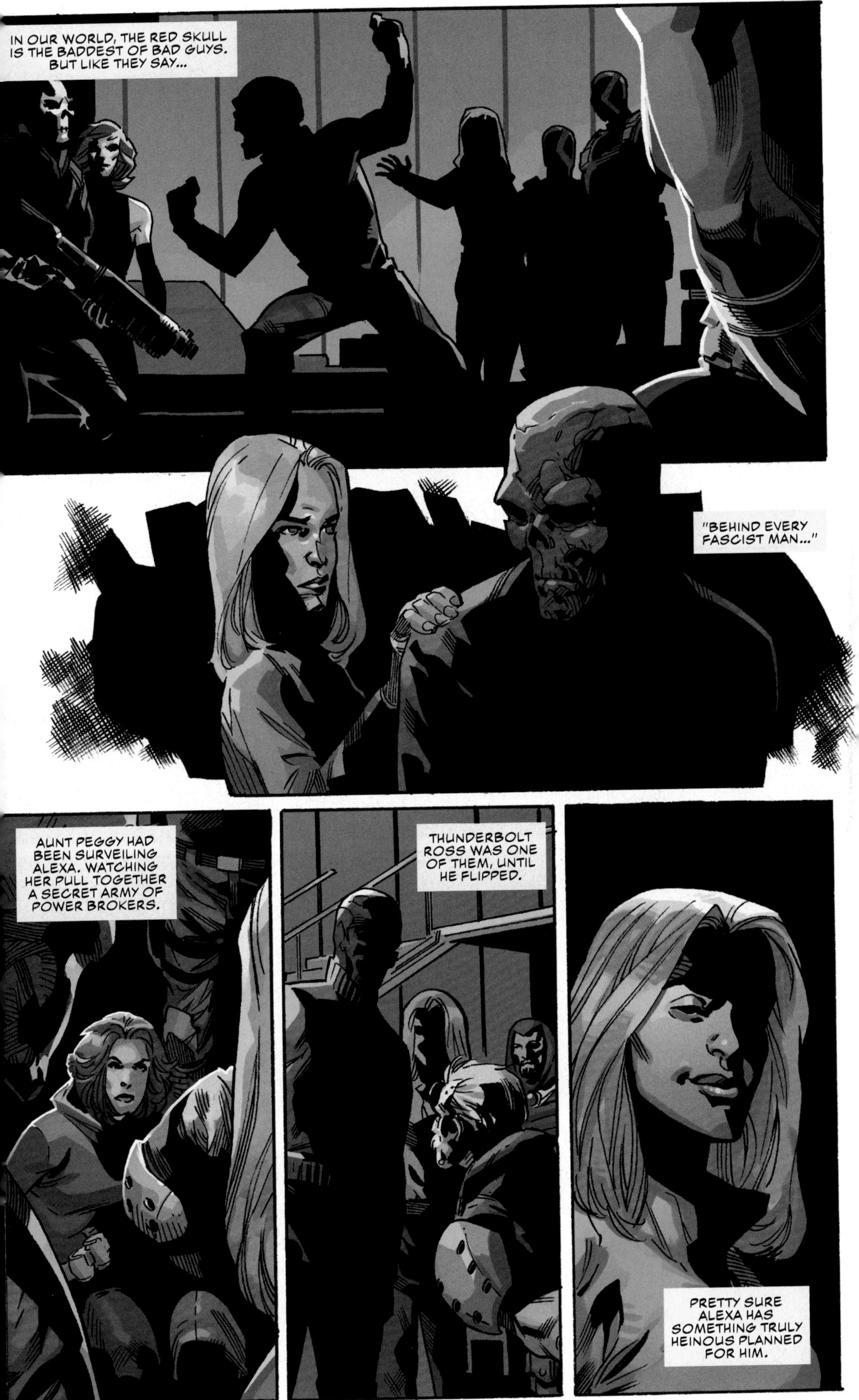
IN OUR WORLD, THE RED SKULL IS THE BADDEST OF BAD GUYS. BUT LIKE THEY SAY...
"BEHIND EVERY FASCIST MAN..."
AUNT PEGGY HAD BEEN SURVEILING ALEXA. WATCHING HER PULL TOGETHER A SECRET ARMY OF POWER BROKERS.
THUNDERBOLT ROSS WAS ONE OF THEM, UNTIL HE FLIPPED.
PRETTY SURE ALEXA HAS SOMETHING TRULY HEINOUS PLANNED FOR HIM.

SHE WAS ALWAYS RUTHLESS. HELL, SHE TAUGHT AUNT PEGGY HOW TO BE RUTHLESS.

IT WAS ALEX WHO BROUG HER INTO TH DAUGHTERS

SAVED AUNT PEGGY FROM THAT JUNE CLEAVER LIFE.

GAVE HER SOMETHING TO FIGHT FOR, AND EVEN MORE...

...SOMETHING TO BELIEVE IN.

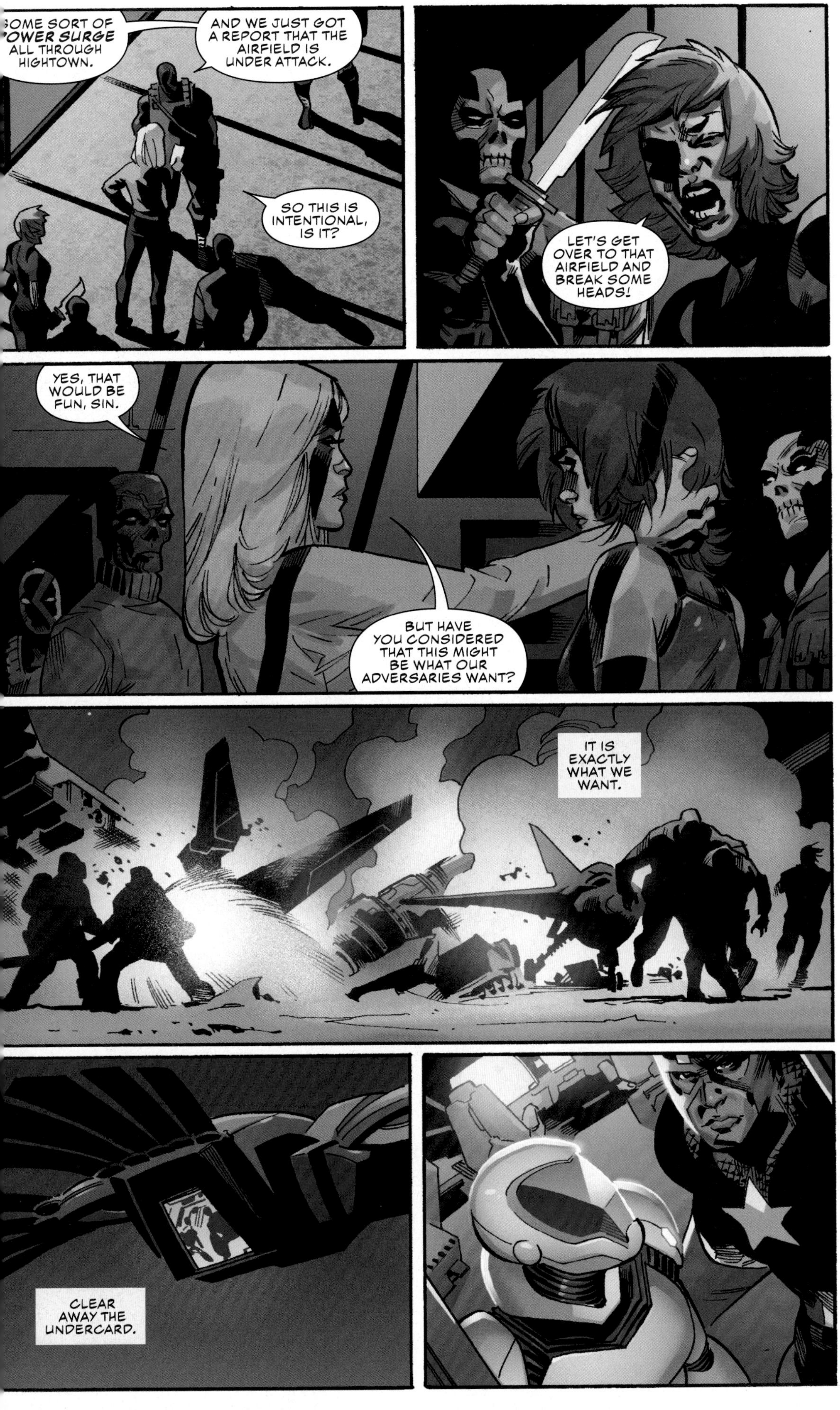
SOME SORT OF POWER SURGE ALL THROUGH HIGHTOWN.
AND WE JUST GOT A REPORT THAT THE AIRFIELD IS UNDER ATTACK.
SO THIS IS INTENTIONAL, IS IT?
LET'S GET OVER TO THAT AIRFIELD AND BREAK SOME HEADS!
YES, THAT WOULD BE FUN, SIN.
BUT HAVE YOU CONSIDERED THAT THIS MIGHT BE WHAT OUR ADVERSARIES WANT?
IT IS EXACTLY WHAT WE WANT.
CLEAR AWAY THE UNDERCARD.

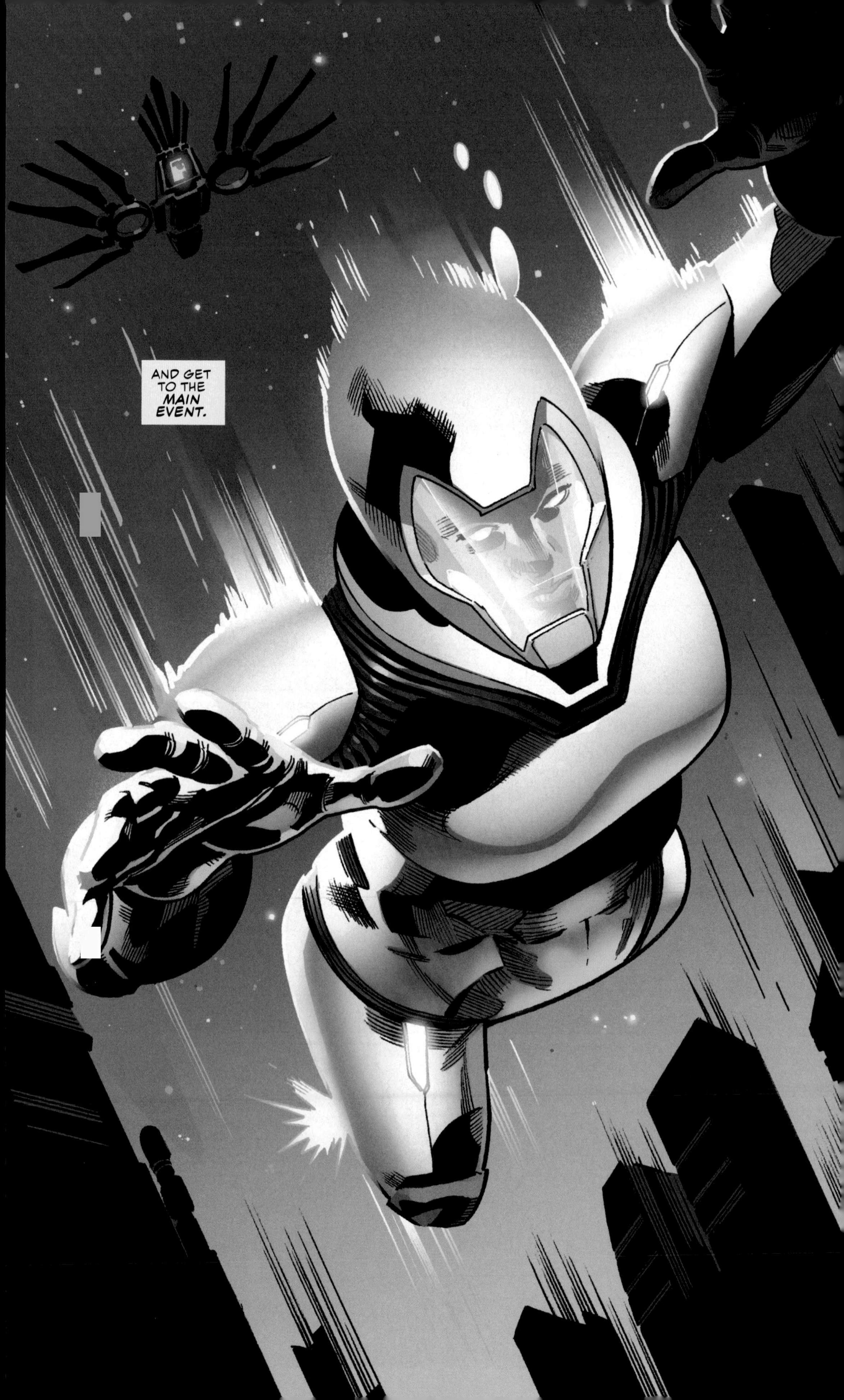
AND GET TO THE MAIN EVENT.

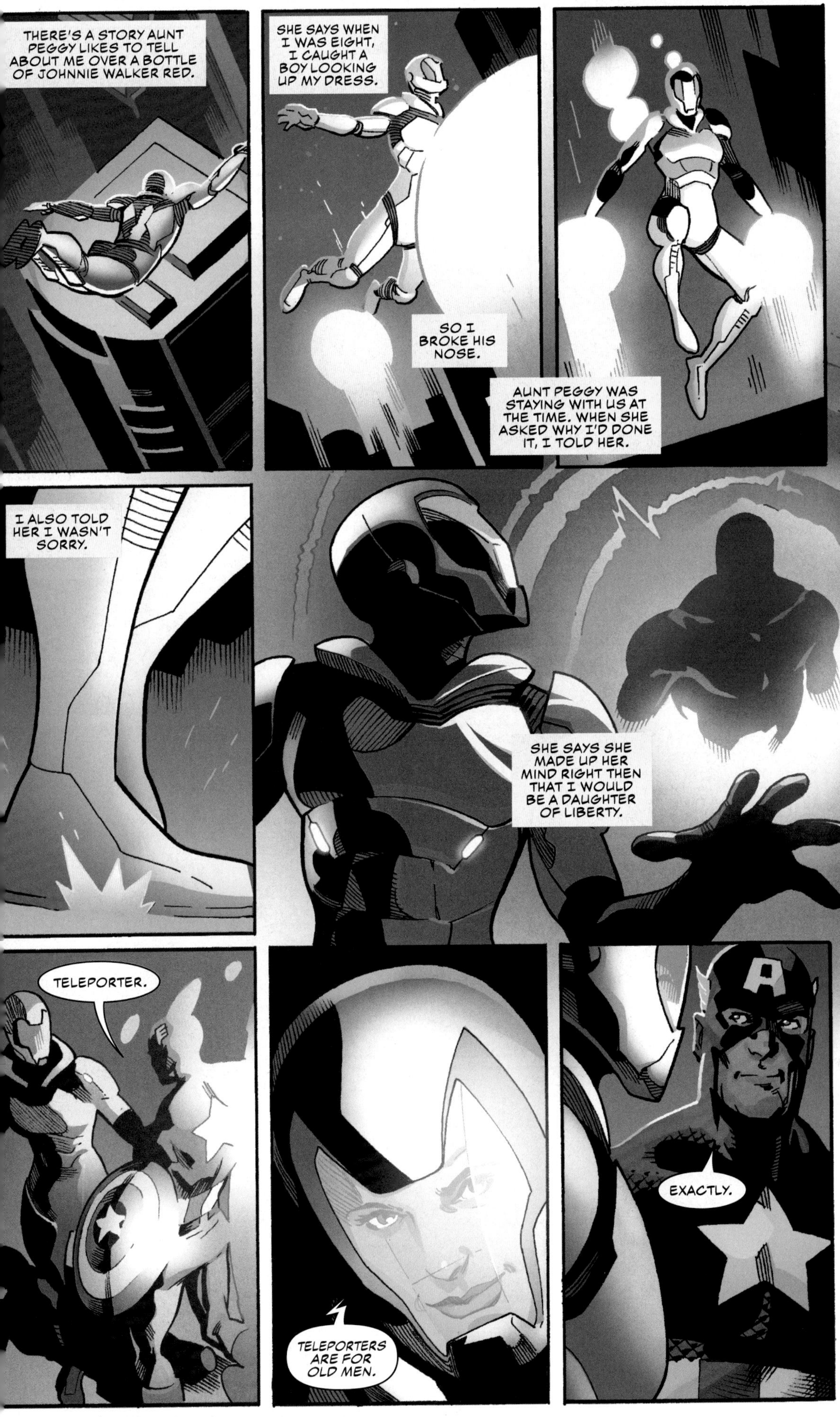
THERE'S A STORY AUNT PEGGY LIKES TO TELL ABOUT ME OVER A BOTTLE OF JOHNNIE WALKER RED.
SHE SAYS WHEN I WAS EIGHT, I CAUGHT A BOY LOOKING UP MY DRESS.
SO I BROKE HIS NOSE.
AUNT PEGGY WAS STAYING WITH US AT THE TIME. WHEN SHE ASKED WHY I'D DONE IT, I TOLD HER.
I ALSO TOLD HER I WASN'T SORRY.
SHE SAYS SHE MADE UP HER MIND RIGHT THEN THAT I WOULD BE A DAUGHTER OF LIBERTY.
TELEPORTER.
TELEPORTERS ARE FOR OLD MEN.
EXACTLY.

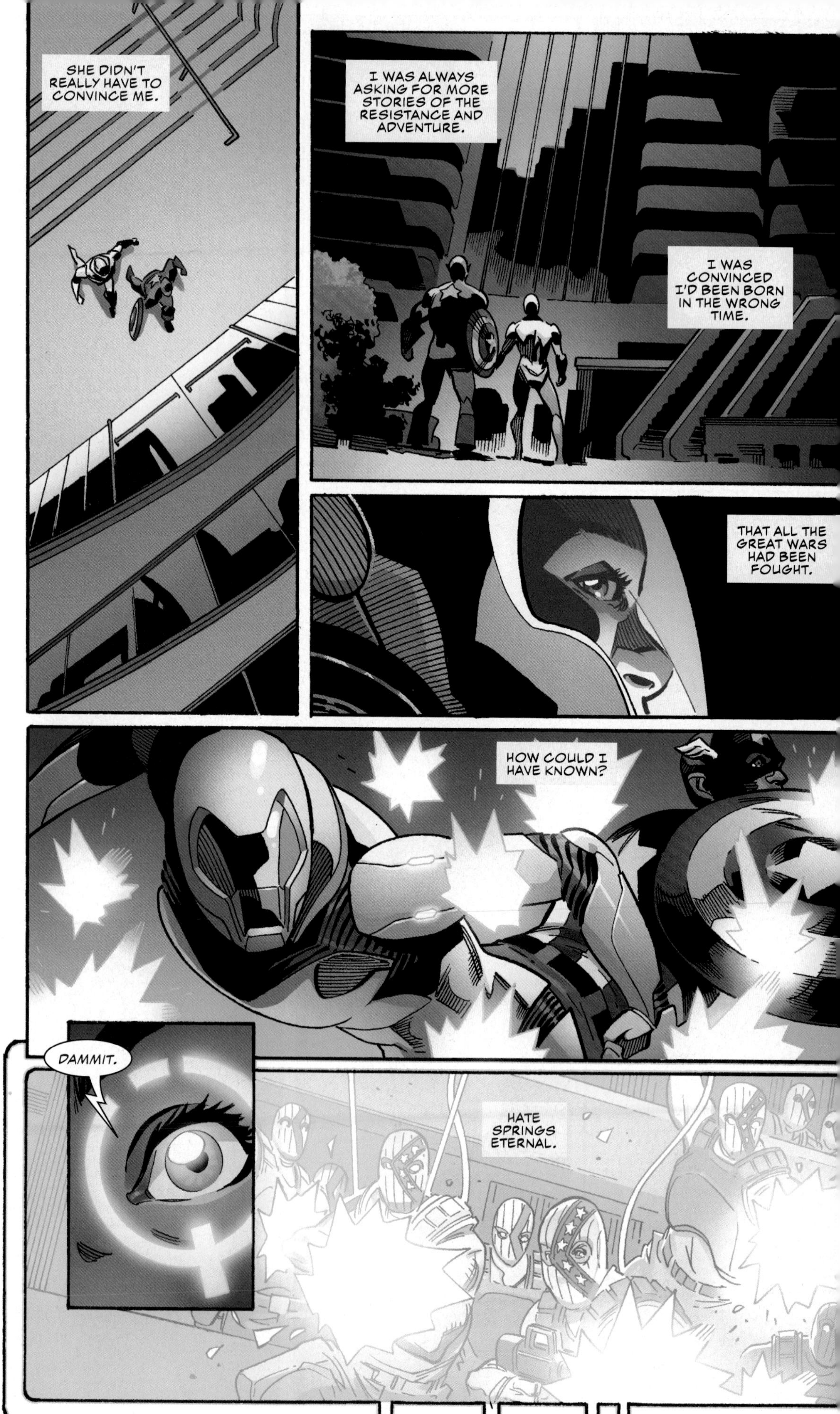
SHE DIDN'T REALLY HAVE TO CONVINCE ME.
I WAS ALWAYS ASKING FOR MORE STORIES OF THE RESISTANCE AND ADVENTURE.
I WAS CONVINCED I'D BEEN BORN IN THE WRONG TIME.
THAT ALL THE GREAT WARS HAD BEEN FOUGHT.
HOW COULD I HAVE KNOWN?
DAMMIT.
HATE SPRINGS ETERNAL.

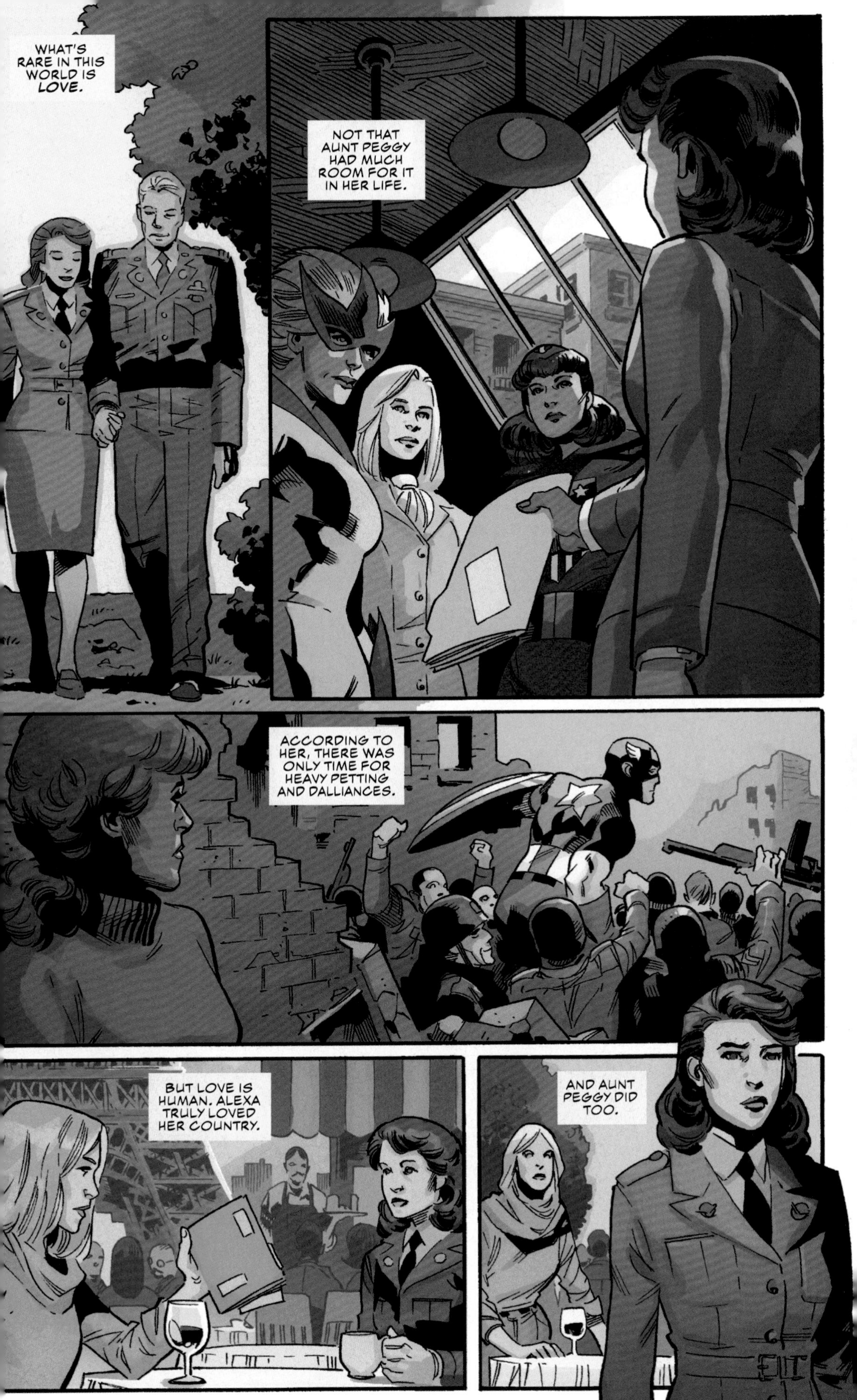
WHAT'S RARE IN THIS WORLD IS LOVE.
NOT THAT AUNT PEGGY HAD MUCH ROOM FOR IT IN HER LIFE.
ACCORDING TO HER, THERE WAS ONLY TIME FOR HEAVY PETTING AND DALLIANCES.
BUT LOVE IS HUMAN. ALEXA TRULY LOVED HER COUNTRY.
AND AUNT PEGGY DID TOO.

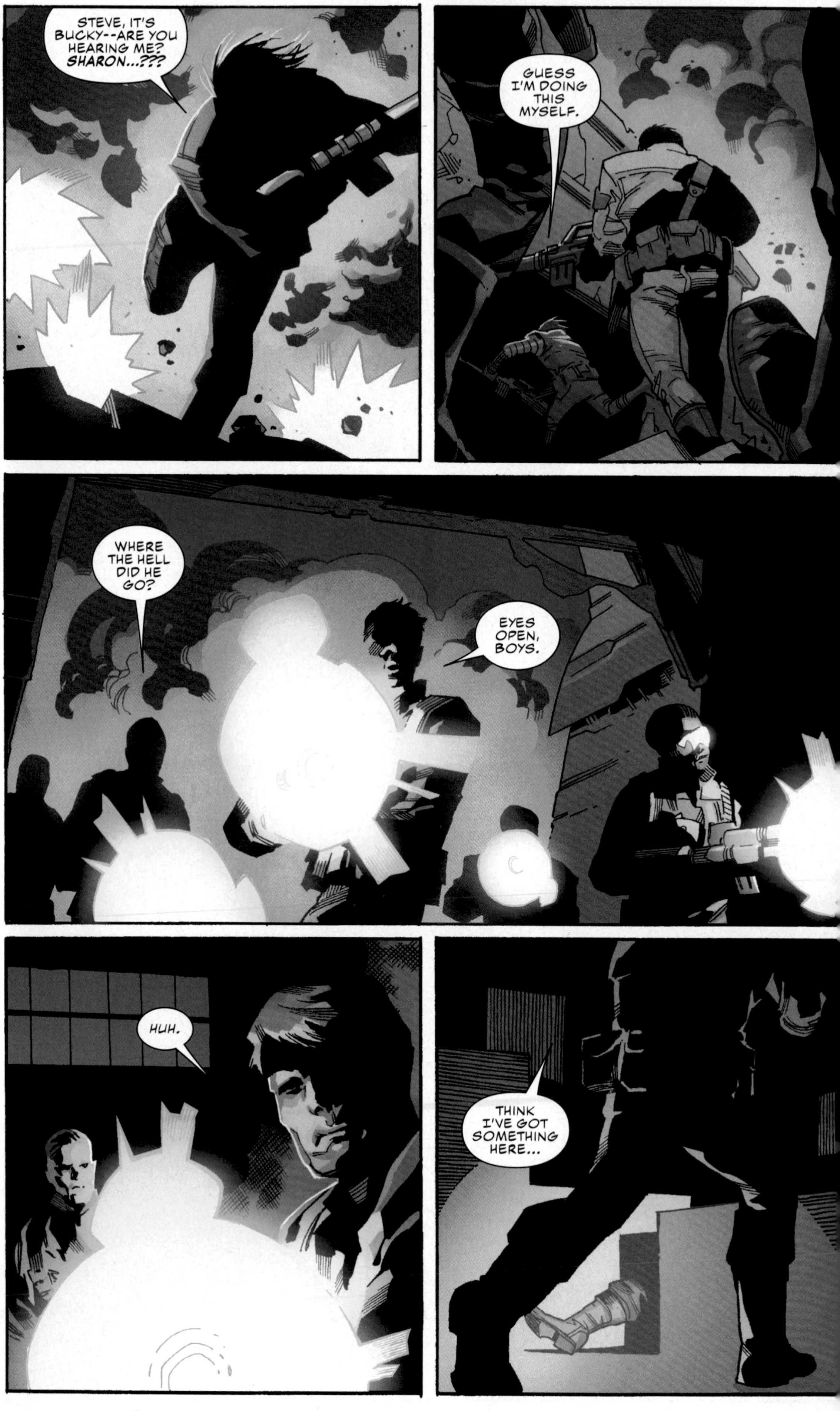
STEVE, IT'S BUCKY--ARE YOU HEARING ME? SHARON...???
GUESS I'M DOING THIS MYSELF.
WHERE THE HELL DID HE GO?
EYES OPEN, BOYS.
HUH.
THINK I'VE GOT SOMETHING HERE...

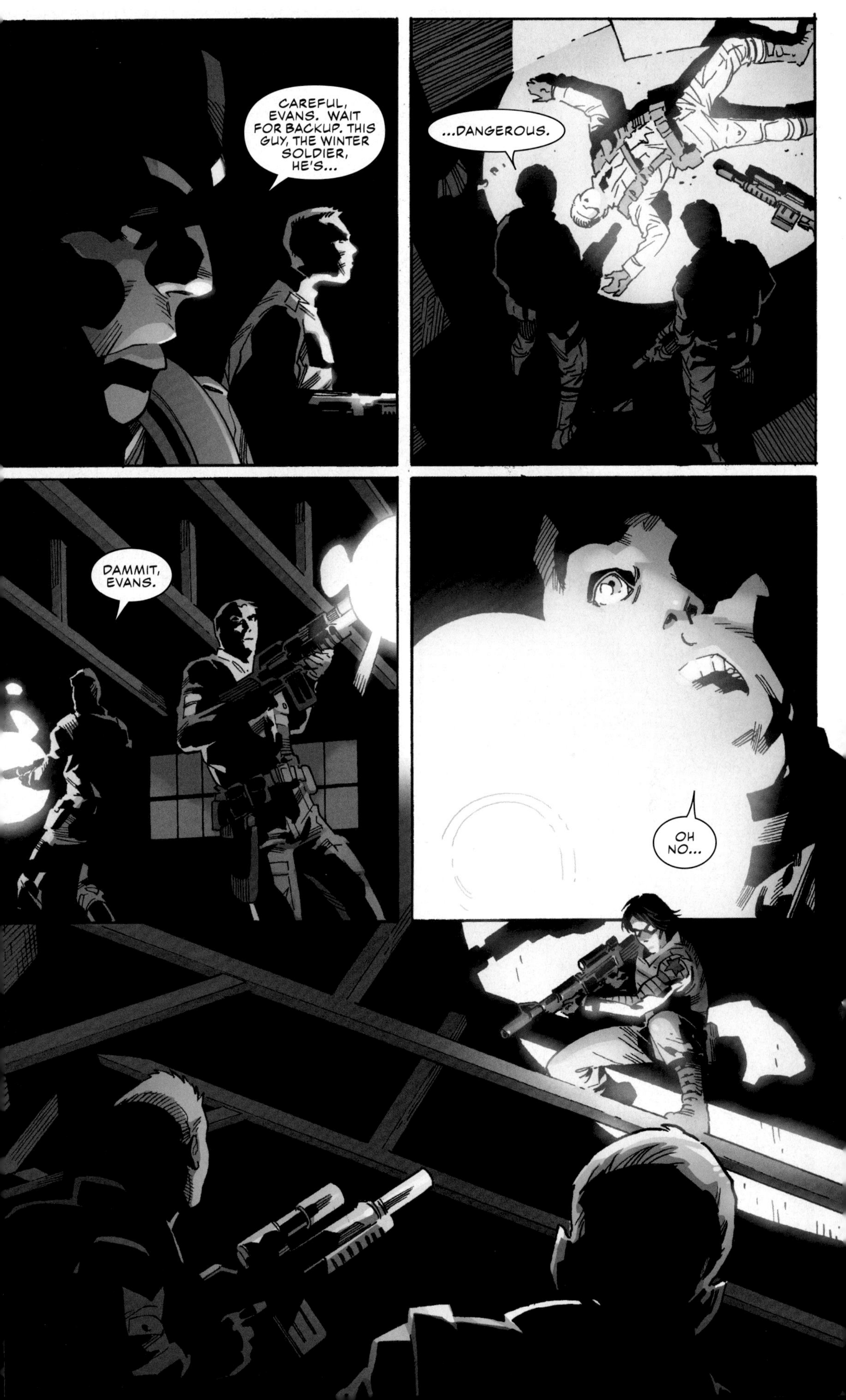
CAREFUL, EVANS. WAIT FOR BACKUP. THIS GUY, THE WINTER SOLDIER, HE'S...
...DANGEROUS.
DAMMIT, EVANS.
OH NO...

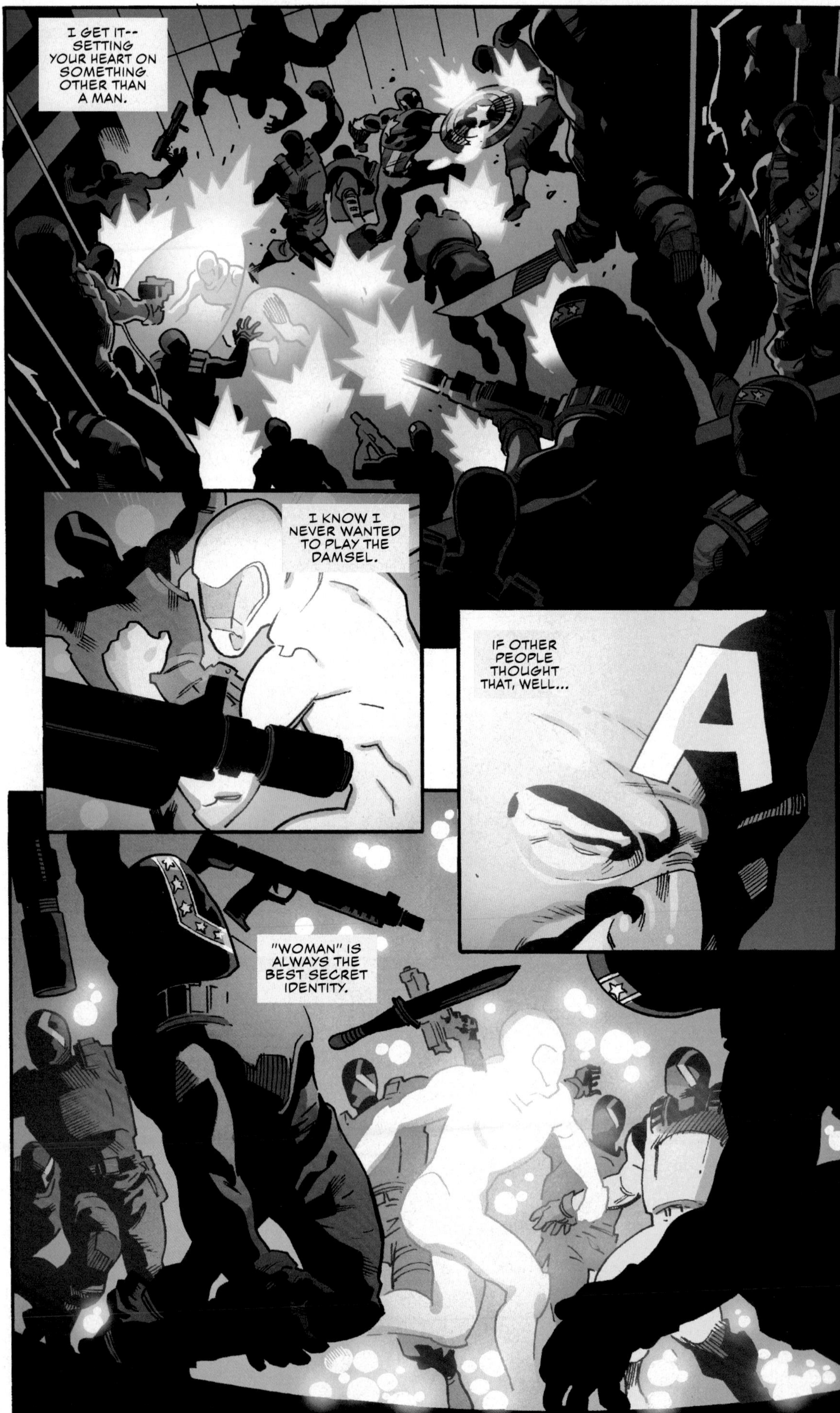
I GET IT--
SETTING YOUR HEART ON SOMETHING OTHER THAN A MAN.
I KNOW I NEVER WANTED TO PLAY THE DAMSEL.
IF OTHER PEOPLE THOUGHT THAT, WELL...
"WOMAN" IS ALWAYS THE BEST SECRET IDENTITY.

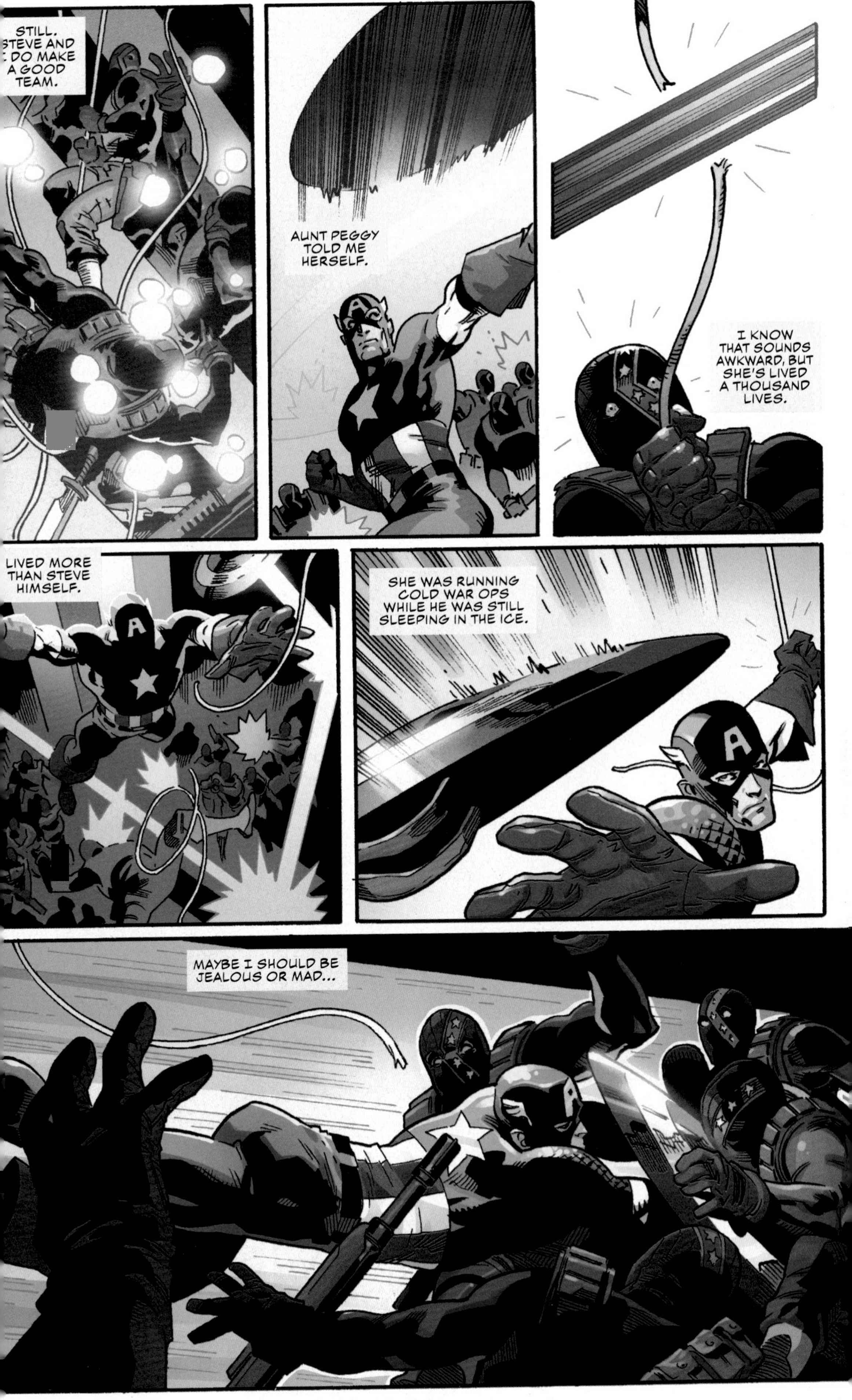
STILL. STEVE AND I DO MAKE A GOOD TEAM.
AUNT PEGGY TOLD ME HERSELF.
I KNOW THAT SOUNDS AWKWARD, BUT SHE'S LIVED A THOUSAND LIVES.
LIVED MORE THAN STEVE HIMSELF.
SHE WAS RUNNING COLD WAR OPS WHILE HE WAS STILL SLEEPING IN THE ICE.
MAYBE I SHOULD BE JEALOUS OR MAD...

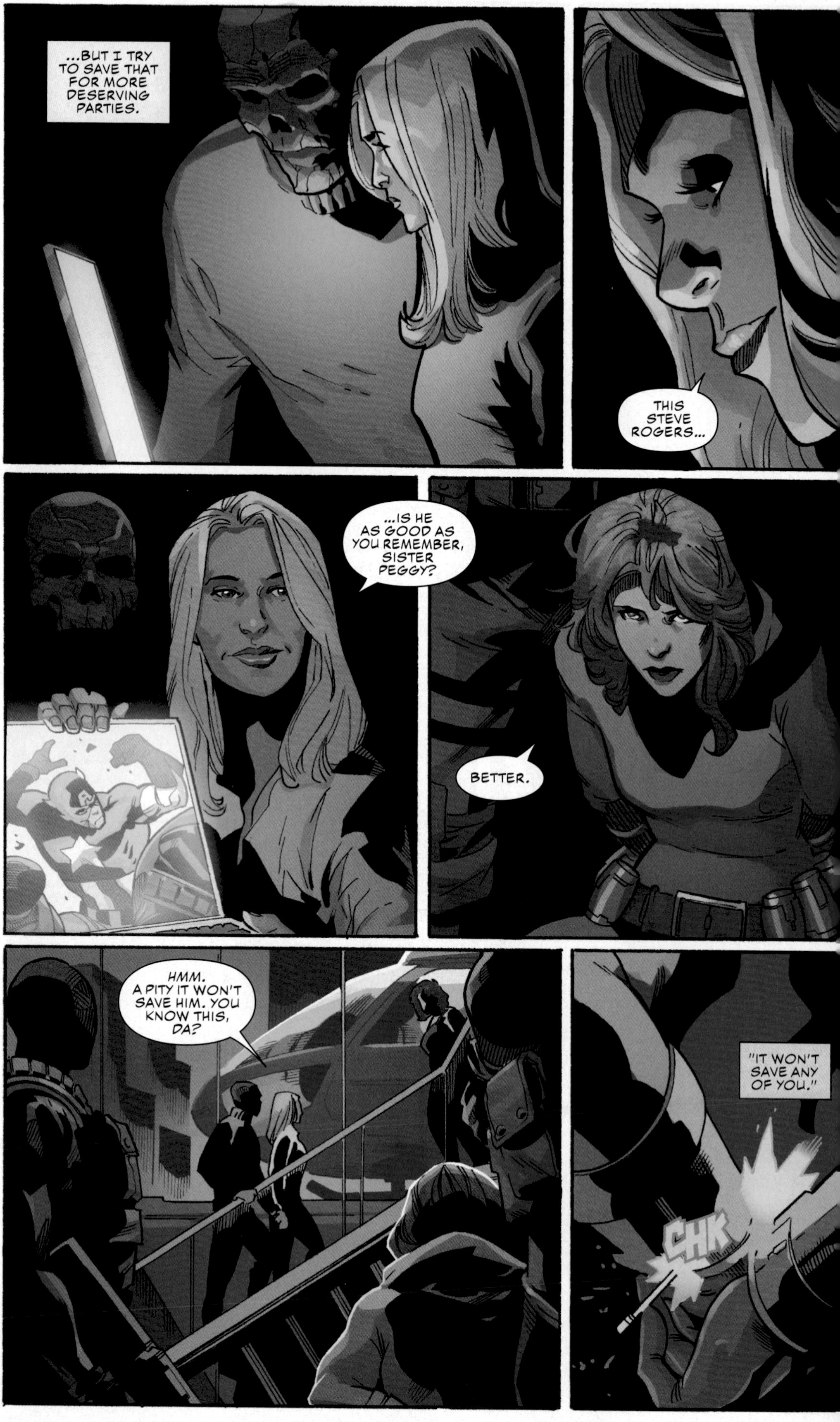
...BUT I TRY TO SAVE THAT FOR MORE DESERVING PARTIES.
THIS STEVE ROGERS...
...IS HE AS GOOD AS YOU REMEMBER, SISTER PEGGY?
BETTER.
HMM. A PITY IT WON'T SAVE HIM. YOU KNOW THIS, DA?
"IT WON'T SAVE ANY OF YOU."
CHK

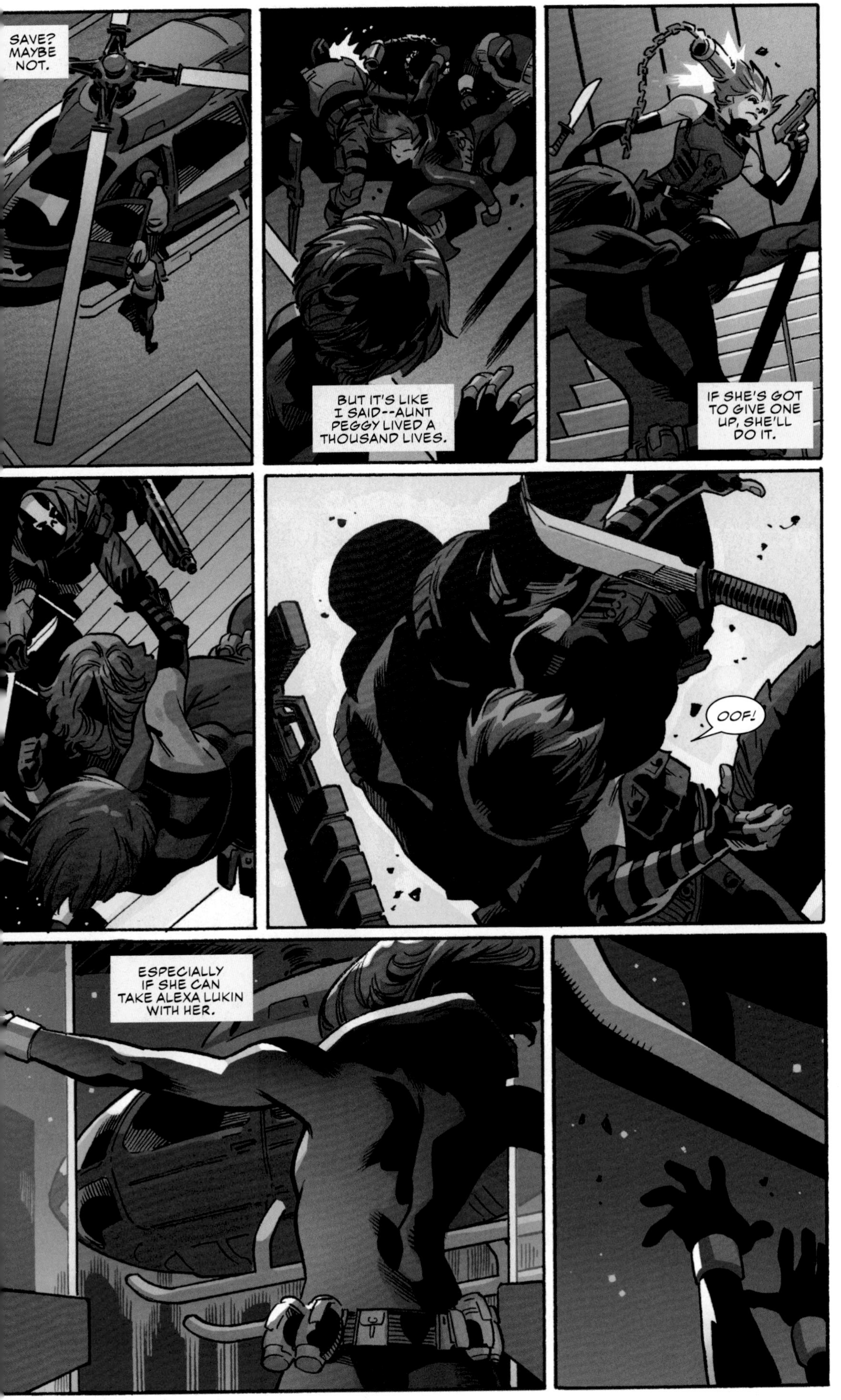
SAVE? MAYBE NOT.
BUT IT'S LIKE I SAID--AUNT PEGGY LIVED A THOUSAND LIVES.
IF SHE'S GOT TO GIVE ONE UP, SHE'LL DO IT.
OOF!
ESPECIALLY IF SHE CAN TAKE ALEXA LUKIN WITH HER.

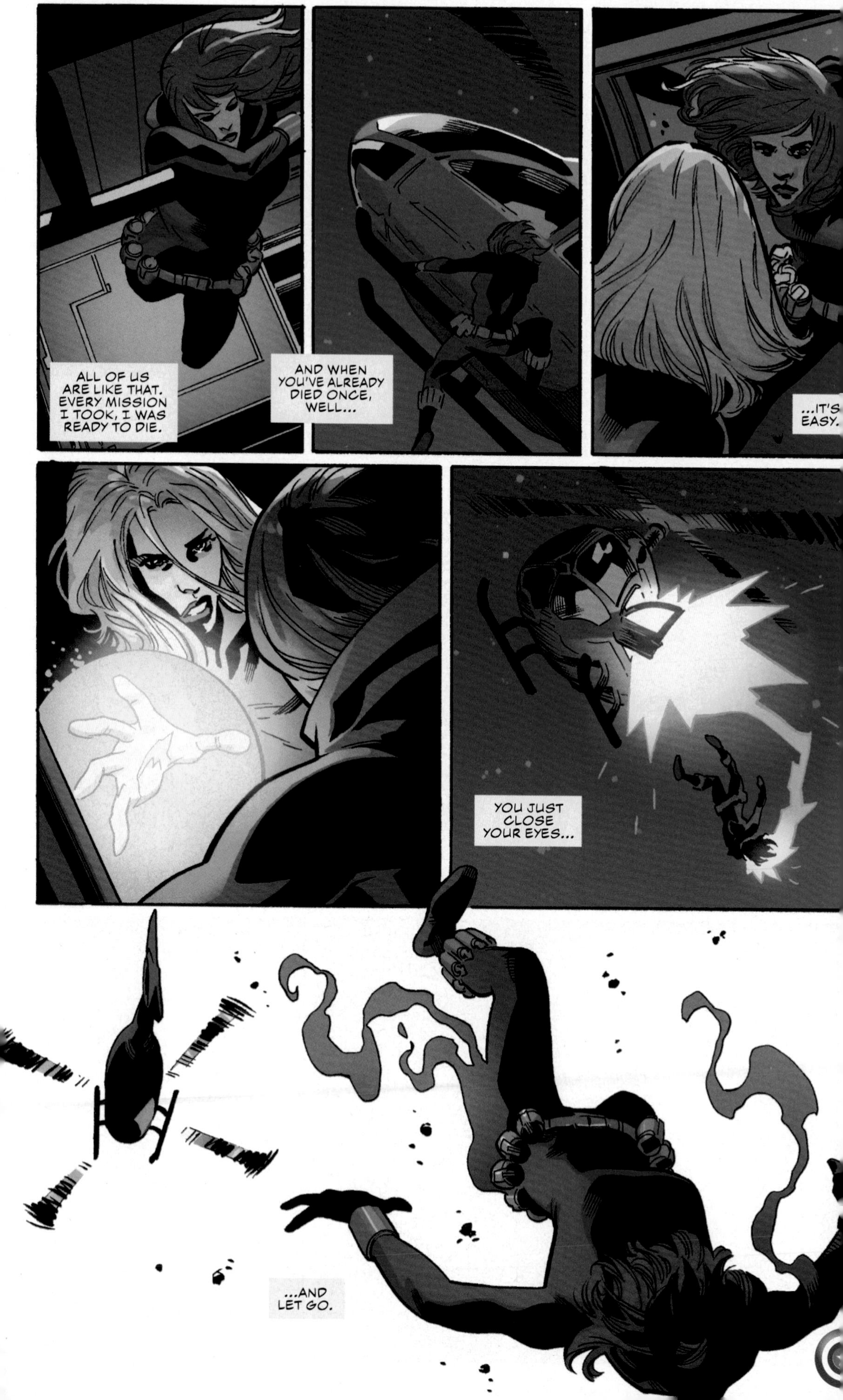
ALL OF US ARE LIKE THAT. EVERY MISSION I TOOK, I WAS READY TO DIE.
AND WHEN YOU'VE ALREADY DIED ONCE, WELL...
...IT'S EASY.
YOU JUST CLOSE YOUR EYES...
...AND LET GO.

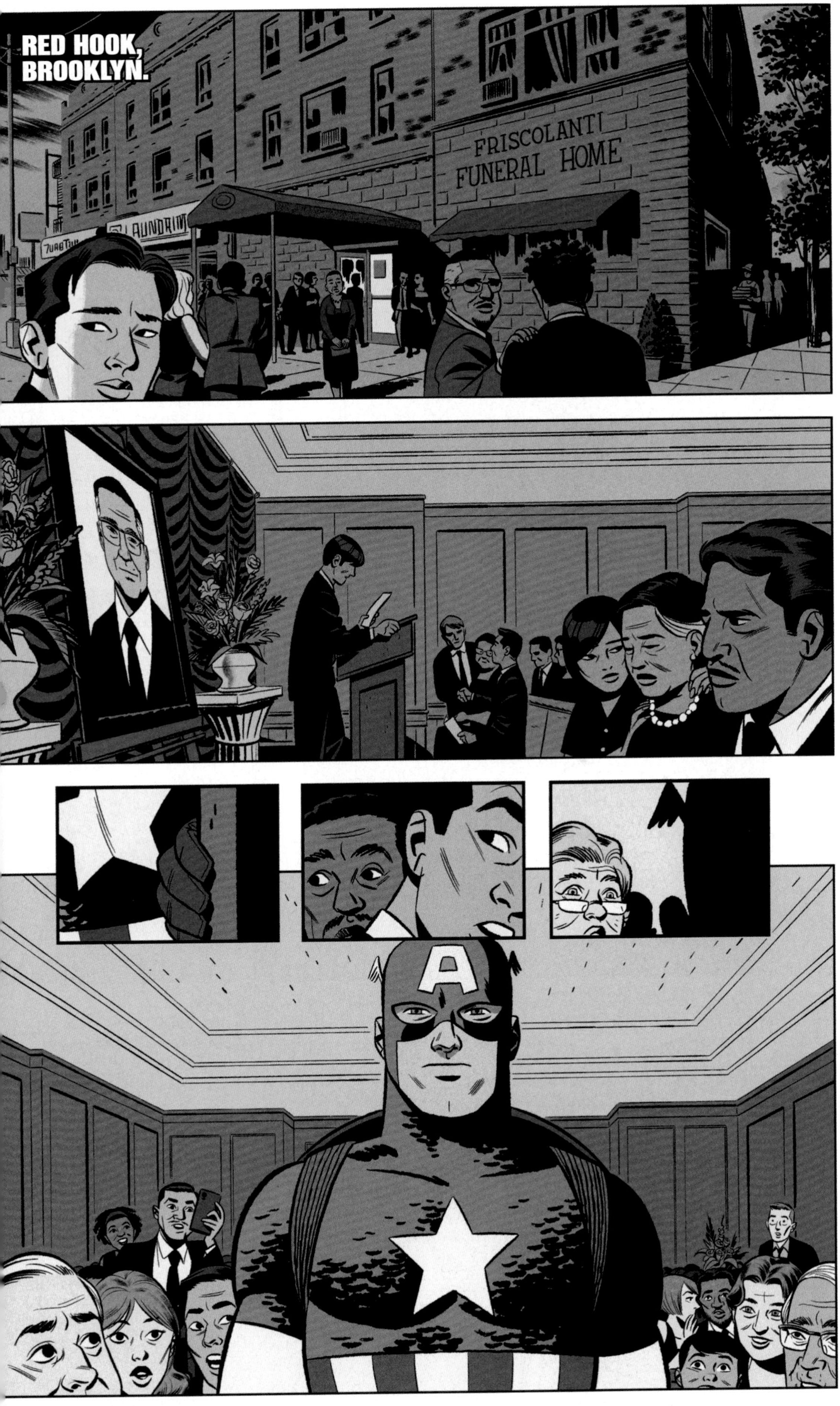
RED HOOK, BROOKLYN.
FRISCOLANTI FUNERAL HOME

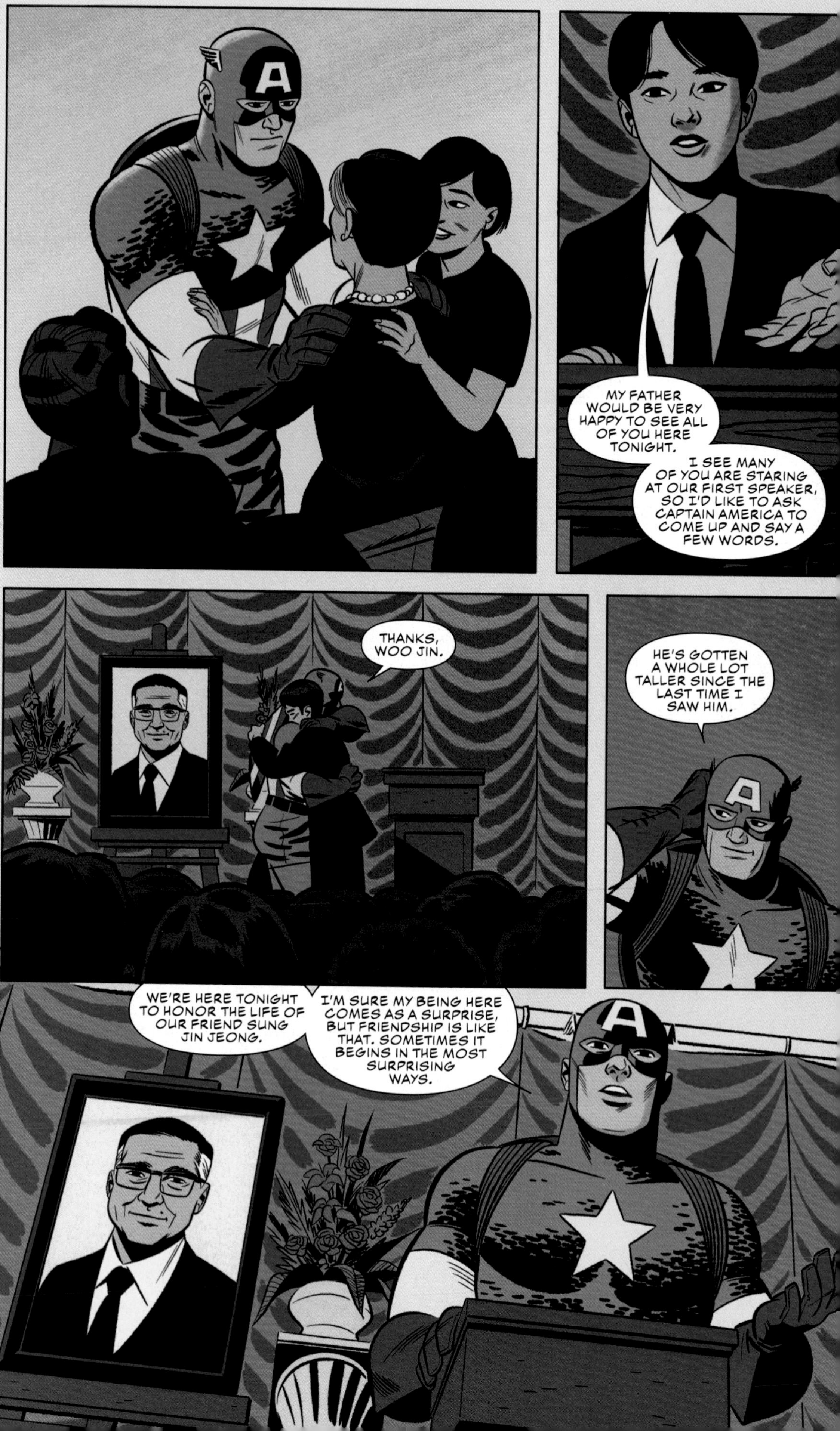
MY FATHER WOULD BE VERY HAPPY TO SEE ALL OF YOU HERE TONIGHT.
I SEE MANY OF YOU ARE STARING AT OUR FIRST SPEAKER, SO I'D LIKE TO ASK CAPTAIN AMERICA TO COME UP AND SAY A FEW WORDS.
THANKS, WOO JIN.
HE'S GOTTEN A WHOLE LOT TALLER SINCE THE LAST TIME I SAW HIM.
WE'RE HERE TONIGHT TO HONOR THE LIFE OF OUR FRIEND SUNG JIN JEONG.
I'M SURE MY BEING HERE COMES AS A SURPRISE, BUT FRIENDSHIP IS LIKE THAT. SOMETIMES IT BEGINS IN THE MOST SURPRISING WAYS.

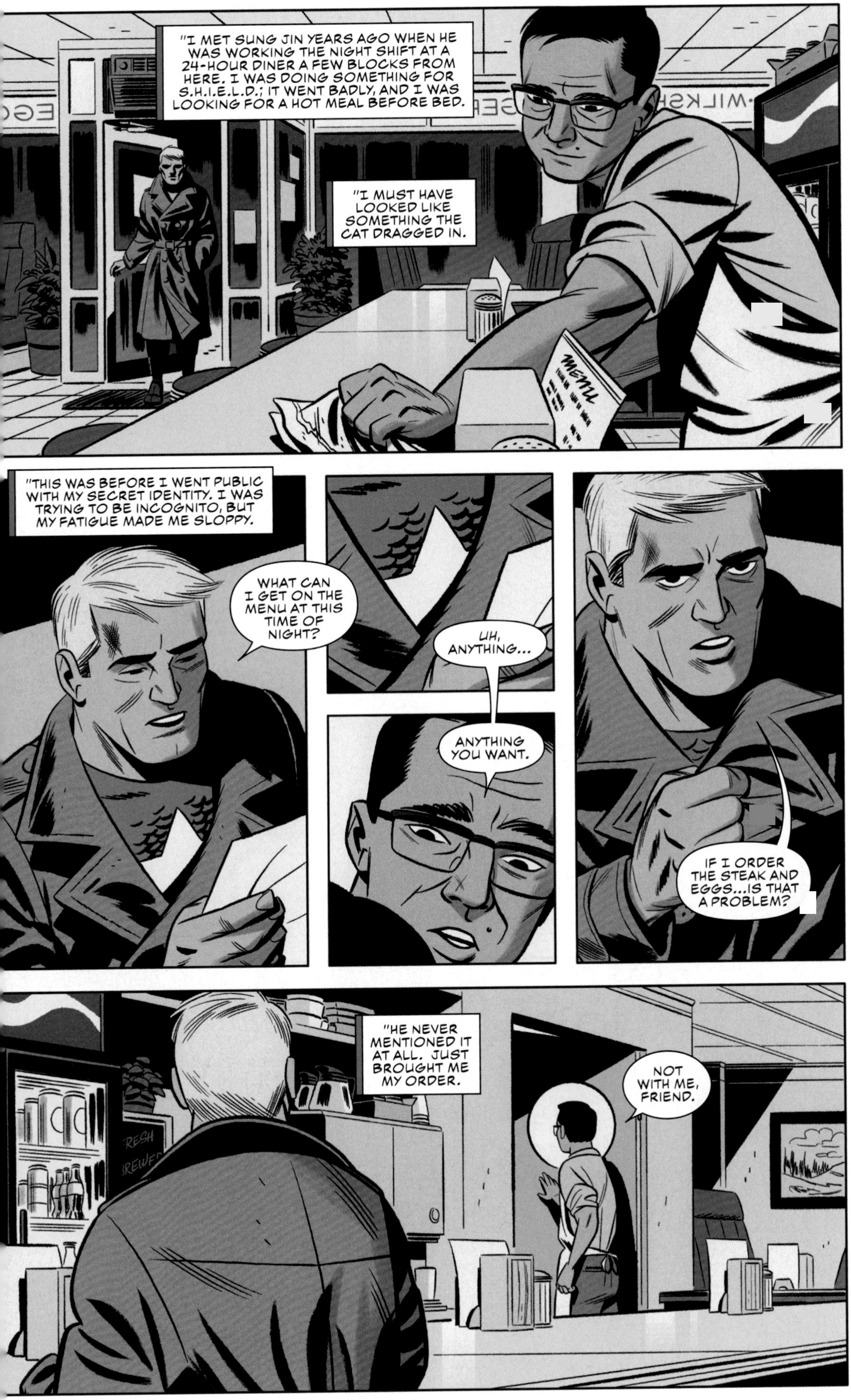
"I MET SUNG JIN YEARS AGO WHEN HE WAS WORKING THE NIGHT SHIFT AT A 24-HOUR DINER A FEW BLOCKS FROM HERE. I WAS DOING SOMETHING FOR S.H.I.E.L.D.; IT WENT BADLY, AND I WAS LOOKING FOR A HOT MEAL BEFORE BED.
"I MUST HAVE LOOKED LIKE SOMETHING THE CAT DRAGGED IN.
MENU
"THIS WAS BEFORE I WENT PUBLIC WITH MY SECRET IDENTITY. I WAS TRYING TO BE INCOGNITO, BUT MY FATIGUE MADE ME SLOPPY.
WHAT CAN I GET ON THE MENU AT THIS TIME OF NIGHT?
UH, ANYTHING...
ANYTHING YOU WANT.
IF I ORDER THE STEAK AND EGGS...IS THAT A PROBLEM?
"HE NEVER MENTIONED IT AT ALL. JUST BROUGHT ME MY ORDER.
NOT WITH ME, FRIEND.

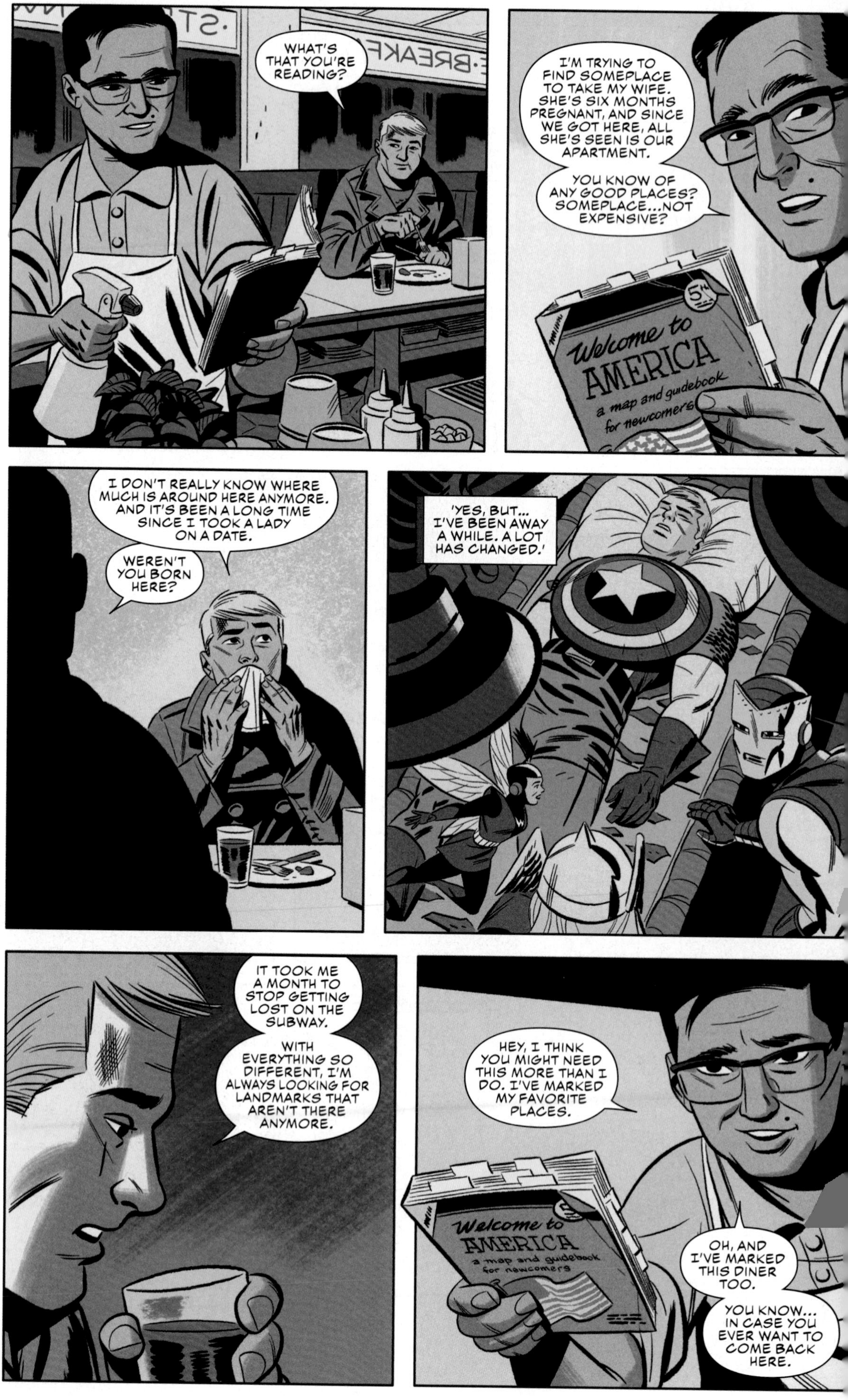

WHAT'S THAT YOU'RE READING?
I'M TRYING TO FIND SOMEPLACE TO TAKE MY WIFE. SHE'S SIX MONTHS PREGNANT, AND SINCE WE GOT HERE, ALL SHE'S SEEN IS OUR APARTMENT.
YOU KNOW OF ANY GOOD PLACES? SOMEPLACE...NOT EXPENSIVE?
Welcome to AMERICA a map and guidebook for newcomers
I DON'T REALLY KNOW WHERE MUCH IS AROUND HERE ANYMORE. AND IT'S BEEN A LONG TIME SINCE I TOOK A LADY ON A DATE.
WEREN'T YOU BORN HERE?
'YES, BUT... I'VE BEEN AWAY A WHILE. A LOT HAS CHANGED.'
IT TOOK ME A MONTH TO STOP GETTING LOST ON THE SUBWAY.
WITH EVERYTHING SO DIFFERENT, I'M ALWAYS LOOKING FOR LANDMARKS THAT AREN'T THERE ANYMORE.
HEY, I THINK YOU MIGHT NEED THIS MORE THAN I DO. I'VE MARKED MY FAVORITE PLACES.
Welcome to AMERICA a map and guidebook for newcomers
OH, AND I'VE MARKED THIS DINER TOO.
YOU KNOW... IN CASE YOU EVER WANT TO COME BACK HERE.

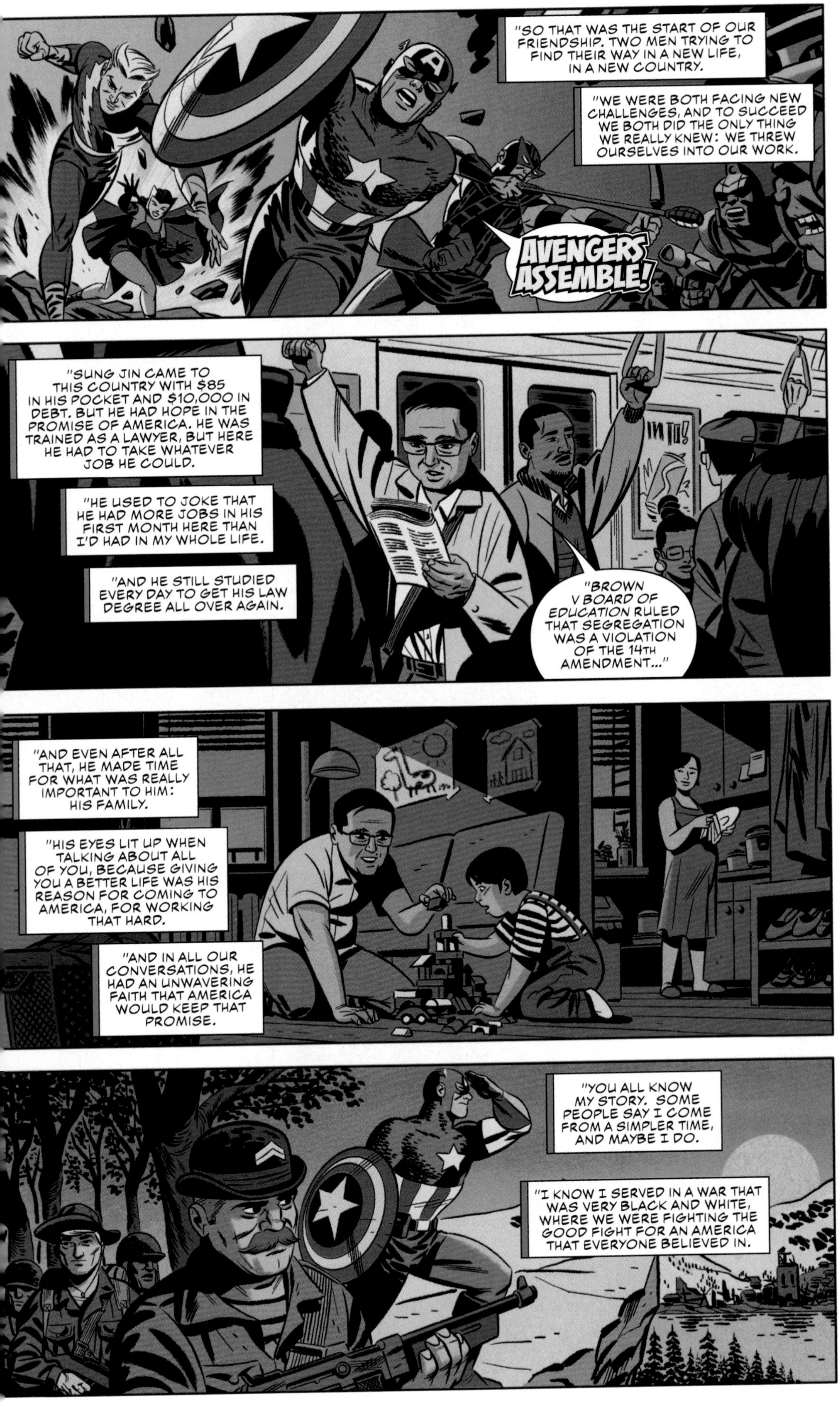
"SO THAT WAS THE START OF OUR FRIENDSHIP. TWO MEN TRYING TO FIND THEIR WAY IN A NEW LIFE, IN A NEW COUNTRY.
"WE WERE BOTH FACING NEW CHALLENGES, AND TO SUCCEED WE BOTH DID THE ONLY THING WE REALLY KNEW: WE THREW OURSELVES INTO OUR WORK.
AVENGERS ASSEMBLE!
"SUNG JIN CAME TO THIS COUNTRY WITH $85 IN HIS POCKET AND $10,000 IN DEBT. BUT HE HAD HOPE IN THE PROMISE OF AMERICA. HE WAS TRAINED AS A LAWYER, BUT HERE HE HAD TO TAKE WHATEVER JOB HE COULD.
"HE USED TO JOKE THAT HE HAD MORE JOBS IN HIS FIRST MONTH HERE THAN I'D HAD IN MY WHOLE LIFE.
"AND HE STILL STUDIED EVERY DAY TO GET HIS LAW DEGREE ALL OVER AGAIN.
"BROWN V BOARD OF EDUCATION RULED THAT SEGREGATION WAS A VIOLATION OF THE 14TH AMENDMENT..."
"AND EVEN AFTER ALL THAT, HE MADE TIME FOR WHAT WAS REALLY IMPORTANT TO HIM: HIS FAMILY.
"HIS EYES LIT UP WHEN TALKING ABOUT ALL OF YOU, BECAUSE GIVING YOU A BETTER LIFE WAS HIS REASON FOR COMING TO AMERICA, FOR WORKING THAT HARD.
"AND IN ALL OUR CONVERSATIONS, HE HAD AN UNWAVERING FAITH THAT AMERICA WOULD KEEP THAT PROMISE.
"YOU ALL KNOW MY STORY. SOME PEOPLE SAY I COME FROM A SIMPLER TIME, AND MAYBE I DO.
"I KNOW I SERVED IN A WAR THAT WAS VERY BLACK AND WHITE, WHERE WE WERE FIGHTING THE GOOD FIGHT FOR AN AMERICA THAT EVERYONE BELIEVED IN.

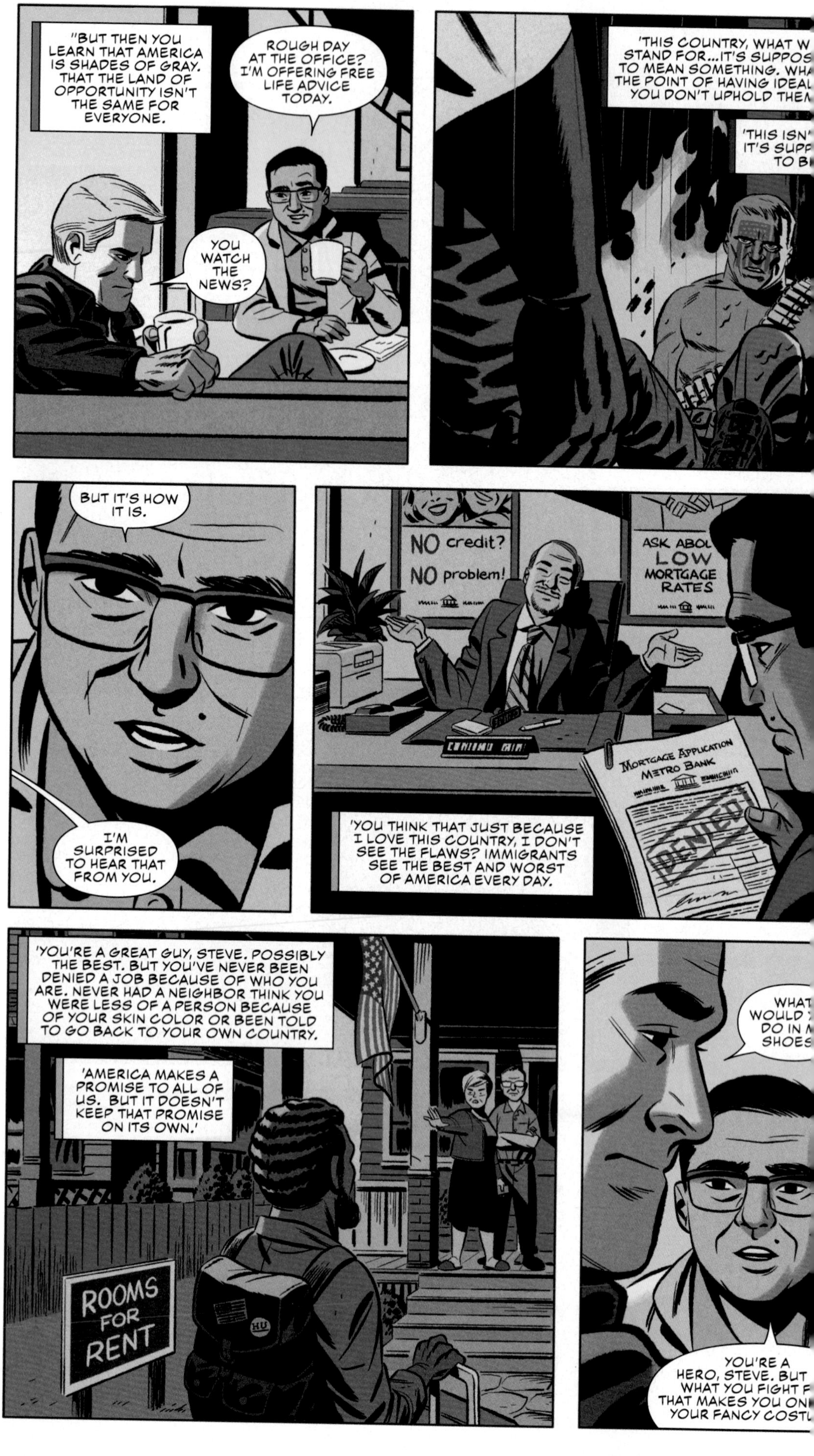

"BUT THEN YOU LEARN THAT AMERICA IS SHADES OF GRAY. THAT THE LAND OF OPPORTUNITY ISN'T THE SAME FOR EVERYONE.
ROUGH DAY AT THE OFFICE? I'M OFFERING FREE LIFE ADVICE TODAY.
YOU WATCH THE NEWS?
'THIS COUNTRY, WHAT W
STAND FOR...IT'S SUPPOS
TO MEAN SOMETHING. WHA
THE POINT OF HAVING IDEAL
YOU DON'T UPHOLD THEM
'THIS ISN'
IT'S SUPP
TO B
BUT IT'S HOW IT IS.
I'M SURPRISED TO HEAR THAT FROM YOU.
NO credit?
NO problem!
ASK ABOU
LOW
MORTGAGE
RATES
MORTGAGE APPLICATION
METRO BANK
DENIED
'YOU THINK THAT JUST BECAUSE I LOVE THIS COUNTRY, I DON'T SEE THE FLAWS? IMMIGRANTS SEE THE BEST AND WORST OF AMERICA EVERY DAY.
'YOU'RE A GREAT GUY, STEVE. POSSIBLY THE BEST. BUT YOU'VE NEVER BEEN DENIED A JOB BECAUSE OF WHO YOU ARE. NEVER HAD A NEIGHBOR THINK YOU WERE LESS OF A PERSON BECAUSE OF YOUR SKIN COLOR OR BEEN TOLD TO GO BACK TO YOUR OWN COUNTRY.
'AMERICA MAKES A PROMISE TO ALL OF US. BUT IT DOESN'T KEEP THAT PROMISE ON ITS OWN.'
ROOMS FOR RENT
HU
WHAT
WOULD
DO IN M
SHOES
YOU'RE A
HERO, STEVE. BUT
WHAT YOU FIGHT F
THAT MAKES YOU ON
YOUR FANCY COSTU

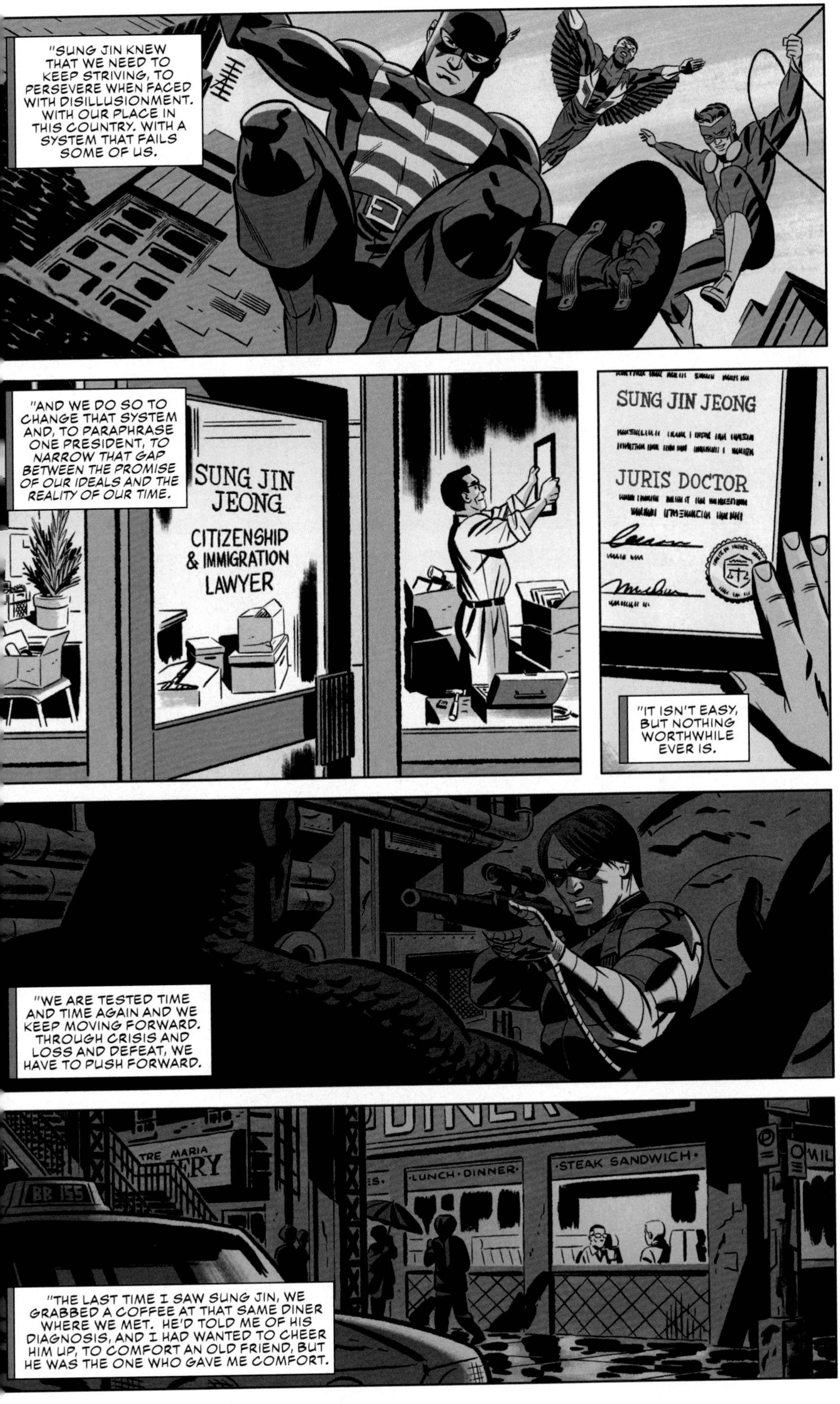
"SUNG JIN KNEW THAT WE NEED TO KEEP STRIVING, TO PERSEVERE WHEN FACED WITH DISILLUSIONMENT. WITH OUR PLACE IN THIS COUNTRY. WITH A SYSTEM THAT FAILS SOME OF US.
"AND WE DO SO TO CHANGE THAT SYSTEM AND, TO PARAPHRASE ONE PRESIDENT, TO NARROW THAT GAP BETWEEN THE PROMISE OF OUR IDEALS AND THE REALITY OF OUR TIME.
SUNG JIN JEONG
CITIZENSHIP & IMMIGRATION LAWYER
SUNG JIN JEONG
JURIS DOCTOR
"IT ISN'T EASY, BUT NOTHING WORTHWHILE EVER IS.
"WE ARE TESTED TIME AND TIME AGAIN AND WE KEEP MOVING FORWARD. THROUGH CRISIS AND LOSS AND DEFEAT, WE HAVE TO PUSH FORWARD.
DINER
TRE MARIA
ERY
BB 155
LUNCH·DINNER
STEAK SANDWICH
"THE LAST TIME I SAW SUNG JIN, WE GRABBED A COFFEE AT THAT SAME DINER WHERE WE MET. HE'D TOLD ME OF HIS DIAGNOSIS, AND I HAD WANTED TO CHEER HIM UP, TO COMFORT AN OLD FRIEND, BUT HE WAS THE ONE WHO GAVE ME COMFORT.

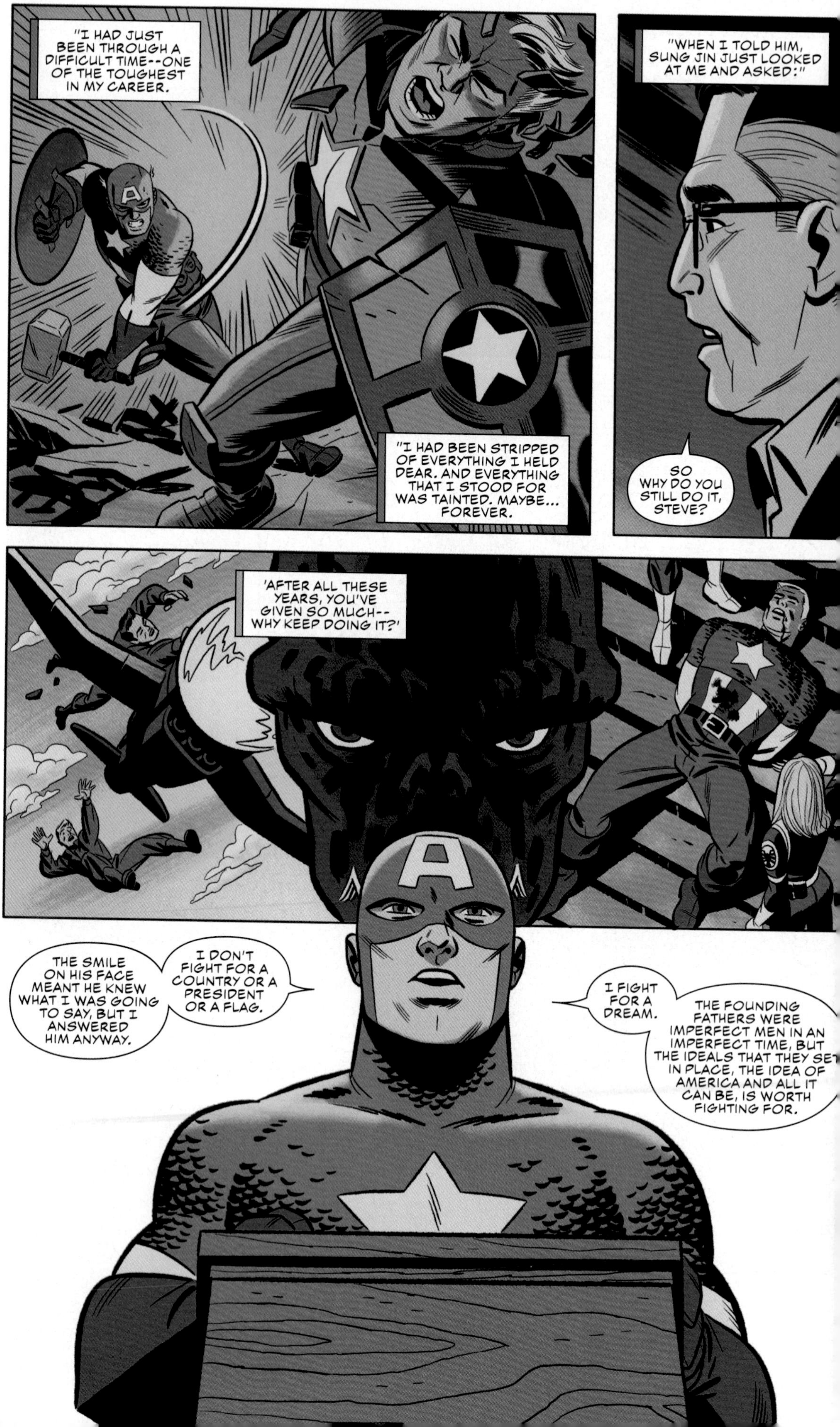
"I HAD JUST BEEN THROUGH A DIFFICULT TIME--ONE OF THE TOUGHEST IN MY CAREER.
"I HAD BEEN STRIPPED OF EVERYTHING I HELD DEAR. AND EVERYTHING THAT I STOOD FOR WAS TAINTED. MAYBE... FOREVER.
"WHEN I TOLD HIM, SUNG JIN JUST LOOKED AT ME AND ASKED:"
SO WHY DO YOU STILL DO IT, STEVE?
'AFTER ALL THESE YEARS, YOU'VE GIVEN SO MUCH-- WHY KEEP DOING IT?'
THE SMILE ON HIS FACE MEANT HE KNEW WHAT I WAS GOING TO SAY, BUT I ANSWERED HIM ANYWAY.
I DON'T FIGHT FOR A COUNTRY OR A PRESIDENT OR A FLAG.
I FIGHT FOR A DREAM.
THE FOUNDING FATHERS WERE IMPERFECT MEN IN AN IMPERFECT TIME, BUT THE IDEALS THAT THEY SET IN PLACE, THE IDEA OF AMERICA AND ALL IT CAN BE, IS WORTH FIGHTING FOR.

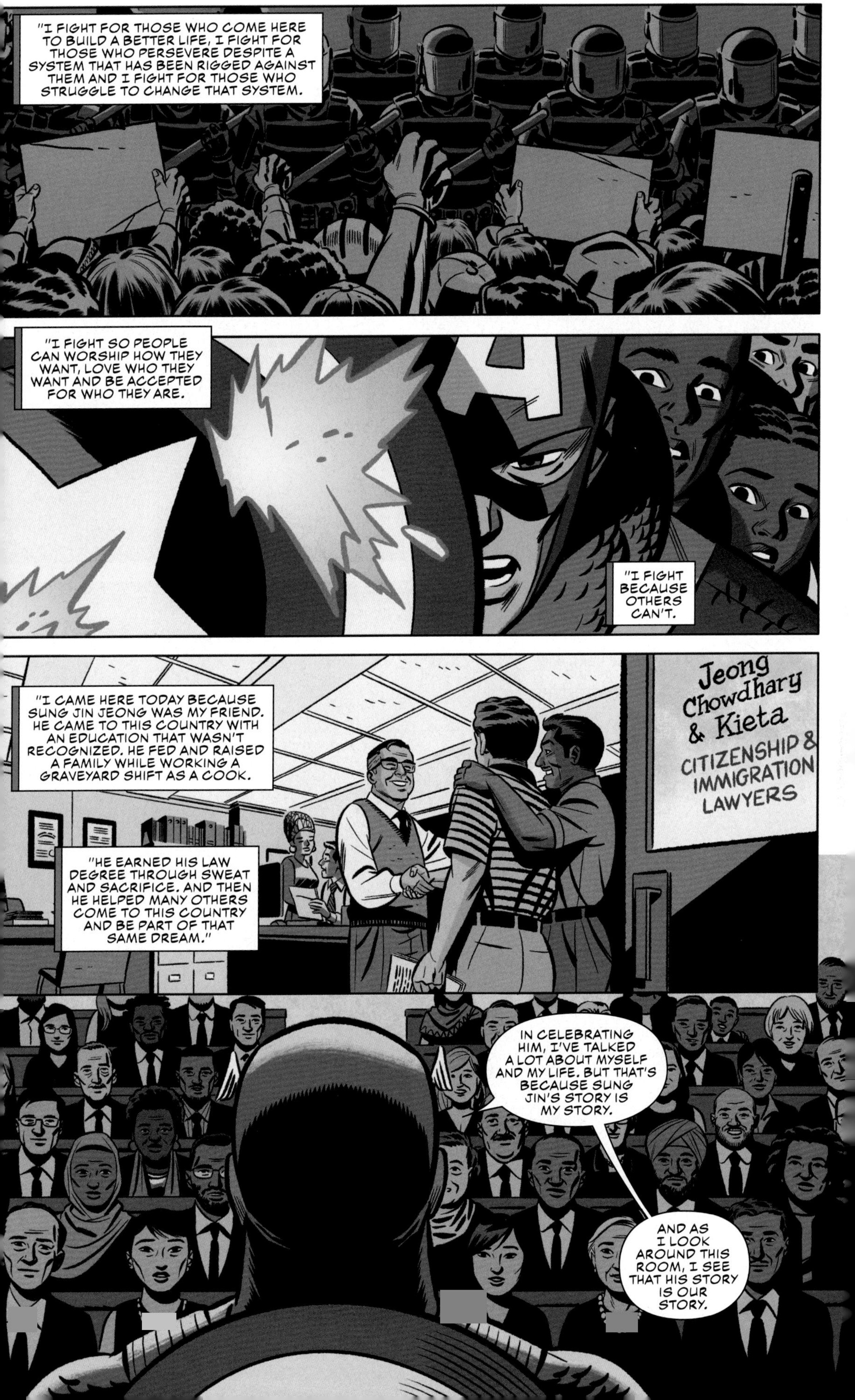
"I FIGHT FOR THOSE WHO COME HERE TO BUILD A BETTER LIFE, I FIGHT FOR THOSE WHO PERSEVERE DESPITE A SYSTEM THAT HAS BEEN RIGGED AGAINST THEM AND I FIGHT FOR THOSE WHO STRUGGLE TO CHANGE THAT SYSTEM.
"I FIGHT SO PEOPLE CAN WORSHIP HOW THEY WANT, LOVE WHO THEY WANT AND BE ACCEPTED FOR WHO THEY ARE.
"I FIGHT BECAUSE OTHERS CAN'T.
"I CAME HERE TODAY BECAUSE SUNG JIN JEONG WAS MY FRIEND. HE CAME TO THIS COUNTRY WITH AN EDUCATION THAT WASN'T RECOGNIZED. HE FED AND RAISED A FAMILY WHILE WORKING A GRAVEYARD SHIFT AS A COOK.
Jeong Chowdhary & Kieta
CITIZENSHIP & IMMIGRATION LAWYERS
"HE EARNED HIS LAW DEGREE THROUGH SWEAT AND SACRIFICE. AND THEN HE HELPED MANY OTHERS COME TO THIS COUNTRY AND BE PART OF THAT SAME DREAM."
IN CELEBRATING HIM, I'VE TALKED A LOT ABOUT MYSELF AND MY LIFE. BUT THAT'S BECAUSE SUNG JIN'S STORY IS MY STORY.
AND AS I LOOK AROUND THIS ROOM, I SEE THAT HIS STORY IS OUR STORY.

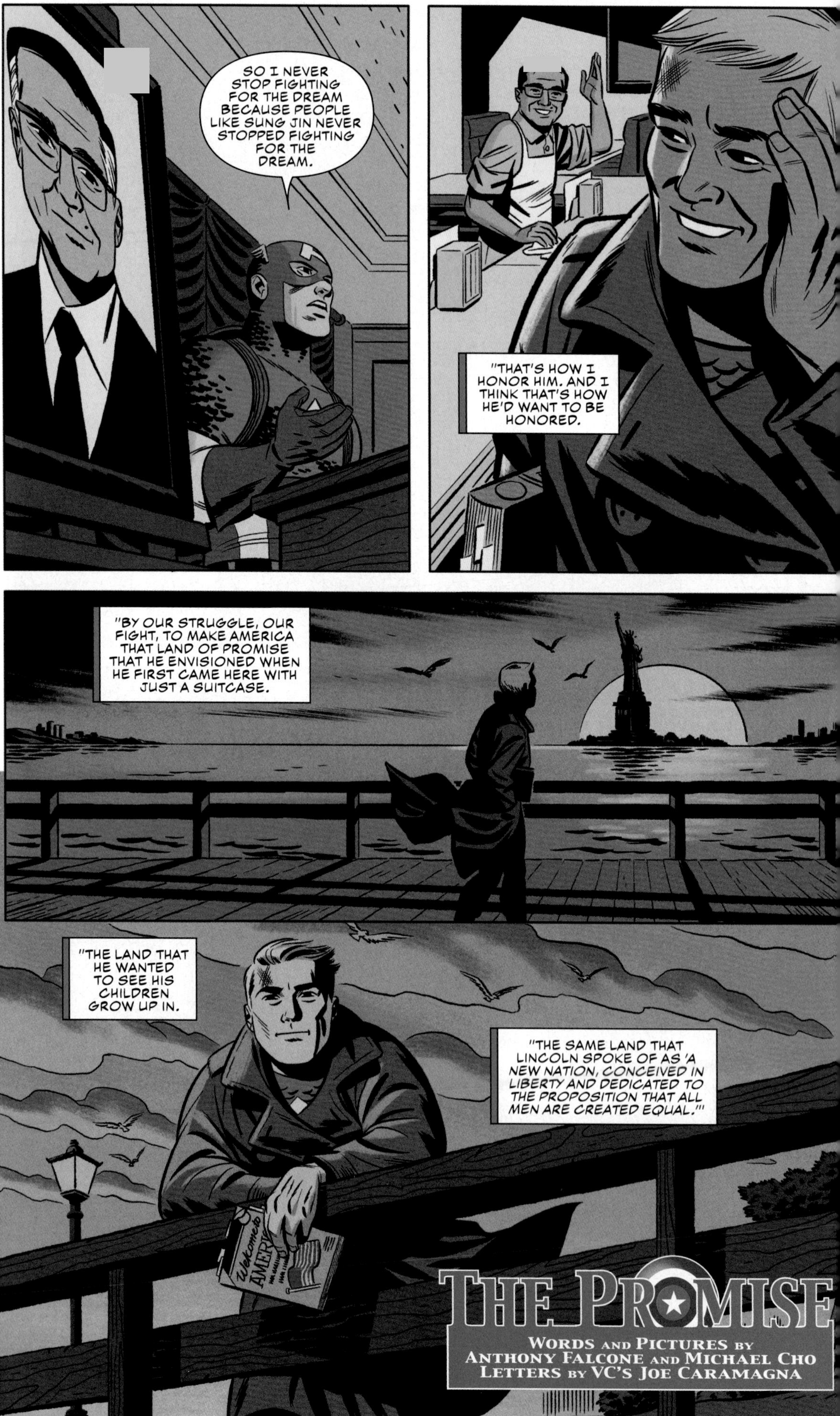
SO I NEVER STOP FIGHTING FOR THE DREAM BECAUSE PEOPLE LIKE SUNG JIN NEVER STOPPED FIGHTING FOR THE DREAM.
"THAT'S HOW I HONOR HIM. AND I THINK THAT'S HOW HE'D WANT TO BE HONORED.
"BY OUR STRUGGLE, OUR FIGHT, TO MAKE AMERICA THAT LAND OF PROMISE THAT HE ENVISIONED WHEN HE FIRST CAME HERE WITH JUST A SUITCASE.
"THE LAND THAT HE WANTED TO SEE HIS CHILDREN GROW UP IN.
"THE SAME LAND THAT LINCOLN SPOKE OF AS 'A NEW NATION, CONCEIVED IN LIBERTY AND DEDICATED TO THE PROPOSITION THAT ALL MEN ARE CREATED EQUAL.'"
THE PROMISE
WORDS AND PICTURES BY ANTHONY FALCONE AND MICHAEL CHO
LETTERS BY VC'S JOE CARAMAGNA

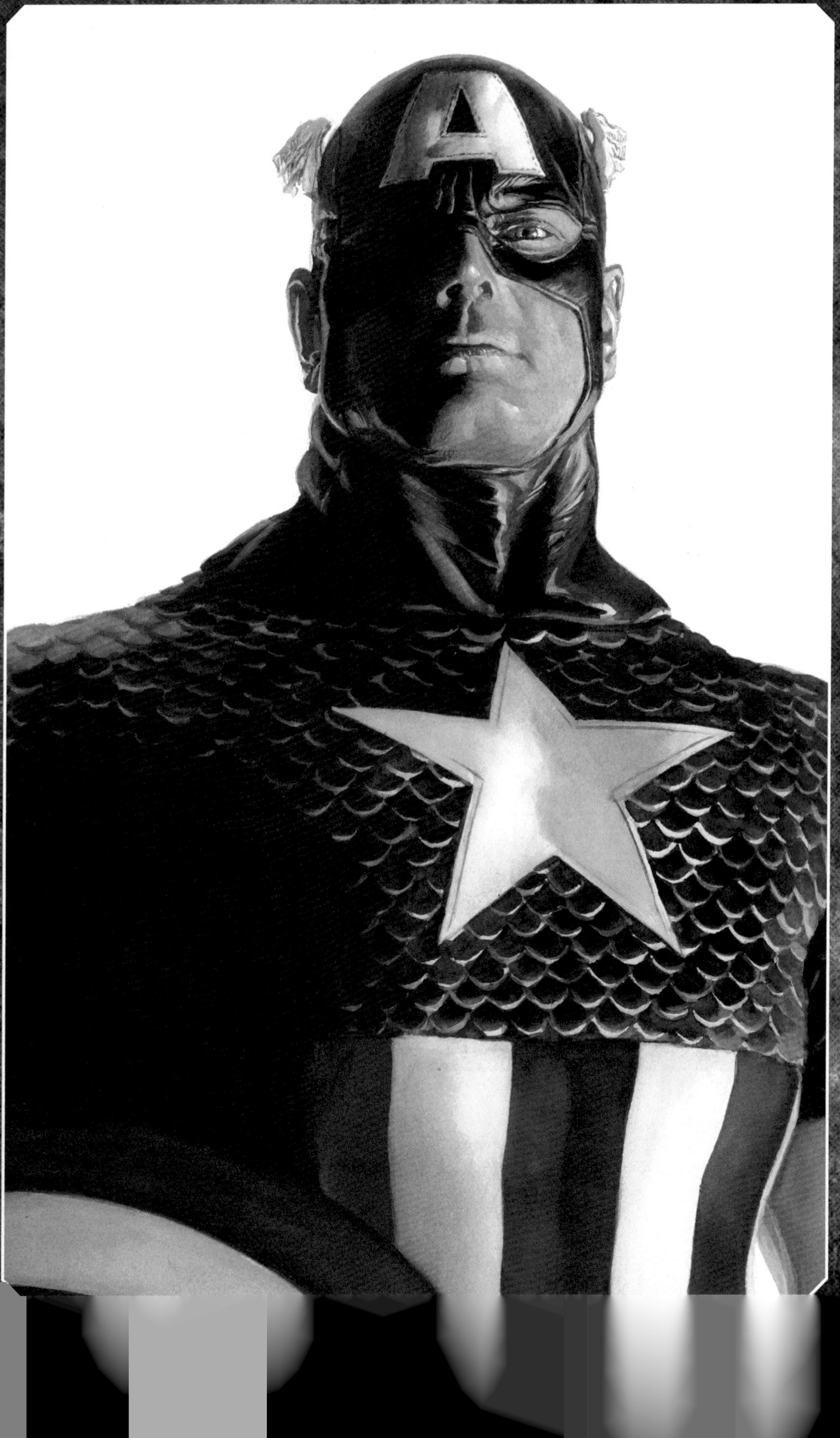

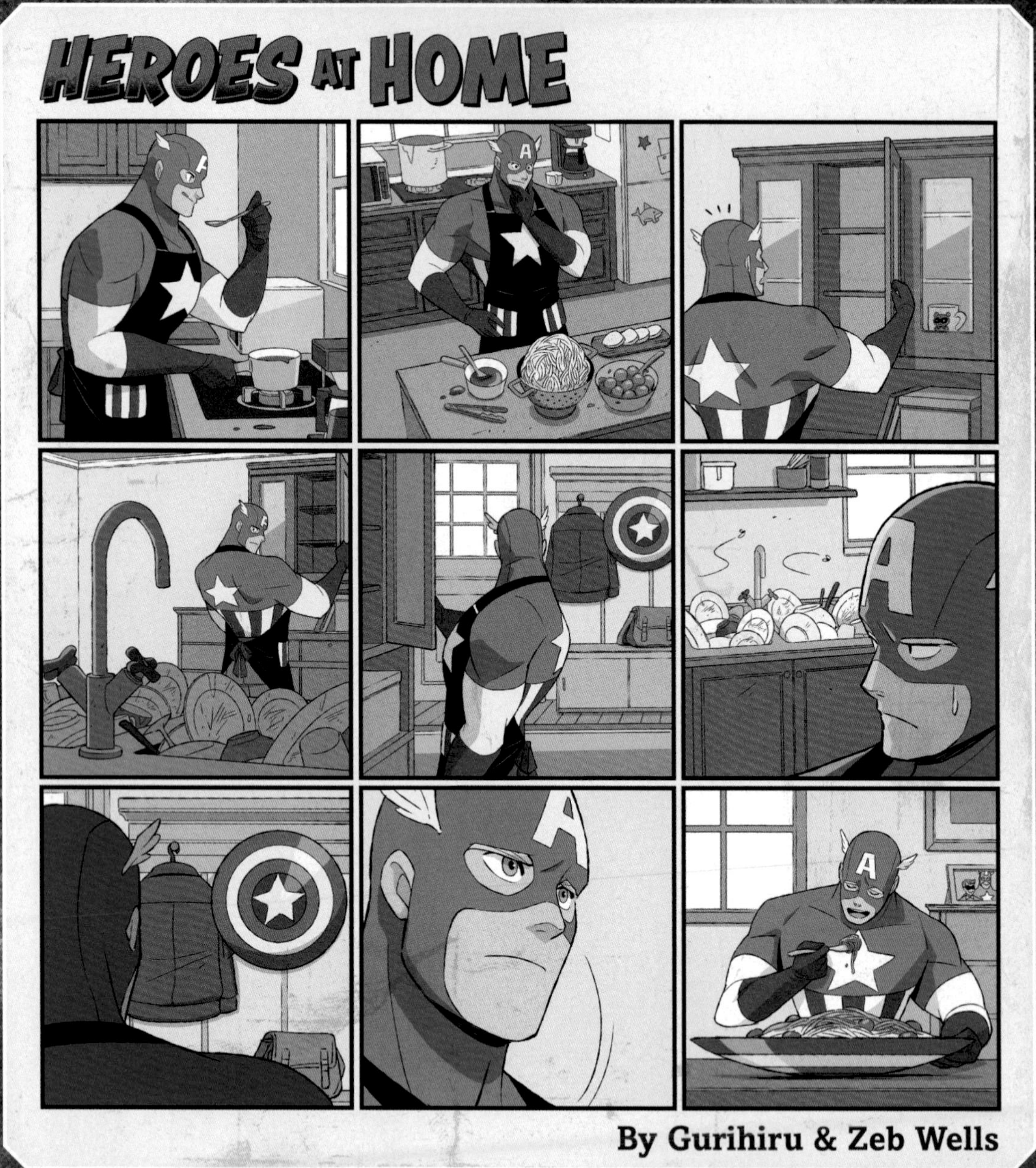
HEROES AT HOME
By Gurihiru & Zeb Wells

GURIHIRU & ZEB WELLS

23 HEROES AT HOME VARIANT

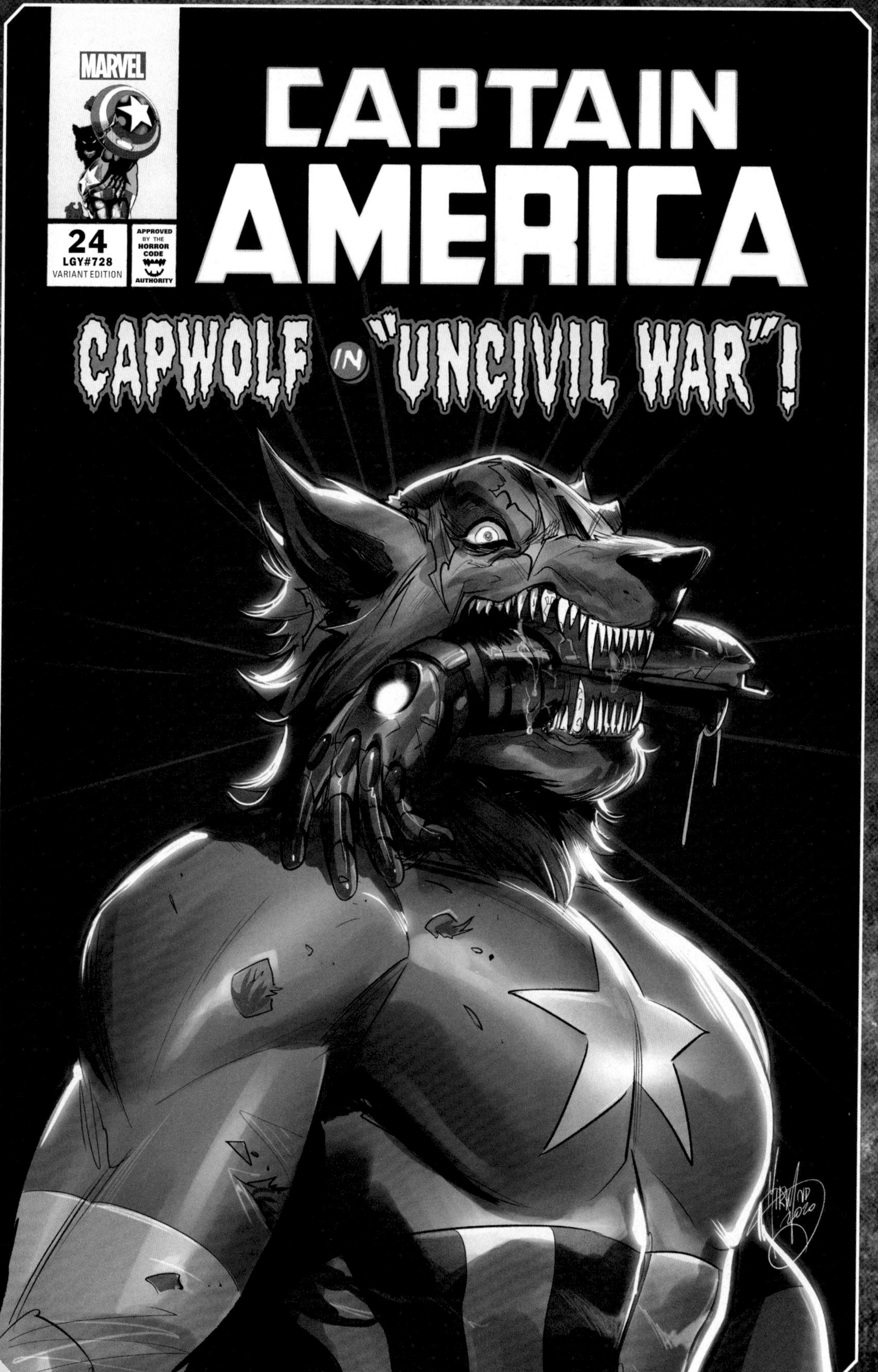

MARVEL
CAPTAIN AMERICA
24
LGY#728
VARIANT EDITION
APPROVED BY THE HORROR CODE AUTHORITY
CAPWOLF IN "UNCIVIL WAR"!

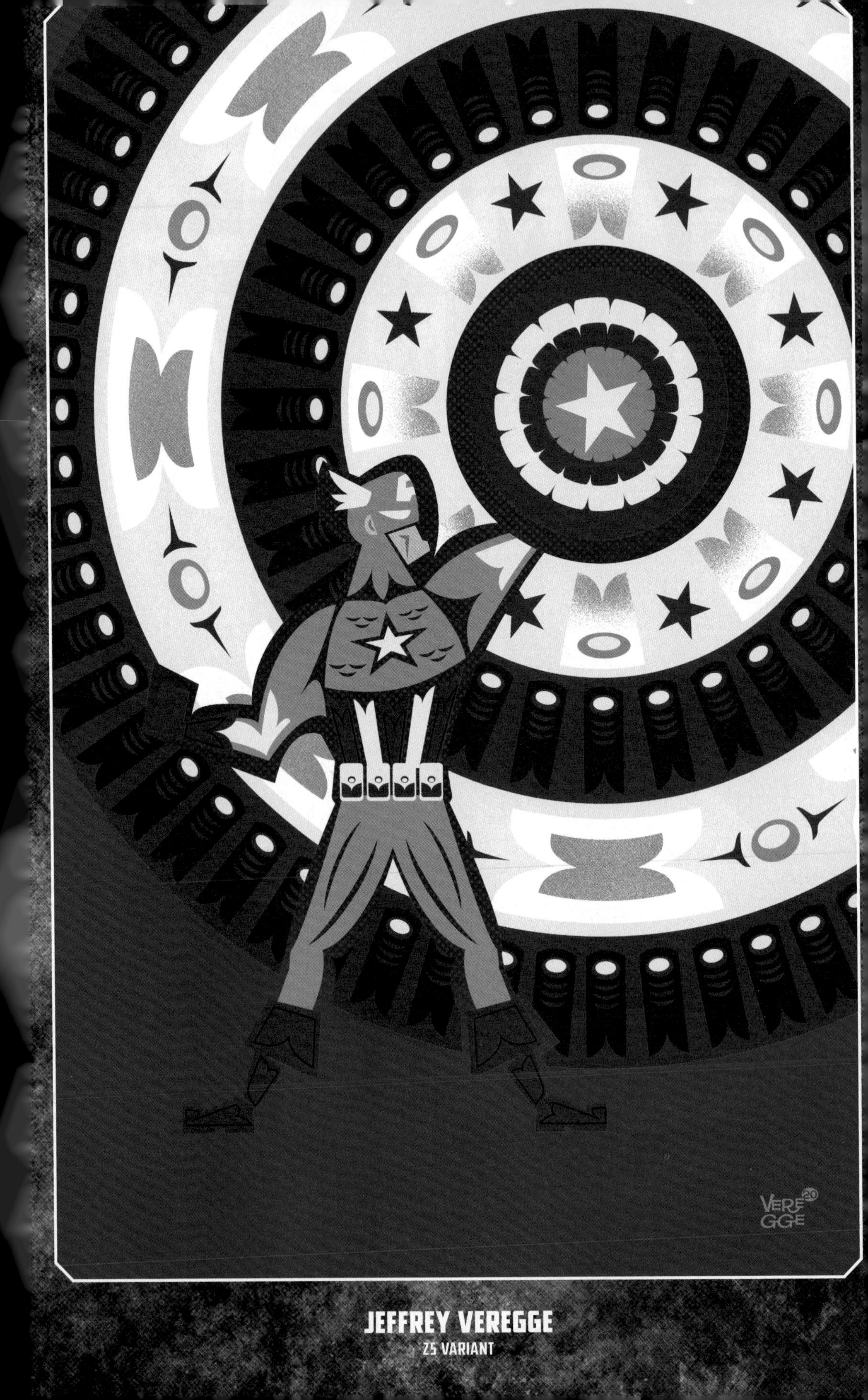
VEREGGE 20

JEFFREY VEREGGE
25 VARIANT

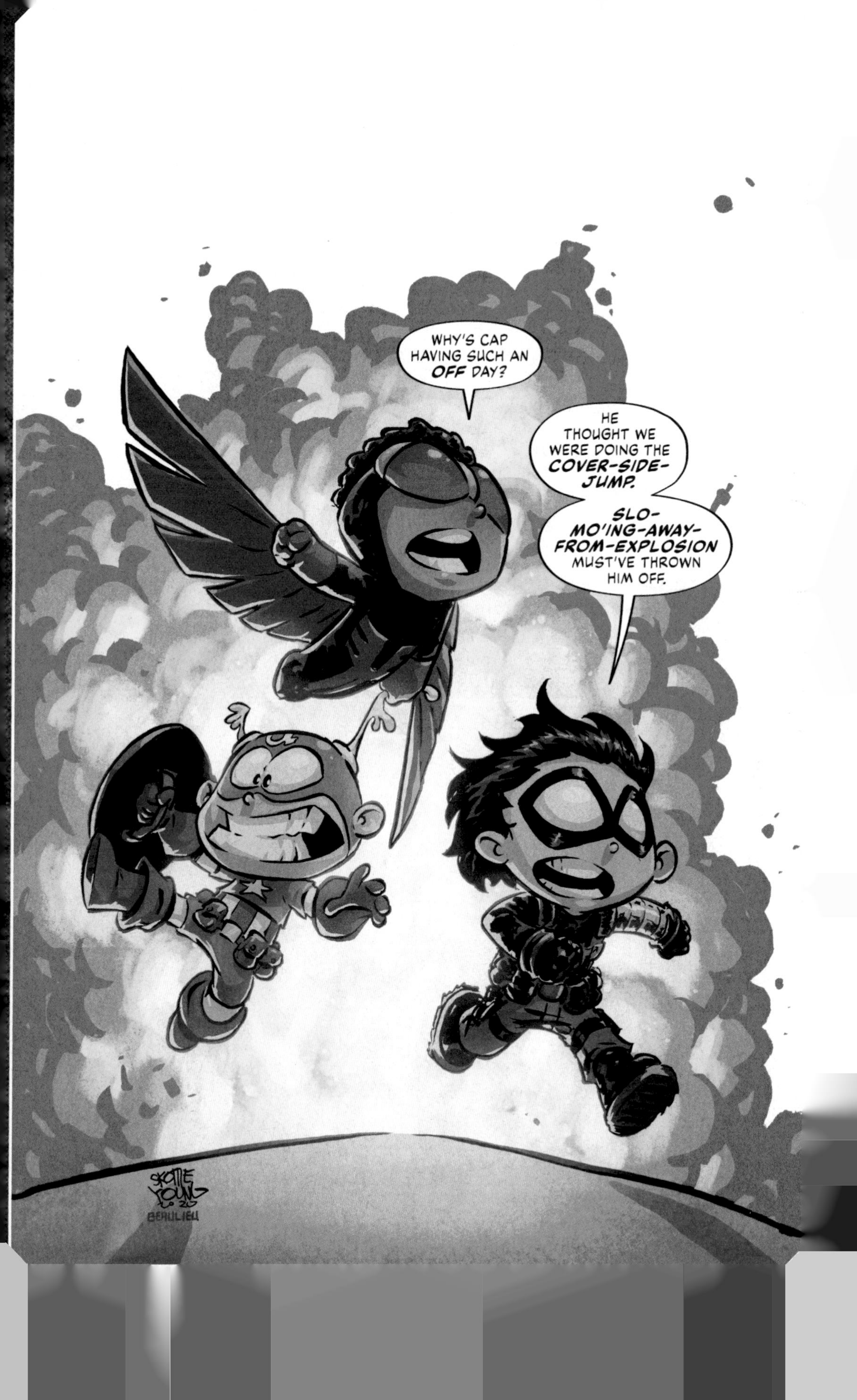
WHY'S CAP HAVING SUCH AN OFF DAY?
HE THOUGHT WE WERE DOING THE COVER-SIDE-JUMP.
SLO-MO'ING-AWAY-FROM-EXPLOSION MUST'VE THROWN HIM OFF.
SKOTTIE YOUNG '20
BEAULIEU

BEN CALDWELL
ZD SPIDER-WOMAN VARIANT

PATCH ZIRCHER & EDGAR DELGADO
Z1 ZOMBIES VARIANT

SALVADOR LARROCA & FRANK D'ARMATA